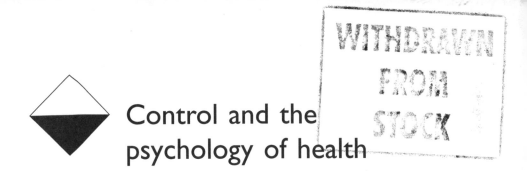

Control and the
psychology of health

Health Psychology

Series editors Sheila Payne and Sandra Horn

Published titles

Control and the psychology of health
Theory, measurement and applications

Jan Walker

Open University Press
Buckingham · Philadelphia

Open University Press
Celtic Court
22 Ballmoor
Buckingham
MK18 1XW

email: enquiries@openup.co.uk
world wide web: www.openup.co.uk

and
325 Chestnut Street
Philadelphia, PA 19106, USA

First Published 2001

Copyright © Jan Walker, 2001

A catalogue record of this book is available from the British Library

ISBN   0 335 20264 0 (pb)   0 335 20265 9 (hb)

Library of Congress Cataloging-in-Publication Data
Walker, Jan, 1946–
    Control and the psychology of health : theory, measurement, and applications / Jan Walker.
        p.   cm. – (Health psychology)
    Includes bibliographical references and index.
    ISBN 0–335–20265–9 – ISBN 0–335–20264–0 (pbk.)
    1. Health psychology.   2. Control (Psychology)–Health aspects.   3. Mind and body–Health aspects.   I. Title.   II. Series.

R726.5.W35 2001
610′.1′9–dc21   2001021147

Typeset by Graphicraft Limited, Hong Kong
Printed in Great Britain by St Edmundsbury Press Limited,
Bury St Edmunds, Suffolk

I dedicate this book to Professor Justus Akinsanya who, with so much else, taught me the value of using flow diagrams to explore theoretical relationships.

 # Contents

Series editors' foreword

This series of books in health psychology is designed to support postgraduate and postqualification studies in psychology, nursing, medicine and healthcare sciences, as well as the study of health psychology at undergraduate level. The framework in which the books are set is psychosocial rather than a medical disease, physiological systems or organic disease approach. Health psychology is growing rapidly as a field of study and a profession. Concerned as it is with the application of psychological theories and models in the promotion and maintenance of health, and the individual and interpersonal aspects of adaptive behaviour in illness and disability, health psychology has a wide remit and an important part to play in the future.

In this book, Jan Walker presents a comprehensive overview of concepts related to control. She covers such topics as perceived and personal control, locus of control, self-efficacy, mastery, social support and the emotional states that accompany them. The origins of these psychological concepts are explored and set within the context of developing ideas and theory in psychology. The reader can therefore understand how the ideas are both a product of their times and also influential in developing new ways to construe the world. The book is well referenced back to original sources. For health psychologists and other health professionals working with today's problems and issues, it is enlightening to realize that others have struggled with these concerns. However, this is not merely a theoretical book, it is also concerned with issues of measurement and practical applications, and is rich with examples drawn from Jan's practice as a nurse working predominantly with elderly people in Pain Clinics. The final chapter offers a new integrative model, which will challenge readers to explore the concept of control in more depth. The past few years have witnessed an important rethink about the way we approach the concept of control; this book aims to contribute to the debate.

Sheila Payne and Sandra Horn

 # Preface

Introduction

This book serves two key purposes. The first is to clear up many personal confusions and frustrations about terms and variables associated with the concept of control. The word 'control' is so much part of our everyday language that we all take its meaning for granted. When we read about 'control' in psychological terms, many of us tend to impose our own interpretation on it. Yet it is clear from the literature that it conceals a variety of different meanings, each of which has important theoretical implications. The information explosion means that students rarely have time to conduct extensive literature searches that go back beyond the past ten years. Obtaining recent material is a matter of some ease. But while recent research findings are clearly important, their interpretation requires knowledge of the theoretical and empirical contexts in which they are situated. In this book, I have set out a fairly comprehensive review of each of the main control-related concepts. I have explored the origins of each concept, together with subsequent theoretical and empirical developments, anomalies and dilemmas. In so doing, I have been able to focus on important and relevant information that is in danger of being lost to a new generation of students and researchers.

My second purpose is to offer a new theoretical analysis of the concept of control. This is one that seeks to account for the apparent anomalies identified by previous researchers and links each of the concepts reviewed in this book. Ultimately, I have sought to enhance theoretical clarity and generate testable hypotheses. I hope that this will inform improvements in research designs and generate new ideas for applications in health and health care.

Who is the book intended for?

The book is intended for undergraduate and postgraduate students who already have a reasonable understanding of basic psychological theories. It is aimed particularly at those who are preparing dissertations or research studies on topics related to health and well-being, for which the concepts in this book are of relevance.

How to use this book

Chapter 1 presents a brief overview of the key concepts included in this book, explaining briefly how each relates to a theory of control. Chapters 2 to 7 focus on each of these concepts in turn. In each chapter, I have set out the origins and development of the concept, drawing on contributions from key theorists, research studies and review articles. I have presented this material in a relatively raw form so that readers can trace the chronology of theoretical development and judge for themselves the nature and value of each contribution. This has also enabled me to set out the theoretical dilemmas, conflicts and resolutions or outstanding problems that have developed over time. Chapter 8 is devoted to my own contribution to theory development. It contains a critical review of some of the existing theoretical interpretations and offers a way of integrating the concepts previously reviewed. There I am able to explain some of the theoretical dilemmas identified. I also offer some new hypotheses and pointers for future research.

Each chapter contains a section on measurement and health care applications. While these are not exhaustive, they will provide the reader with an idea of the range of measurements and applications in the field of health and health care. At the end of each chapter are some recommendations for further reading. Some of the recommended texts are out of print, but they should not be considered out of date and are worth obtaining for those who wish to gain a deeper understanding of a particular concept.

Readers will note that in some places I have referred to the first name of a theorist or researcher. This is to enable the reader to identify the gender of certain key authors and also attempts to break down the sense of 'facelessness' that pervades some psychology texts.

# Acknowledgements

My sincere gratitude is given to: Sheila Payne and Sandra Horn for giving me the opportunity and impetus for writing this book and for their helpful comments; my husband, Mike, who encouraged, cajoled and supported me when the task seemed overwhelming; Hugh Baldwin, Brenda Goddard and the staff in the Postgraduate Library at the Royal Hampshire County Hospital, Winchester, without whose help the material could not possibly have been gathered; Helena Morton, for her encouraging review and very useful observations.

Summary of control concepts

CHAPTER 1

Overview of contents

- Control theory
- Control research
- Perceived or personal control
- Locus of control
- Self-efficacy
- Learned helplessness
- Social support
- Emotional states and responses
- A unifying theory of control
- Further reading

Control theory

Control is a key concept in the psychology of health. It has important applications in the fields of stress, coping and adaptation, health promotion, health education, rehabilitation and care in acute and chronic illness, disability and terminal illness. It also has important implications for the management of the relationship between patients or clients, carers and health care professionals in all health care settings.

Control is used predominantly to refer to the attainment of a desired outcome or, using the language of systems theory, the system goal or 'reference criterion' (Hyland 1987). Desired outcomes thus encompass those that assure the survival of the individual and the species, protect individual health and well-being, and meet cultural, ideological, social and material demands. The term control is commonly used to refer to both process (of attainment) and outcome.

Although 'control' is frequently used to refer to personal control, I will illustrate later in this book how control may be achieved through the activities of either self or others, or even belief in an external force. 'Others' in a health context may include family, relatives, friends, doctors and other professionals, employers and support agencies. Control is normally associated with positive outcomes and with adaptation, yet control may in some circumstances be associated with deviant or maladaptive consequences. The classification of an outcome as adaptive or maladaptive may depend on the different perspectives of the actor and the observer.

Although frequent reference is made in the literature to 'control theory', there is to date no accepted unifying theory of control. Rather, there is a multiplicity of theories and concepts associated with control. These include perceived control, personal control, locus of control, self-efficacy and learned helplessness. While these concepts have provided useful heuristics in health and health care, the search for a theory of control has remained illusive. Systems theory has come closest to achieving this and I refer to this again in Chapter 8, where I offer a theoretical framework that integrates all the concepts reviewed in this book.

Control research

The development and testing of control-related concepts has involved a number of different approaches over time. Research in the 1940s and 1950s involved objective testing of the effects of giving or withholding of control over aversive stimuli, much of which took place in the animal laboratory (Lefcourt 1966a, b). The theory of learned helplessness emerged directly from this type of research. The 1960s saw a general shift towards relatively small-scale human experiments involving university undergraduates. Hypotheses were developed and tested in a reductive way, but with considerable attention to methodological rigour. Meanwhile, research into control beliefs emerged from studies of the responses of human participants in health care and education settings. From the mid-1970s onwards, most researchers favoured field-based experiments and surveys in naturalistic settings. However, it has proved difficult to demonstrate the power of variables associated with the concept of control to predict health outcomes. Important reasons put forward in this book include the lack of a clear distinction between independent, mediating and dependent variables, the neglect of most researchers to consider the interaction between perceived personal control and different types of social support, as well as the failure to provide unambiguous definitions of concepts and terms.

Below is an overview of each of the concepts reviewed in this book, together with a brief rationale for inclusion.

Perceived or personal control

Perceived control reflects the beliefs of an individual about the actual or potential availability of control achievable by self or others in different types of situation. Perceived control may differ from the actual level of personal control available within an environment, since it is influenced by the actor's frame of reference, knowledge and skills, past history of control or lack of control in similar situations, personality traits and cultural beliefs. Under normal circumstances it appears that most people demonstrate an illusion of control, with attribution bias towards personal control.

Most researchers, when referring to perceived control, imply perceived personal control, omitting the possibility that perceived control may also be achieved with assistance from others. Most research supports the view that perceived personal control is generally advantageous in relation to physical and psychological health outcomes. However, total reliance on personal control is likely to be maladaptive in uncontrollable situations. Hence, it is argued during the course of this book that a balance of personal control and social support is desirable when an individual is in difficulties, sick or disabled. Perceived or personal control, unlike other control-related concepts, is not associated with a key theorist or group of theorists. The terminology used is very variable and there is little or no agreement about appropriate forms of measurement. Despite this, the concept has had a profound impact on a range of health care practices; for example, in the field of pain management.

Locus of control

Locus of control refers to beliefs about responsibility for outcomes. The concept accounts for different sources of control, including self, others and chance. However, its conceptualization has changed over the years as a result of research, reviews and reanalysis. Starting as a unidimensional concept (internal–external), it was revised in the 1970s to reflect three orthogonal dimensions: internal, external (powerful others) and external (chance). More recently, it has been suggested that chance beliefs are not independent of internal locus of control, but reflect the opposite pole of the same dimension.

Research findings in relation to locus of control have proved somewhat contradictory. Despite its initial promise, locus of control has been shown to be a relatively weak predictor of health-related behaviour. The most consistent finding is that chance locus of control is associated with poor motivation to engage in preventive or protective health behaviours, and poor health outcomes. Logically, high scores on both internal and external (powerful others) locus of control would appear to be most adaptive in terms of health outcomes. Such scores indicate a belief in personal responsibility for health but a willingness to seek help from others and take advice when necessary. Beliefs in luck, fate or chance are generally associated with failure to engage in health-protective behaviours and depression in the face of chronic illness.

Self-efficacy

Self-efficacy is fundamental to the achievement of internal or personal control. It refers to the ability/capability of the individual to achieve a desired outcome. Hence it implies a body of requisite knowledge and skills. However, in order to achieve a desired outcome, it is necessary for people not only to have the knowledge and skills, but also to believe that they have them. Therefore self-efficacy normally refers to sense of self-efficacy or perceived self-efficacy. Self-efficacy is particularly important when a task requires specific knowledge and skills. Therefore, specific rather than general measures of self-efficacy are usually used and a wide range of these is currently available. The concept of self-efficacy emerged from research by Albert Bandura on social learning theory. Bandura has, over the past three decades, remained at the centre of research to develop and test the concept in a variety of health-related contexts.

Self-efficacy has proved to be an important variable, in conjunction with other variables, in predicting health-related behaviours and behaviour change. The importance of promoting beliefs in self-efficacy is central to many health care interventions, particularly in the field of chronic disease. Sense of self-efficacy is a good indicator of motivation and a measure of self-efficacy may therefore be a useful indicator of the sustainability of interventions designed to enhance personal control.

Learned helplessness

Learned helplessness refers to the belief that one's actions have no effect on outcomes. It is thus a belief in total lack of personal control over the situation. In the experimental context, a period of exposure to total loss of control leads subsequently to the total failure to attempt any response that could lead to a desired outcome or to the cessation of an aversive or undesired outcome. The concept originated from observations in the animal laboratory and is most commonly associated with Martin Seligman. Seligman and his colleagues demonstrated that learned helplessness is associated with three deficits: behavioural, cognitive and motivational. Seligman subsequently presented learned helplessness as an analogue for human depression.

The concept of learned helplessness has undergone numerous revisions over the past three decades. It was reformulated using attribution theory to represent human beliefs about helplessness. More recently, it was revised again to account only for a hopelessness subtype of depression. The literature reveals a concept that has failed to live up to its original promise in terms of theoretical prediction and appears, according to recent reviews, to have lost its way.

Nevertheless, despite recent threats, the concept of learned helplessness continues to hold great intuitive appeal for health care professionals and has been extensively used as an explanatory framework within health care. It implies that what is learned can be unlearned, a prediction supported by early experimental evidence. Learned helplessness appears to imply situational, rather than personal, causes, thus avoiding victim-blaming. However, some applications in general health care settings have been based on theoretical misunderstandings. For example, most health care professionals from non-psychology backgrounds use the term 'learned helplessness' to refer to a state of induced dependence. This is an inference which, though logical, goes beyond its original conceptual meaning.

The term 'learned helplessness' appears ripe for a thorough review and this I attempt to do in Chapter 8 in this book. There I examine loss of control in a social context to refer to a failure to achieve desired outcomes through the actions of either self or others. This reanalysis allows for a distinction between hopelessness and helplessness. According to this reanalysis, hopelessness is associated with prolonged failure to gain control by any means (self or others) and failure to foresee any possibility of so doing. Helplessness refers to the perception of threat of loss of control brought about by perceptions of persistent uncertainty or unpredictability, or in response to an episode of sudden temporary but total loss of control, as in post-traumatic stress. In accordance with these definitions, I propose that a generalized sense of 'learned hopelessness' is associated with clinical depression. A generalized sense of 'learned helplessness' is associated with chronic anxiety states, with or without depression.

Social support

Social support appears to be the missing variable in our current under-standing of control. Based on the definitions and propositions presented in this book, it is evident that control may be achieved through the actions of others as well as those of self. The actions of others, whether through helping, sharing or giving information or advice, constitute social support.

Social support would appear to serve a number of distinct control functions. It can remove or replace personal control, or it can enhance or increase it. Instrumental social support may exert direct control on behalf of, or over, the individual. This can complement the personal control of the individual or usurp it. It may therefore be beneficial or deleterious, depend-ing on circumstances or context. Similarly, informational support may be used to exert power over an individual or to facilitate personal control. Emotional support is usually considered to bolster individual sense of personal control and self-efficacy and enhance self-esteem. This explains why informational and emotional support, in health care contexts, are usually found to have a positive impact on health and well-being. Instrumental support, in contrast, has been found to be associated with dependence and increased depression.

Researchers must therefore distinguish between different types of support if they are to make sense of the direct and buffering effects of social support in different circumstances. It is also necessary to take account of individual desire for control and the controllability of the situation. Placing social support in the context of a theory of control enables researchers to understand how different types of support are likely to impact on health outcomes. Failure to do so will continue to lead to conflicting and confusing research findings.

Emotional states and responses

Control has a direct effect on emotional states (and possibly vice versa). Perceived lack or loss of control is associated with both anxiety and depression, and measures of depression and/or anxiety are commonly used in studies of perceived control and self-efficacy. However, little attention has been given to the positive emotional impact of perceived control, including feelings of confidence and satisfaction. The causal relationship between emotional state and control remains unclear. Some researchers use the term 'affect', implying a causal link between emotional state and beliefs and behaviours. Other researchers have assumed that emotional states such as depression and anxiety are effects of loss of control. In reality, feedback loops between physiological state, cognitive set and behavioural pattern make it difficult if not impossible to distinguish between cause and effect. The possible relationship between event, arousal, cognition and action are illustrated in Chapter 8, Figure 8.8.

A unifying theory of control

In Chapter 8 of this book, I present a theoretical framework that proposes a direct link between control beliefs, social support and emotional states. In it I illustrate how a range of mood states may be mapped on to different beliefs about control and support. In Figure 8.9, I present a flow diagram that illustrates the likely relationships between each of the concepts reviewed in this book and summarizes a proposed new unifying theory of control. I believe that this has important implications for the development of health care interventions based on the enhancement of both personal control and social support. It also assists in guiding the selection of dependent and independent measures for use in future health care research.

Further reading

Baum, A., Newman, S., Weinman, J., West, R. and McManus, C. (eds) (1997) *Cambridge Handbook of Psychology, Health and Medicine.* Cambridge: Cambridge University Press.
This text provides brief but comprehensive overviews of the key concepts contained in this book (and much else) by authors who are well recognized in their respective fields.

Perceived or personal control

CHAPTER 2

Overview of contents

- Theories of personal control
- Perceived control, personal control or both?
- Experimental approaches
- Control, pain and endurance
- The distinction between cognitive and behavioural control
- Information and control cover stressful situations
- Prediction, control and the Minimax hypothesis
- Choice and control
- Desirability of control
- Relinquishing control
- Perceived control: actual or illusory?
- Control, personality and cultural expectations
- Life-span influences on perceived control
- Control or confusion?
- Measuring perceived or personal control
- Health applications
- Concluding comments
- Further reading
- Notes.

Theories of personal control

The hypothesis that people are intrinsically motivated to achieve a sense of mastery over the environment is embedded in twentieth-century Western psychology. It has been variously attributed (e.g. Lefcourt 1966a) to Adler's proposition, from the 1920s, that striving for competence and superiority is a motivational force; to Erikson and Piaget in the 1950s on the developmental understanding of causality; and to R. W. White's research (see White 1959) into competence and effectance. This notion of personal control is to be found in the works of psychologists from most of the mainstream traditions in psychology, including behavioural, developmental, humanistic, psychoanalytic and social psychology. Influential theorists have included Fritz Heider (1944) for his work on social perception and causality; George Kelly (1955) and his conceptualization of man-as-scientist whose aim is to predict and control events; B. F. Skinner (1953) through his theoretical account of personal control and self-management; Michotte (1963) on the perception and understanding of causal relationships; Richard DeCharms (1968) with his analysis of personal causation; and Harold Kelley (1973) in his work on attribution theory. In some of the earlier writings on control, there appears to emerge an infinite regress of related concepts, ideas and theories from philosophy and psychology. These reveal a general consensus about the importance of the role of self in causal relationships and the ability to predict and influence actions (those of self and others) and outcomes.

White and Janson (1986: 298) defined (personal) control as: 'the ability to cause or influence intended outcomes by differential responding, resulting in a sense of mastery.' In other words, people initiate appropriate action to achieve a desired outcome and gain a sense of mastery or control in so doing. This defines personal control in terms of causation, action and outcome. In order to produce an intended outcome, I need to know that I have the power to initiate appropriate action, the ability to implement that action and the belief that I can achieve the intended outcome as a result of my action. Some theorists have preferred to differentiate between these aspects. DeCharms (1968, 1979) is one of the few theorists to devote specific attention to the issue of personal causation, concluding that personal manipulation of the environment is intrinsically motivating. He drew on the work of such philosophers as McLelland, Atkinson and Ryle, as well as psychological theorists including Skinner, Piaget, Freud, Maslow and Heider, to present a balanced analysis of how human beings try to understand the nature of causation and their role in it. Perceptual processes and the role of attributional inferences are central to DeCharms's thesis. His work cautions against a simplistic approach to understanding perceived control, highlighting the complexities of perception in the social environment. His work is too detailed to do justice to in this book, but is well worth reading for its contribution to the topic.

Rothbaum *et al.* (1982) reviewed evidence from anthropology, philosophy and psychology that supports an innate motivation towards personal control. They referred, for example, to observations by Groos in 1901 that children derive pleasure from controlling stimulation; Malinowski in 1955 that primitives [*sic*] need to believe that they can master the world; and De-Charms's (1968) proposition that to be effective in changing the environment is 'man's primary motivational propensity'. These assumptions were supported by early experiments that demonstrated the advantages of perceptions of personal control. For example, Janis conducted extensive research on the topic from the 1950s, concluding that perceived control is a core concept in understanding reactions to stressful life events (Janis 1983). White and Janson (1986) reported that people who possess a greater sense of control are better adapted and have a greater sense of well-being, that people threatened with loss of control will make efforts to regain it, while loss of sense of control may result in mental and physical pathologies.

Perceived control, personal control or both?

Hyland (1987) examined control from a systems theory perspective in an attempt to present a unifying theory of control. He explained that behaviour in response to the goal or purpose of the system corresponds to motivated behaviour. A negative feedback loop reduces discrepancy between the system's purpose and the system's perception of the environment, and directs behaviour toward the goal. Thus, 'the system does not control its environment, instead, it controls its perception of the environment' (Hyland 1987: 110). This highlights the importance of perceptual processes in achieving desired outcomes.

The terms control, personal control and perceived control are frequently used interchangeably even though there are subtle and sometimes important differences in meaning. Indeed, Lacey commented that 'theories of perceived control are marred by an important ambiguity in their usage of the concept of control' (Lacey 1979: 15). In the same publication, Seligman and Miller (1979) referred to a 'terminological mare's nest'. The following definitions are given to aid clarification:

- ◆ *Control*: the responsiveness of an event to human intervention (things are 'under control': see Antonovsky 1979; Schultz *et al.* 1991).
- ◆ *Perceived control*: the extent to which an event is believed to be under control (things are believed to be under control).

A situation may be perceived to be 'under control' with or without any direct intervention on the part of the actor; for example, when responsibility for control is shared among members of a team or where it is assumed that organizational structures are in place to maintain control on our behalf. In contrast, personal control is based directly on personal action.

- ◆ *Personal control*: self-determination of an event (things are under my control).

The literature normally uses the term perceived control to imply personal control. For example, Lefcourt defined perceived control as: 'perception of the ability to "do something" ' (Lefcourt 1982: 3). The emphasis in this definition on both perception and personal action indicates that it should perhaps be more correctly referred to as:

◆ *Perceived personal control*: the belief held by an individual that he or she is able to determine or influence important events or situations (I believe that things are under my control).

The importance of these distinctions becomes apparent later in this book when personal control is reviewed within the context of a reciprocal social environment. However, throughout this chapter, the term 'perceived control' reflects common usage and should be taken to mean 'perceived personal control'.

Experimental approaches

Most experiments on perceived or personal control have focused on control over noxious or aversive stimuli and it is perhaps surprising to find little or no attention given to control over pleasant stimuli. Human experimental research into the ability to predict and control (terminate or tolerate) noxious stimuli began in the 1940s. Haggard (1943) used electric shock as a stimulus, though the most common stimulus used prior to the 1960s was the cold pressor test in which the hand is plunged into a bucket of ice cold water. This provides a good test of willingness to endure pain under the influence of different types of condition and instruction. Studies conducted during the 1960s and early 1970s were more inclined to use electric shock or noise as the noxious stimulus. Most of the subjects of these early experiments were psychology undergraduates who, whether as paid volunteers or as part of their degree programmes, endured discomfort to advance our scientific knowledge.

A selection of findings from experimental studies conducted over this period and into the 1980s is highlighted in Table 2.1. In deciding which to include, I have drawn on authors and studies cited in the literature as having contributed to theoretical developments or clarifications. The culture of the time was to conduct and publish a series of experiments. These typically started with a preliminary hypothesis designed to test a key theoretical position. Following a review of the findings and methodology, the authors or other researchers would critique the findings, conduct further experiments to address emergent issues or ambiguities and review their theoretical relevance. Periodic review articles aided conceptual and methodological consideration. In this way, theory was fairly rapidly developed, tested, supported or falsified, and exposed to wide academic debate.

A wide range of important issues emerged from these experiments, including: the importance of predictability as a safety signal; the relationship between choice and personal control; the phenomenon of the illusion of personal control; the adaptive importance of skill and efficacy; the

Table 2.1 Experimental studies of aspects of perceived or personal control

Topic	Date	Authors	Findings and implications
Predictability and control over aversive stimuli	1943	Haggard	Series of experiments on a small group of paid college students showed that those who knew most about the conditions and took an active role in facing the delivery of electric shock consistently showed less autonomic disturbance.
Predictability and control in situations of threat	1963	Pervin	Predictability is more desirable in new and highly threatening situations (electric shock); some unpredictability is desirable in repetitive, less threatening situations.
Judgements of contingency between responses and outcomes	1965	Jenkins and Ward	People have difficulty in distinguishing between their ability to manipulate outcomes and their ability to predict them. They seem to attribute successful outcomes to their own actions in the absence of another predictable or known cause.
Review of personal control	1966a	Lefcourt	The accomplishment of tasks that require skill, compared to tasks described as requiring luck, leads to more adaptive responses (achievement orientation, self-monitoring) in terms of future expectations.
Tolerance using the cold pressor test	1966	Kanfer and Goldfoot	Tolerance greatest where subjects had control over a means of distraction. Tolerance poorest when encouraged to verbalize their sensations. Distraction has a potentially important role in improving pain tolerance.
Association between pain tolerance and control	1968	Bowers	Study based on pain theories of Beecher and Melzack. Perceived control over shock was associated with increased pain tolerance. A causal link between anxiety and pain was not supported.

Title	Year	Author	Description
Illusion of control and anxiety	1970	Geer et al.	Illusion of control (over shock) sustains the belief that the individual is not helpless, thereby providing emotional comfort and reducing physiological signs of anxiety.
Effect of choice on perceptions of noxiousness stimulus (noise)	1970	Corah and Boffa	Choice reduced reported aversive qualities of stimulus and physiological arousal. Lack of control in the form of lack of the choice to escape from an unpleasant situation leads to appraisals of threat.
Effect of prediction and control on endurance and perceived discomfort	1971	Staub et al.	Prediction and control (over shock) increased endurance and reduced ratings of self-administered discomfort (rather than escape). Control and predictability act interchangeably as safety signals to reduce threat and impact of aversive stimuli.
Effects of indirect control (over noise) on cognitive performance	1971	Glass et al.	Uncontrollability impairs subsequent cognitive function. But knowledge that one can contact someone with the power to act on one's behalf to terminate an unpleasant stimulus (proxy control) ameliorates the adverse effects.
Do individuals feel in control if they 'cause' outcomes and know what they hope to achieve?	1975	Wortman	The effects of perceived control (in games of chance) are mediated by feelings of choice and responsibility. Those randomly allocated to groups in experimental designs will view treatments more favourably if they are led to believe that they have some control over the process.
Impact of illusions of control in gambling-type situations	1975	Langer	Findings indicated that people tend to approach chance situations as if they require skill. Langer suggested that this might occur because positive outcomes are most often attributed to the action that precedes them.
Effect of positive and negative outcomes on perceptions of control	1975	Harvey and Harris	Authors claim support for hypothesis that perceived choice and expectancy of personal control is greater when the decision involves positive (enjoyable) options rather than negative options.

Table 2.1 *cont'd*

Topic	Date	Authors	Findings and implications
Effect of residential density on choice and control	1976	Rodin	Children from higher density housing took longer to learn solvable problems (this deficit was corrected by pretraining). High-density living may foster conditions in which events are perceived to be less predictable and/or controllable and thereby reduce feelings of choice and control.
Effects of perceived control over noise	1977	Sherrod *et al.*	Control over initiation and termination of noise improved performance of cognitive tasks during and after the aversive event. Perception of personal control can ameliorate the effects of aversive environments.
Effects of crowding on supermarket shopping	1977	Langer and Saegert	Shopping speed and efficiency adversely affected by crowding. Performance improved when informed about the adverse psychological effects of crowding. Information may provide individuals with explanations for adverse feelings and free them to concentrate on the task in hand.
Role of lack of control over noise on report of physical symptoms	1977	Pennebaker *et al.*	Lack of control was associated with a range of physical arousal symptoms (from checklist) – these may be labelled as emotional responses.
Effect of control over termination/continuation of noise on cognitive performance	1977	Hage *et al.*	Being able to initiate or terminate noise improved performance (proofreading). Results fit deCharms (1968) finding that originators of events perceive themselves to possess more control because they see themselves as competent manipulators of the environment.

	Year	Author(s)	Description
Effects of crowding on perceived attractiveness of neighbours	1978	Baum et al.	Students in long corridors expressed more negative views of their accommodation, interpersonal goals and feelings about neighbours. Crowding may threaten both personal control and social regulation.
Relationship between fear and control in infants	1978	Gunnar-Vongnechten	Reaction of one-year-olds to a frightening event is a function of their control over that event. Control reduces fear.
Self-control training and pain tolerance (cold pressor)	1979	Girodo and Wood	Tested the effects of self-control training, with or without task-motivational instructions (TMI), on tolerance of pain. TMI produced ceiling effects on endurance for all groups. Positive self-statements were effective, provided accompanied by a rationale to give meaning and purpose.
Effects of desire for control on illusions of control (game of chance)	1979	Burger and Cooper	Illusion of control was observed in those scoring high on desire for control, but only in anticipatory conditions. Individuals who become hooked on gambling may be those who are highly motivated to control their environments.
Influence of mood and mood induction on control beliefs	1981	Alloy et al.	Depressed students (natural and induced) gave relatively accurate judgements of having little control; non-depressed students and depressed students with induced elation showed illusions of control.
Choice and personal control	1982	Skowronski and Carlston	Individuals found to infer more personal control when positive outcomes attained as a result of behavioural choice than when attained without choice.
Developmental processes and perceived control	1982	Weisz and Stipek	Measured changes in magnitude of perceived contingency (action–outcome) and processes by which contingency judgements were formed. Younger children made absolute judgements about skill; older children tended to use social comparisons with peers to judge their own level of skill.

Table 2.1 *cont'd*

Topic	Date	Authors	Findings and implications
Control in uncontrollable situations	1983	Langer et al.	Used problem-solving under conditions focusing on process and outcome. Estimates of personal ability to achieve success were higher after consideration of strategies. Emphasis on outcomes at expense of process may foster 'mindlessness'. Process orientation emerges as superior to outcome orientation.
Effects of behavioural control over positive outcomes in captive monkeys	1985	Mineka and Hendersen	Monkeys with control over access to food, water and treats were later found to be bolder, more eager to explore novel situations and environments, and better adapted to stress. The authors considered the role of control in the development of attachment relationships, possibly due to the provision of contingent, controllable stimulation.
Control (over noise) and coronary-prone (type A) behaviour	1985	Miller et al.	Most type Bs were happy to relinquish control. Half type As preferred to retain control even though not advantageous. Remainder relinquished control to ensure better outcome, or from trust of partner. Males were more inclined to opt for control than females.
Choice and motivation in children	1986	Perlmuter et al.	Choice enhances motivation in young and older learners, though choice alone is insufficient to strengthen perceptions of control. To achieve this, choice must be meaningful, involve comparable alternatives and require some degree of effort in execution.
Causal beliefs in children	1988	Skinner et al.	Tested distinction between control beliefs (control over outcomes), agency beliefs (agent controls means or process) and means–end beliefs (certain action leads to certain outcomes). Children were able to distinguish between these three aspects of causality.

possibility of proxy (external other) control as a substitute for personal control; negative effects of crowding on personal control; and personal control, self-control training and distraction as means of enabling personal control over pain and discomfort. These findings, along with many others, have done much to inform our current understanding of the importance of personal control in health and social care settings.

Control, pain and endurance

Early studies focused predominantly on pain and stress. Indeed, most contemporary practices in the management of pain and reduction of stress in hospitals were informed by early experimental work and theory development. For example, the development of patient-controlled analgesia has been attributed to the research of Kenneth Bowers (1968; see Table 2.1). In 1973, Lefcourt confirmed, following a review of the available research, that people are more likely to tolerate aversive stimuli such as noise and pain if they believe that they have some means of terminating it or minimizing its impact. He observed: 'Endurance through hope of relief is familiar to medical settings . . . conceivably, it is the fear of unendurable pain that is debilitating' (Lefcourt 1973: 422).

By this time it had become evident that the ability to predict the occurrence of an aversive event and belief in the ability to control it can ameliorate its adverse effects. However, there remained some anomalous findings. Both Lefcourt (1973) and Averill (1973) reviewed the study of Brady *et al.* (1958), which appeared to demonstrate that 'executive' monkeys controlling the delivery of electric shock experienced more gastrointestinal problems than yoked monkeys that had no control. This was at odds with theoretical predictions of the advantages of personal control. These reviews revealed that the study and its findings were seriously flawed by the selection criteria used. But by then the Brady study had given rise to the pervasive myth of the stress-prone business executive.

The distinction between cognitive and behavioural control

Averill (1973), in his review of the literature, identified the need to distinguish between:

◆ Behavioural control: direct action to influence outcomes.
◆ Cognitive control: reinterpretation of events as less threatening.
◆ Decisional control: choice.

Thompson (1981) elaborated on the distinction between behavioural and cognitive control:

♦ Behavioural control is the belief that one has a behavioural response available that can affect the aversiveness of an event – terminate it, make it less probable or less intense, or change its duration or timing. Thompson included decisional control and choice under the heading of behavioural control.

♦ Cognitive control is the belief that one has a cognitive strategy available that can affect the perceived aversiveness of an event.

Thompson concluded that perceived behavioural control lessens anticipatory anxiety and arousal and thereby increases tolerance (though not experience) of noxious stimuli. Cognitive control reduces the immediate impact of the stimulus. The distinction between cognitive and behavioural control has therapeutic implications that are considered below in relation to information, choice, illusions of control and the relationship between cognition and action.

Folkman (1984) examined the multifaceted relationships between personal control, stress, cognitive appraisal and coping. According to her analysis, control beliefs influence primary appraisals of harm, loss, threat or challenge. The greater the situational ambiguity, the more inference is required and the greater the influence of belief systems on perceptions of controllability or uncontrollability. Secondary appraisal involves an evaluation of coping resources, influenced by outcome and efficacy expectancies (after Bandura 1977a). Folkman pointed out that control might take different forms to fulfil different objectives, including:

♦ reduce harm or enhance recovery;
♦ maintain self-esteem or positive self-image (see also Kelley and Michela 1980);
♦ avoid anxiety;
♦ maintain satisfactory relationships with others.

Folkman defined coping in terms of control: the cognitive and behavioural efforts to master, reduce or tolerate internal and/or external demands. In so doing, she distinguished between two types of coping:

♦ *Problem-solving coping*. This is used to control the troubled person–environment relationship through problem-solving, decision-making and/or direct action.
♦ *Emotion-focused coping*. This is used to control distressing emotion; for example, by altering the meaning of the outcome or by manipulating others to achieve a favourable outcome.

In essence, these types of coping are synonymous with behavioural and cognitive control.

Folkman argued that (personal) control was not always beneficial but could be a mixed blessing:

the match between the person's appraisals of controllability in a stressful encounter and the extent to which the outcome is actually controllable provides a key to understanding. An adaptive appraisal should fit reality reasonably well.

(Folkman 1984: 848)

According to Folkman, the risk of maladaptive outcomes should be greater when appraisals of controllability fail to match reality.[1] She also cited evidence that using problem-solving approaches in the face of uncontrollable situations such as chronic illness militates against acceptance.

Information and control over stressful situations

Averill (1973) distinguished between 'gaining information' that predicts events and provides a safety signal, and 'appraisal' in which the individual actively interprets or imposes meaning on events (after Lazarus 1966). Averill drew on the work of Janis who, as early as 1958, had demonstrated that surgical patients who were moderately fearful prior to surgery showed a more rapid recovery than those who were either extremely fearful or not at all fearful. Averill (1973) concluded from his review of the available literature that the relationship between stress and control is complex. It depends on the predictability and controllability of the situation, the number of choices available and the cognitive set of the individual. Averill had also proposed that there might be certain conditions in which (personal) control increases rather than decreases stress. Of particular importance, he suggested, is the desire for, or acceptance of, responsibility for decisional control and preference for information about the aversive nature of the situation. Those with little or no desire for control may be exposed to increased stress by having information thrust upon them.

Thompson (1981) linked information with predictability. Information enables people to predict the occurrence and nature of the event and the sensation likely to be experienced. Based on a review of the available evidence, she concluded:

- information used as a warning signal may lead to negative or positive outcomes, depending on the strategies and goals evoked;
- information about procedures did not appear particularly helpful;
- information about sensations appeared to reduce distress, though not necessarily symptoms such as pain;
- information about the causes of a past traumatic event appeared to be useful only if ways of participating in recovery are provided.

An important omission from the above list is the beneficial effect of information about effective ways of coping (Langer *et al.* 1975; see Table 2.2). Nevertheless, Thompson highlighted the facts that not all types of information have equal value, and information is not necessarily beneficial in all circumstances.

which they had personal control) more favourably than uncontrolled ones (those over which they had no causal influence), whether the outcome was positive or negative.[2] Wortman (1976) examined the view that people make causal attributions in order to enhance their own feelings of control over their environment. Her article contains an informed review of a number of important theoretical contributions, including Kelley's attribution theory and Lerner's 'just world theory'. She pointed out that belief in the desirability of personal control might lead individuals or society to blame or punish those who fail to control their own outcomes. Of particular interest is Wortman's review of studies by Walster in the 1960s that indicate that the more severe the outcome of an accident, the less willing people are to attribute the accident to chance.

Thompson *et al.* (1988) identified a number of problematic characteristics of perceived control:

- perceptions of control may or may not be veridical;
- available control is probabilistic, since outcomes are rarely certain;
- desired outcomes are often multidimensional (e.g. health outcomes may include self-esteem, interpersonal relationships and valued activities);
- potential benefits may be balanced by potential costs (such as financial loss, personal effort).

These, they argued, had particular relevance in such situations as chronic illness, but had received little attention. Having examined a variety of situations in which control *may* be undesirable or ineffective, Thompson *et al.* concluded that control might not be intrinsically motivating, desirable or adaptive in situations when:

- using control is difficult;
- there is insufficient information to use control effectively;
- control is contrary to preferred coping style;
- control options do not have a high probability of success or result in failure or disconfirmation of control;
- a more effective agent is available (Thompson *et al.* 1988: 81).

The authors also considered a number of particular contextual problems in health care:

- health-related behaviours often demand considerable effort;
- health outcomes are uncertain;
- compliance with medical advice may involve other risks or side-effects;
- information-giving and treatment choices frequently fail to take account of individual preferences for control.

Burger (1989) added that personal control might have negative consequences when increase in perceived control leads to a high level of concern for self-presentation. He agreed that increasing personal control in, for example, those who are sick might be unhelpful for some.

Relinquishing control

Miller (1980) suggested that although individuals generally choose to retain control over aversive stimulation, they do so only as long as they believe that their own response is the most stable factor for limiting the maximum danger to themselves. People normally choose to relinquish control at the point they believe another individual to have a more stable response for minimizing danger. Those who refuse to relinquish control under such circumstances demonstrate higher levels of anxiety and hostility. This finding is incompatible with the view that internality is best under all circumstances, but supportive of the Minimax hypothesis. This proposition also fits well with the theoretical analysis presented in Chapter 8 of this book.

Rothbaum *et al.* (1982) examined the notion that passivity, withdrawal and submissiveness are signs of relinquishing perceived control. In so doing, they distinguished between what they referred to as:

◆ *Primary control* – attempts to change the world to fit in with individual needs (this appears analogous to personal control).
◆ *Secondary control* – attempts to fit in with the world and 'go with the flow'. This may be more appropriate in situations where the individual is unable to gain primary control.

Rothbaum *et al.* challenged the simplistic definition of control as contingency between actions and outcomes and drew further distinctions between:

◆ *Predictive control* – the ability to predict whether outcomes are controllable or uncontrollable, which leads to adjustment of expectations.
◆ *Illusory control* – the individual takes or shares the credit for chance outcomes.
◆ *Vicarious control* – individuals associate themselves with powerful others and share in the glory of their control.
◆ *Interpretive control* – the individual derives meaning from, and learns to accept, otherwise uncontrollable experiences.

They drew up a table of active and passive behaviour patterns associated with each of these types of control, according to primary or secondary control processes. Each was supported by a wide-ranging review of the evidence available at that time, drawing on behavioural, cognitive, psychoanalytic and anthropological research and theory. Crucially, they considered the adaptiveness of primary and secondary control and considered how the correct balance might be determined. They argued that a distinction between primary and secondary processes and different types of control may have important therapeutic implications in terms of matching clients to interventions most likely to be adaptive in given circumstances.

Moch (1988) proposed that acceptance of lack of power over uncontrollable events may be adaptive for some people in certain health care situations. She responded to the growing literature on information-giving in health care important component of what Kobasa (1979) termed the 'hardy' personality. This represents a buffer that enables people to withstand high levels of stress without falling ill. Kobasa based her hypothesis on the work of Averill (see Averill 1973) proposing that healthier people have decisional control (exercise autonomy or discretion), cognitive control (have the ability to choose a suitable course of action) and coping skill (possess a behavioural repertoire that enables them to achieve a successful outcome). The concept of hardiness has proved a fertile source of research in health care, where it has gained some support. But it has not been without its critics, largely because of difficulties in obtaining valid and reliable measurements (Jennings and Staggers 1994).

Antonovsky (1985) introduced the term 'sense of coherence' to describe persistent beliefs in control as an adaptive characteristic of the individual. He defined coherence as: 'the enduring dynamic feeling of confidence that one's internal and external environments are predictable and that there is a high probability that things will work out as well as can reasonably be expected' (Antonovsky 1985: 123). Antonovsky referred to case studies in which people's worlds were suddenly turned upside down through environmental catastrophe or sudden illness, demanding rapid readjustment to regain sense of coherence or resulting in disintegration into helplessness or hopelessness (post-traumatic stress disorder). Some appeared better able to retain or regain a sense of coherence than others. He also provided a fascinating analysis of the importance of coherence, or rather its absence, in the development of schizophrenia. Antonovsky highlighted the importance of cross-cultural perspectives, since autonomy and control are not equally valued in all societies. He noted that, whereas Western societies emphasize the importance of personal responsibility for health, other cultures place more emphasis on collective responsibility, or are happy to hand over responsibility to shamans or gods. He also explored the relevance of childhood experiences and child-rearing patterns in the development of perceptions of autonomy and control. His work indicates that ability to resist the effects of stress depends on personality and early life experiences as well as the unpredictability or uncontrollability of the situations to which people are exposed.

Life-span influences on perceived control

Weisz and Stipek (1982) investigated the relationship between developmental processes and perceived control in relation to children. They drew attention to the possibility that young children might not distinguish between external and internal attributions, but believe they are lucky people. These authors distinguished between quantitative and qualitative changes in perceived competence. While younger children make absolute judgements about skill, older children tend to use social comparisons with peers to judge their level of skill.

Manipulation of control in institutional care settings

Two important field experiments into the effects of manipulating control among elderly people in institutional settings were reported in 1976 (Langer and Rodin 1976; Schultz 1976). Langer and Rodin (1976) sought to demonstrate that increased control would result in increased physical and mental activity, satisfaction and sociability among elderly care home residents. Control in the form of responsibility was induced in an experimental group through instructions from the home administrator. These provided increased choice, involvement in decision-making and voluntary involvement in the care of plants. Measurements were collected blind and it is stated that care staff were unaware of the experimental conditions. Compared to the control group, those with increased responsibility reported feeling happier and more active, and were rated as more alert and as spending more time on visiting others and talking to staff. They demonstrated general improvement, compared to decline in the control group.

Rodin and Langer (1977) returned after 18 months to re-evaluate the effects of their intervention. The most startling finding was that the death rate among those with induced responsibility was 15 per cent, compared to 30 per cent in the comparison group. A number of possible explanations for this were considered, including lack of randomization. If increased control was indeed the main reason for the finding, there could be little doubt that the improvement had been sustained during the interim period.

Schultz (1976) tested the impact of increased control in a similar context by providing residents with visits over which they could exert choice in terms of frequency and duration (control). Comparison groups received similar input, either with instructions about the timing and duration of visits (prediction) or no advanced warning at all (random) and there was an additional 'no visit' group (no treatment). At the end of the study period, those in both the prediction and increased control groups were found to score consistently and significantly higher on all measures of physical and psychological status, including level of activity, with little evidence of differentiation between the two conditions. Those who received random visits appeared to report higher levels of loneliness and boredom than those who received no visits.

The situation that confronted Schultz and Hanusa (1978) when they returned after 18 months contrasted dramatically with that of Rodin and Langer. The group that had been given control for the duration of the study showed substantial declines in psychological and health status following its termination. Fourteen of 20 in the predict and control group showed reduced zest for life compared with six of 20 in the no-treatment and random visits groups. The withdrawal of the visitors over whom subjects had been given control and with whom they had built a close relationship appeared inadvertently to have induced symptoms of learned helplessness. Schultz and Hanusa are perhaps to be congratulated for their bravery in publishing negative findings that serve as a strong warning to future field researchers.

Readers may care to reflect on these findings in the light of the analysis presented in Chapter 8. It is clear that, following the termination of the Schultz and Hanusa experiment, the residents in the experimental group suffered a significant loss of both support and control which was likely to make them liable to hopelessness and depression.

At the other end of the lifespan, Rodin (1986) reviewed possible mechanisms by which control and health appear to be related in later life. Citing research to indicate that those with less control complain of more physical symptoms, Rodin suggested the possibility that control (or lack of it) affects the labelling of symptoms. She identified low social status as a causal factor in both reduced sense of control and poor health, and suggested that physiological mechanisms may mediate between control and health, notably through the endocrine and immune systems. Rodin is perhaps best known for her involvement in research into the effects of control institutional settings.

The literature on control and ageing grew substantially during the 1980s and included two key edited texts (Baltes and Baltes 1986; Fry 1989). In the first of these, Lachman (1986a) presented an overview of conflicting and often contradictory findings (mostly from cross-sectional studies) concerning changes in personal control in later life (Lachman 1986a: 212–13). She concluded that the evidence favoured an association between personal control and intellectual functioning but further research was required to advance thinking on these issues. In the second text, Reid and Stirling (1989) pointed out that despite an extensive literature on psychological control, little research had focused on the process of change. They expressed alarm and dismay at the emphasis, in the literature on control and ageing, on the findings of Langer and Rodin (1976) and Schultz (1976). Having reviewed these pieces of work critically, they concluded that we still have little idea about what 'having control' means to the individuals in institutional settings. They pointed out that although instrumentalism is itself rewarding, people learn as they grow older that there are some situations or variables over which they have a lot of control and others over which they have little influence. Therefore, generalized beliefs in control are not adaptive. Older individuals may realize that there are others who have the expertise, energy or resources to help and who can be trusted to act in their best interests. In these circumstances, Reid and Stirling suggested, participatory control is preferred to the relinquishment of control. Participatory control implies that agency is negotiated and boundaries are agreed, allowing the individual to retain some decisional control. Thus Reid and Stirling emphasized the importance of partnership between professionals and patients, and patient involvement in care and decision-making.

Schultz *et al.* (1991) reviewed control and adaptive functioning across the life span, suggesting that while biological decline from middle age onwards affects ability to exercise control over important outcomes, retirement increases demands for self-initiated activities. Most individuals come to terms with biological decline and socio-cultural impoverishment associated with ageing through, they suggested, a shift from action-based strategies to cognitive strategies. They suggested that it is useful to draw the distinction (as did Antonovsky 1979) between 'having control over things' (personal control) and 'things being under control'. Schultz *et al.* suggested that action-outcome experiences in children allow the development of competence and self-efficacy beliefs but, as people grow older, they gradually become more selective in the domains over which they perceive control and more optimistic in their perceived competence within those domains. From middle age onwards, people make increasing use of secondary control strategies. As individuals approach the end of their lives they may find it helpful to focus on mental representations of past competencies rather than changing the future (see also Ross 1989). Thus, while primary control is preferred, secondary control substitutes in situations where primary control is no longer a viable option. As a result of their analysis, Schultz *et al.* recommended two further distinctions between orthogonal dimensions of control:

♦ veridical–illusory (referring to the validity of expectancy–behaviour links);
♦ functional–dysfunctional (referring to adaptive value).

They also identified the future importance of considering self-esteem maintenance, social comparison processes and self-enhancing bias mechanisms and their impact on control strategies across the life span.

More recently, Krause (1993) investigated the relationship between parental loss due to death, divorce or separation before the age of 16 and feelings of personal control among those aged 65 and over. Although no direct association was found, Krause observed an indirect effect of early parental loss on personal control, mediated by respondent education and financial strain. The findings suggest that lower levels of parental education and early parental loss erode the resources (education) needed to ensure financial security in later life and highlight the importance of ongoing socio-economic factors (alongside other life stressors) in determining perceptions of control.

Control or confusion?

A number of issues related to perceived control remain unexplained and a number of confusions remain unresolved. Wallston *et al.* (1987) presented a review of perceived control and the implications for health and distinguished between two more dimensions of control.

Control over what (see also Skinner *et al.* 1988 in Table 2.1):
♦ our behaviour and our internal states (agency) – see self-efficacy;
♦ processes (means), situations or environments;
♦ outcomes – see locus of control.

Control over time:
♦ future, present or past events.

Wallston *et al.* pointed out that whether individual differences in perceived control are state-like or trait-like had divided investigators for over 20 years. They noted that the evidence pointed to a fair degree of stability over time. Personal control is not easily manipulated in health care settings since perceptions of control over health vary depending upon whether or not outcomes are already known. Giving patients choice does not necessarily increase perceived control. Self-efficacy appears to be an important component in those with high expectations of perceived control. Wallston *et al.* concluded that health consequences are multiply determined such that personal control must operate in conjunction or interaction with other factors to produce an effect. In short, 'Perceived control may be a central psychological construct, but it does not act in isolation from other important constructs' (Wallston *et al.* 1987: 21).

The issue of causal relationships between perceived control and other variables remains somewhat confusing. For example, Arntz and Schmidt (1989) presented a theoretical model linking environmental stress with low perceived control and depression in chronic pain. In their model, they identified low pain tolerance as an independent variable, leading to decreased motivation to learn controlling responses, and hence chronic pain and depression. Yet it is equally possible that low pain tolerance is a result of lack of perceived control over uncontrollable pain. These different causal assumptions can have profound implications for research designs and for the ways in which patients are treated and labelled within the health care system.

Another important issue is that of terminology. Reid and Stirling (1989) commented on

the proliferation of control-related constructs . . . with a growing list of terms including: internal–external locus of control, controllability, cognitive control, learned helplessness, personal efficacy, secondary control, primary control, personal causation, proxy control, illusory control, mindlessness–mindfulness, powerlessness and empowerment.

This led them to ask: 'would the real control please stand up?' (Reid and Stirling 1989: 220). Zuckerman *et al.* (1996) highlighted a range of words commonly used to describe control or perceived control and reviewed the terminology used by various authors. Based on these and other sources, terms commonly associated with control and control beliefs are given in Table 2.2.

Measuring perceived or personal control

It is questionable whether there is a need at all for a measure of perceived (personal) control. If perceived control refers to perceived control over outcomes, then a measure of internal locus of control (see Chapter 3) is adequate. If it refers to control over action, a measure of self-efficacy (see Chapter 4) will suffice. Indeed, most studies of perceived and/or personal control have tended to use locus of control or self-efficacy measures. One attempt to measure personal control is the 'Beliefs in Personal Control over Life' scale (Krause 1993). This consists of just three items that reflect a global assessment of ability to influence the course events in respondents' lives and appears to combine internal locus of control with self-efficacy. The items reflect:

1 Life will work out the way respondent wants.
2 When respondent plans ahead, things work out as expected.
3 Respondent can run his or her own life the way he or she wants (Krause 1993: 980).

There are two other approaches worth mentioning. First, it might be expected from the work of Skinner (1985), Rothbaum *et al.* (1982) and others that personal control is an active process. Therefore, individuals who demonstrate a sense of personal control would be expected to make use of active, as opposed to passive, coping strategies (see Table 2.2). The Vanderbilt Pain Management Inventory was designed and tested with rheumatoid arthritis patients as a measure of active and passive coping (Brown and Nicassio 1987). As predicted, active coping strategies were found to be associated with less pain, depression and functional impairment. The correlation with internal health locus of control was significant though modest.

Second, it has been suggested that not all people share the same desire for personal control. It may therefore be relevant in health care to assess individual desire for control. Measures of desire for control are given in Table 2.3.

Table 2.2 Concepts and definitions commonly associated with control (actual or perceived)

Concepts associated with personal control	Concepts associated with lack of personal control	Reference
Internal locus of control	External locus of control	Rotter (1966)
Active control/coping	Passive control/coping	Brown et al. (1989a)
Mastery	Incompetence	White and Janson (1986)
Action	Inaction	Skinner (1985)
Does things for self	Relies on others	Miller (1979)
Self-care	Dependent care	Orem (1995)
Instrumentalism	Fatalism	Mirowsky and Ross (1990)
Behavioural control	Cognitive control (cognitive reinterpretation)	Averill (1973)
Primary control, including predictive, anticipatory control	Secondary control, including vicarious, illusory control, interpretive control	Rothbaum et al. (1982)
Problem-focused coping	Emotion-focused coping	Folkman (1984)
Mindfulness	Mindlessness	Piper and Langer (1986)
Personal control	Uncontrol	Moch (1988)
Coherence	Disintegration	Antonovsky (1985)
Autonomy	Alienation	Seeman and Seeman (1983)

Table 2.3   Measures of desire for control

Author(s)	Date	Title	Details
Burger and Cooper	1979	The Desirability of Control Scale (DC) (complete scale given in text p. 384)	20-item scale, including: 'When it comes to orders, I would rather give them than receive them'; 'I try to avoid situations where someone else tells me what to do.'
Reid and Ziegler	1980, 1981	Desire for Control (full scales given, 1981, pp. 153–7)	35 items plus short-form 16 items. Two components: desire for outcomes (importance) and beliefs and attitudes (extent to which the individual believes he or she can obtain these outcomes).
Wallston *et al.*	1983	Desire for Control of Health Care (DCON)	General scale related to health care. Scale not given.
Krantz *et al.*	1980	Krantz Health Opinion Survey (p. 980)	Two subscales: information and behavioural involvement, consisting of 7 and 9 items respectively.

Wallston *et al.* (1983) compared their Desire for Control of Health Care (DCON) scale with the Burger and Cooper DC Scale and the Krantz Health Opinion Survey for use in preparation for childbirth and a group concerning preparation for death and dying. The Krantz Health Opinion Survey emerged as the most consistent discriminator of desire for control in health settings.

Health applications

Table 2.4 contains a selection of studies in applied settings, together with some additional review papers. These illustrate some of the different methodologies and approaches used to investigate personal control and are presented in chronological order. I have made no attempt to offer a critique of these but would draw attention to at least two important issues. First is the apparent lack of theoretical clarity about what is meant by perceived control. Does it refer only to personal control and, if so, does this imply personal control over causation, actions and/or outcomes? Second is the

Table 2.4 Selected studies and reviews of perceived control and health

Topic	Date	Authors	Methods used	Findings
Reduction of psychological stress in surgical patients	1975	Langer et al.	Experimental design involving presentation of cognitive coping strategy, preparatory information and controls. Dependent measures included single item anxiety rating scale and nurses' behavioural ratings.	Patients who received information about coping scored higher on stress tolerance, required less analgesics and sedatives. There was a non-significant trend in favour of shorter hospital stay. Procedural information produced no benefits.
Control and mental handicap	1979	Houts et al.	Experimental design. Staff asked to develop action plan for clients. Responses involved: reward/punishment; positive/negative attitude towards controlling behaviour.	Staff attitudes influenced the traits ascribed to clients. When control is viewed negatively, clients are seen as uncooperative. Clients rewarded for behaviour of which staff disapprove are seen an ungrateful. Staff expectations may influence client behaviour.
Responses of blood donors to information and choice	1979	Mills and Krantz	Experimental design: choice manipulation conditions involved low information – low choice, low info. – high choice; high info. – low choice and high info. – high choice. Dependent variables included ratings of pain, discomfort and anxiety.	Both information and choice reduced distress, though these treatments did not combine to give additive effects.
Personal control over activities versus personal control over outcomes	1982	Bazerman	Experimental design involving proofreading task to test congruence between environmental opportunities (pay with or without bonus) and	Congruence was found to lead to improved performance. The logic of this thesis is that increasing job demands (e.g. by providing incentive bonuses) to exceed the performance capabilities of the individual

Title	Year	Authors	Description	Findings
			ability to use control (personal control). Subjects students.	will result in decreased, rather than increased, performance.
Longitudinal study of correlates of changes in desired control	1983	Ziegler and Reid	Longitudinal study of elderly Jewish residents admitted to a sheltered community with facilities for a wide range of social and occupational activities.	Desired control was found to be associated with staff ratings of control (independence, initiative, assertiveness) and vitality (zest for living, happy). Changes in desired control over time were predicted by self-reported activity (socializing, gardening, reading and walking).
Perceived control and diabetes	1986	Dobbins and Eaddy	Patient survey. Investigated relationship between mood (POMS), perceived life control and metabolic control.	Negative mood, health behaviours and perceived life control accounted for 40% of variance of in HbA1c (glycosylated haemoglobin).
Personal control, meaninglessness and drug use in adolescents	1986	Newcomb and Harlow	Survey of school and college students. Measures included uncontrollable stress events, perceived loss of control (novel tool), meaninglessness and substance use.	Perceived loss of control and meaningless mediated between uncontrollable stressful life events and drug use in the younger but not the older sample. Interventions that focus on increasing perceptions of control might be efficacious prior to, or in the early stages of, drug use, but alternative approaches required once a drug habit is acquired.
Choice and motivation	1986	Perlmuter *et al.*	Series of experiments with children.	Choice enhances motivation in young and older learners, though choice alone is insufficient to strengthen perceptions of control. To achieve this, choice must be meaningful, involve comparable alternatives and require some degree of effort in execution.

Table 2.4 *cont'd*

Topic	Date	Authors	Methods used	Findings
Rheumatoid arthritis	1987	Affleck et al.	Patient study using daily pain diary to examine relationship between control appraisals, illness predictability, pain, psychosocial adjustment (Arthritis Impact Measurement Scale), mood (POMS) and illness status.	Perceived personal control over medical care and treatment, rather than the disease process itself, was associated with positive mood and psychosocial adjustment. Recommended active partnership between health professionals and patients.
Perceived control and chronic pain	1989	Arntz and Schmidt	Review and theoretical model.	Loss of physical functioning combined with unrealistic expectations of total pain relief and consequent failure to learn pain coping strategies serve to perpetuate feelings of loss of control.
Coping with disaster	1989	Solomon et al.	Epidemiological study focused on 1982 Missouri flood victims participating in NIMH. Post-disaster distress varied according to type of exposure and explanations for misfortune.	In contrast to other studies, self-blame was associated with more distress, possibly because it interfered with help seeking from relief agencies. Findings indicate that context is an important variable.
Health promotion	1989	Peterson and Stunkard	Review of concepts and research applied to health promoting activities.	

Topic	Year	Author	Methodology	Findings
Patient information	1990	Dennis	Q-methodology.	Understanding diagnosis, treatment and lifestyle implications were central to cognitive control. Patients varied in their desire for control.
Marriage	1991	Ross	Used data from 1985 Illinois Survey of Well-Being. Eight perceived control items included.	All else equal, marriage decreases women's sense of control but not men's. The economic advantage of marriage is, for women, at the expense of personal control. Sense of control declined with age at an accelerating rate. Minority groups had a lower sense of control allowing for education and income.
Chronic pain	1991	Jensen and Karoly	Telephone interviews with pain clinic patients. Examined pain control appraisals, coping strategies, psychological and social functioning.	Personal control over pain and pain management strategies were positively related to activity level and well-being.
Professional attitudes to patient control over dying	1993	Kelner and Bourgeault	Examined the views of health professionals using qualitative methods.	Most salient was their reluctance to give up clinical discretion in the face of patients' wishes to make decisions about their fate. Increased control for patients was seen to reduce control for staff.
Maintaining perceived control in low-control circumstances (cancer)	1993	Thompson et al.	Correlational study based on telephone interviews. Measures included marital satisfaction, functional impairment, CES-D (depression) and nine-item perceived control scale constructed for the study.	Patients reported less depression and anxiety if they perceived themselves to have control over emotional reaction and physical symptoms, had medical information, had a good relationship with family and friends and, but less importantly, physical recovery from cancer.

tendency to use measures designed for specific studies, resulting in dubious validity and reliability.

Concluding comments

Overall, the concept of perceived personal control appears to have had a profound impact on health care in the late twentieth century. Patient information-giving, patient involvement in decision-making, self-care and 'empowerment' all owe much to the research referred to in this chapter. However, there remain significant gaps in our knowledge. Not all people want control and not all benefit from personal control in all circumstances, particularly when they are ill. Therefore, the routine provision of standard-ized information may have an adverse effect on some people. We still need a better understanding of situations in which giving and receiving informa-tion and choice is most beneficial, methods of identifying those most likely to benefit from increased control and ways of negotiating the balance of control between patients and professionals. The need to distinguish between control over outcome and control over process has been highlighted. Some of these issues are addressed in the following two chapters, on locus of control and self-efficacy.

Notes

1 This assertion is challenged by findings that illusions of control are common in psychologically healthy individuals (for example, see Taylor and Brown 1988).
2 Though the study by Harvey and Harris (1975) – see Table 2.1 – cast some doubt on this observation.
3 Reid and Stirling (1989) – see section on lifespan influences on perceived control.
4 Langer used these findings to argue that competitions should involve skill rather than chance.

Further reading

Baltes, M. M. and Baltes, P. B. (eds) (1986) *The Psychology of Control and Aging.* Hillsdale, NJ: Erlbaum.
DeCharms, R. (1981) Personal causation and locus of control: two different traditions and two uncorrelated measures, in H. M. Lefcourt (ed.) *Research with the Locus of Control Construct. Volume 1, Assessment Methods.* New York: Academic Press, pp. 337–58.
Fry, P. S. (ed.) (1989) *Psychological Perspectives of Helplessness and Control in the Elderly.* Amsterdam North-Holland.
Langer, E. J. (ed.) (1983) *The Psychology of Control.* Beverly Hills, CA: Sage.
Contains a number of original and seminal applied research papers on control.

Perlmuter, L. C. and Monty, R. A. (eds) (1979) *Choice and Perceived Control*. Hillsd... NJ: John Wiley.
Contains chapters by a number of important theorists, including DeCharms, Langer and Phares. Also contains chapters relating to locus of control and learned helplessness.

Schultz, R., Heckhausen, J. and Locher, J. L. (1991) Adult development, control and adaptive functioning. *Journal of Social Issues*, 47(4): 177–96.
Review of control across the life span, including age differences.

Wallston, K. A. (1997) Perceived control and health behaviour, in A. Baum, S. Newman, J. Weinman, R. West and C. McManus (eds) *Cambridge Handbook of Psychology, Health and Medicine*. Cambridge: Cambridge University Press.

Wallston, K. A., Wallston, B. S., Smith, S. and Dobbins, C. J. (1987) Perceived control and health. *Current Psychology – Research and Reviews*, 6(1): 5–25.

Locus of control

Overview of contents

Definitions and conceptual origins

Locus of control refers to a relatively stable set of beliefs, held by an individual, about the likely causal relationships between their actions, and those of others, and the outcomes of events and situations. The key distinction between the concept of personal control and that of locus of control is that the former is concerned exclusively with personal ability to 'do something' (Lefcourt 1982) and with personal motivation (DeCharms 1968). Locus of control is equally concerned with beliefs about the influence of external forces on outcomes. The concept of locus of control has its origins in social learning theory (Phares 1976). Rotter (1975) defined social learning theory as a theory of personality that attempts to integrate stimulus–response or reinforcement theory on one hand and cognitive theories on the other. Unlike the deterministic assumptions of the behaviourism of B. F. Skinner, social learning theory recognizes a capacity for self-direction and self-regulatory processes (Bandura 1977a). More recently, locus of control in relation to health has been subsumed within models of social cognition (see Conner and Norman 1995a).

The development of the concept of locus of control is also linked with social psychology through attribution theory. Attribution theory is fundamentally concerned with understanding cause–effect relationships and the formulation of causal inferences (Heckhausen and Weiner 1974). Fritz Heider is frequently credited with being the founding father of attribution theory, though it is of interest to note that many of Heider's own references (Heider 1944) are to the work of Kurt Lewin from the 1930s and to other German sources. According to Weiner (1990), attribution theory, proposed by Heider and later elaborated by Harold Kelley (see Kelley 1973), became the dominant paradigm in social psychology in the 1970s. Heider (1944) described how, just as we attribute the movement of an object to internal or external forces, we locate the origins of our own experiences within ourselves, or other people, or fate. Heider later formed the view that cognitive psychology is founded on 'the idea that our cognitions, expectations and actions are based on a mastery of the causal network of the environment' (Heider 1958: 59). According to Heider, knowledge of the basic constituents of action enables us to interpret that action and predict and control it. In terms of environmental events, we need to identify whether these are controllable (in which case we must take action to prevent or modify them) or uncontrollable (in which case we must seek to avoid them). In terms of the actions of others, we need to be able to infer their intentions towards us in order to know how to respond. Heider pointed out how often, in social perception, 'acts or products are colored by the qualities of the person to whom they are ascribed' (Heider 1944: 364). Heider's analysis focused on 'can' aspects of personal motivation, including ability, effort (trying), task difficulty, needs, intention, responsibility and dealing with hostile others (Heider 1958). This work has had substantial influence on subsequent attribution theorists, notably Bernard Weiner in the field of achievement motivation. Weiner's work, though important and influential in theoretical terms, is perhaps less well recognized in the field of health psychology.

Julian Rotter is the name most commonly associated with the origin of the concept of locus of control, largely because of his development of the Internal–External Scale as a personality variable (Rotter 1966) and applications in the field of health. Rotter was an established figure in the field of social learning theory by the mid-1950s. But Weiner (1990) noted the curious independence of Rotter and Heider, who, in spite of shared origins and interests, failed to cite each other's work. In fact it was Jerry Phares who, through his doctoral research supervised by Rotter, initiated work on the measurement of internal–external control, introduced the term 'locus of control' and set control in a social learning theory framework (Phares 1957, 1990; Rotter et al. 1961; Lefcourt 1966b). Phares (1976) described how his interest in the control construct came about through clinical observations in the field of mental health. He explained how, at that time, 'hints of the [locus of control] concept had been suggested in earlier social learning theory research' (Phares 1976: 5, footnote). Rotter (1966) did not use the term 'locus of control', but persisted in referring to 'generalized expectancy for internal–external control'. He defined expectancy as 'the probability held by the individual that a particular reinforcement will occur as a function of a specific behaviour on his part in a specific situation or situations' (Rotter 1954: 17). The key variables in his social learning theory are:

♦ Expectancy – the subjective probability held by an individual that a particular reinforcement will occur as a function of a specific behaviour.
♦ Reinforcement value – the importance of the reinforcement to the individual.
♦ Psychological situation – contextual cues.

According to Rotter (1966: 1) external control refers to perceptions that an event is contingent upon luck, fate, chance, powerful others or unpredictable forces. Internal control refers to beliefs that the event is contingent upon one's own behaviour or relatively permanent characteristics.

The concept of locus of control proved fertile ground for experimental studies, most of which involved university students, as well as applied research. These are far too numerous to mention here, though a summary of some early relevant studies is given in Table 3.1. These are based on I–E (internal–external) scales developed by Phares, James and Rotter, or derived from these (e.g. Bialer 1961). The Rotter scale is the best known and most widely used to this day. Many of the early studies were applied in socio-cultural contexts that have obvious relevance to health psychology but appear more recently to have been somewhat neglected.

For those interested, Throop and MacDonald (1971) published an exhaustive bibliography related to internal–external locus of control to that date. According to Weiner (1990), from the 1960s onwards locus of control took on a life of its own and began to be associated with good–bad evaluations. It was thought adaptive to be internal, since this was associated with motivational drives towards information-seeking and problem-solving, and 'bad' to be an external.

Theory development

Control and motivation

Doctoral studies by James and Phares at the Ohio State University in the 1950s indicated that beliefs about the causes of success or failure (whether due to chance or skill) had systematic effects on future expectations about outcomes. As a result, Rotter *et al.* (1961) asserted that it was logical to

Table 3.1 Examples of early research using locus of control

Topic	Date	Authors	Overview
Development of LOC in mentally retarded and normal children	1961	Bialer	PhD study. Adapted scale from those constructed by Phares and James. Found ability to conceptualize success and failure, though slower to mature in mentally retarded children, was not qualitatively different.
Effects of ethnicity and social class on control beliefs	1963	Battle and Rotter	Used the Bialer scale. Identified an interaction between social class and ethnicity such that lower-class children were generally more external than middle-class children, while black children with higher IQs tended to show a higher level of externality than white middle-class children with lower IQs.
Information-seeking	1967	Davis and Phares	Found that university students rated as internal using the I–E scale were more likely to actively engage in information seeking than those rated as external.
Gender	1967	Feather	Young first-year female students were more likely to score high on externality than older women or men. Postulated that this may reflect a more dependent role among late adolescent females in American culture.
Gender	1968	McGhee and Crandall	Studied locus of control among high school students and reported gender differences. Girls' performance was consistently related to instrumental attributions for successes and failures while boys' performance was consistently related to beliefs in responsibility for failure.

Table 3.1 *cont'd*

Topic	Date	Authors	Overview
Motivation and games	1968	Julian *et al.*	Examined motivational aspects of I–E in games and found that internals have a higher need to control, resulting in frustration when control was blocked.
Accident and suicide-proneness	1969	Williams and Nickels	Predicted that accident-proneness would be negatively correlated, and suicide-proneness (attempted or threatened suicides) positively correlated, with externality. Both found to be associated with externality. Various explanations proffered – good example of *post hoc* justifications and difficulty in predicting associations in real-life contexts.
Attitude change	1969 1970	Ritchie and Phares Hjelle and Clouser	Examined differences in attitude change as a function of I–E. Both confirmed that externals are more susceptible to attitude change. Ritchie and Phares found that opinions of externals were more likely to change in response to high-prestige sources, while internals appeared to pay more attention to content of communication which supported their previously held opinions.
Psychiatric treatment	1970	Smith	Demonstrated predicted increase in internality among those receiving psychiatric treatment following life crisis, indicating that therapeutic interventions may influence control beliefs.

assume that internals would show more overt striving for achievement than those who felt they had little control over their environment. Experimental evidence tended to support this. Nevertheless, the person most closely associated with work on locus of control and motivation is Weiner for his work on achievement motivation. Weiner *et al.* (1972) reviewed the role of locus of control as a mediator between stimulus conditions and achievement-related behaviour. Their findings appeared to confirm the following:

- achievement motivation is mediated by attributions of success to internal factors (personal effort);
- persistence in the face of failure is mediated by attributions of outcome to unstable factors (lack of effort or bad luck);
- tasks of intermediate difficulty elicited more effort, than tasks of high or low difficulty.

Based on this, Weiner (1974b) presented a conceptual analysis of locus of control (see Table 3.2) in which he argued in favour of two dimensions – causal stability and expectancy of success – the latter influencing affective responses to success and failure. His approach was strongly influenced by Heider's attribution theory and Atkinson's expectancy-value theory of motivation (Weiner 1990). Weiner used the unidimensional concept of locus of control also favoured by Rotter.

Weiner *et al.* (1972) argued that locus of control and stability dimensions had been confounded in the literature on locus of control. They proposed that persistence in the face of failure is mediated by attributions of outcomes to unstable factors such as lack of effort and bad luck, rather than stable factors such as lack of ability. Based on manipulation of reasons for failure, Weiner and Sierad (1975) confirmed that causal beliefs precede and, in part, determine subsequent action. They claimed that their findings were incompatible with the alternative proposition that attitudes are inferred on the basis of observing one's own behaviour (i.e. that thoughts are by-products of behaviour). Weiner's contribution to research into the concept of locus of control and achievement motivation can only be described as prodigious. Weiner (1990) described his own contributions to attribution theory as emphasizing

Table 3.2 Perceived determinants of achievement

Stability	*Locus of control*	
	Internal	*External*
Stable	Ability	Task difficulty
Unstable	Effort	Luck

Source: Weiner (1974b: 107).

dimensions or properties other than causality, notably those of stability and controllability. Given the relevance of Weiner's work to education, it is interesting to note that his work appears to have had little, if any, impact on health education. An important reason may be that the tasks commonly used in the experimental situations used by Weiner and others are relatively uncomplicated and feedback about outcomes is immediate. Health outcomes, in addition to being unpredictable when applied to an individual (as opposed to populations), are rarely if ever immediate. Indeed, people who change health-related behaviours often feel worse before they start to feel better. Such variables may need to be taken into account when judging the significance of control beliefs to health behaviour change.

Locus of causality

Locus of causality has received relatively little attention in the literature on control. This is perhaps surprising, since an experience of personal control over an outcome then becomes an experience of personal causation. DeCharms (1968) distinguished between origins, those who perceive themselves as determined by their own choosing, and pawns, those who perceive their behaviour as determined by external forces, including other people. It appears difficult to distinguish between this concept and that of locus of control, though DeCharms (1981) identified these as two different traditions. He developed a measure of 'origin' by a complex method of scoring stories told by participants about prescribed scenarios. Little relationship was found between origin scores and locus of control scores with respect to academic achievement. This probably reflects the methodology used, but may also highlight potential differences between test scores on locus of control and the ways people talk about personal responsibility in everyday life.

Skinner and Chapman (1984) distinguished between beliefs about:

- ◆ Control – the expectation of producing the intended outcome, controllability.
- ◆ Causality – that certain conditions lead to particular outcomes.
- ◆ Agency – as in the concept of self-efficacy (see Chapter 4), belief in the ability to effect appropriate action.

Skinner and Connell (1986) presented a framework for the development of individual differences and age-related changes in control understanding (people's generalized perceptions about the causes of desired and undesired outcomes in their lives). They emphasized that control understanding refers to knowledge about the causes of outcomes, rather than the causes of the behaviour itself: an understanding of why something happens to me, not why I do something. Similarly, Marshall (1991) sought to distinguish between contingency recognition (knowing that a particular outcome depends on a particular course of action) and personal mastery recognition (the ability to produce the desired outcome), as in Bandura's concept of self-efficacy. Thus it appears that knowledge of causality involves knowledge of context, process, agency and outcome.

Control and adjustment

Many early studies appear to support the view that internal–external orientation is linked to adjustment (see Table 3.1). These studies indicate that, despite gender and other differences, internals are more achievement motivated. Joe (1971) found evidence that depicted externals as relatively anxious, aggressive, dogmatic, less trustful and more suspicious of others, lacking in self-confidence and having low needs for social approval (though this latter characteristic is difficult to reconcile with the analysis presented in Chapter 8). There was some support for Rotter's (1966) predictions that those at extreme ends of the scale are less well adjusted than those scoring in the middle range. Evidence supported ethnic, social class and gender differences in locus of control. Joe concluded that, at that time, further research was required to improve the I–E scale and develop theoretical links between locus of control and other variables.

In a review of the relationship between locus of control and responses to stress, Lefcourt (1982) examined differences in reactions to life-threatening situations and hospitalization. He found evidence that internals make better use of problem-solving in situations of threat, including the use of social support, and experience less depression and anxiety. Beliefs in the hand of God are more likely than the belief 'God helps those who help themselves' to be associated with helplessness and eventually hopelessness and despair in the face of life-threatening events (Lefcourt 1982: 101).[1] In reviewing the role of fatalistic beliefs in mental illness, Lefcourt drew attention to the chicken–egg nature of the problem and concluded that the relationship is probably perpetuated through a vicious cycle.

Control, development and social influence

Joe (1971) reported on several studies that had examined the influence of parent–child relationships and the child's locus of control, indicating that supportive parenting styles (based on warmth, approval, flexibility, consistency, encouraging independence) were associated with internality, while controlling styles (rejecting, punishing, dominating, critical) were associated with externality. MacDonald (1971) confirmed and clarified this relationship (see Table 3.1), but also noted important gender differences. Internality in males was associated with maternal predictability of standards and paternal physical punishment, while internality in girls was associated with maternal achievement pressure. Externality in males was associated with maternal affective punishment (nagging, scolding, making them feel guilty and ashamed). In referring to research into the origins of locus of control within the family context, Lefcourt (1982) concluded that internality is associated with an environment in which children receive warmth and attention, and critical but fair feedback on good and bad performance, and are encouraged to take personal responsibility from an early age. He noted further evidence that membership of lower socio-economic and minority ethnic groups tended to be associated with externality, suggestive that an environment of poverty and deprivation creates a climate of fatalism and helplessness in which there is minimal perceived contingency between quality of effort and quality of reward.

Lefcourt (1982) reviewed a vast research literature, together with many social and literary observations, in describing the development and refinement of the concept of control. As with other post-war psychologists, Lefcourt was particularly interested to explain man's apparent willingness to act in a barbaric manner towards his fellow men. Lefcourt sought to explain findings from studies of conformity and compliance by reviewing evidence that external control beliefs are associated with submission to peer pressure. He concluded that externality is associated with the surrender of a sense of responsibility, which leaves people open to manipulation by authoritarian dictates. It seems reasonable, on this basis, to assume that internals make natural dictators. In contrast, Goodstadt and Hjelle (1973) provided evidence that externals were more likely to use coercive power than internals, who relied more on persuasive powers.

From an early stage, Rotter (1966) drew attention to the potentially culture-specific nature of assumptions about the primacy of internal control. Lefcourt (1966a) drew attention to the political implications of such assumptions for ethnic minorities (Lefcourt 1966a: 218). Lefcourt (1966b) also reviewed the significance of internal–external control in understanding psychopathology. Based on studies that included schizophrenics, children and tuberculous patients, he concluded that:

> external-control orientation characterizes groups that are marginal in our society . . . In general, internal-control individuals learn more and behave in ways that would facilitate personal control more than external-control persons.
>
> (Lefcourt 1966b: 189–90)

On the other hand, Hjelle (1971) challenged the meaning of locus of control outside Western cultures. He suggested that the endorsement of internal statements might reflect social desirability, rather than personal preference, because attributes of independence and industriousness are valued within American culture.

Internality–externality and health care

A useful overview of the origins of research into health locus of control is given by Lau (1982). The establishment of links between beliefs about control and health-related behaviours goes back to about 1960. Strickland (1978) reviewed a range of studies that identified that internals are more likely to engage in preventive behaviours to improve their health, such as giving up smoking, obtaining vaccination, using birth control and reducing their weight. Strickland identified evidence that internals adapt better to debilitating illness and that externality is associated with mental health problems. She concluded that beliefs about locus of control of reinforcement appear to be influential in relation to health. Lefcourt reported on research evidence that internals are 'more inquisitive, more curious and efficient processes of information than are externals' (Lefcourt 1982: 80). From this it follows that internals are more likely to require information and explanations in health care settings.

Strickland (1978) identified a number of problems at that time. It was evident from published results that the I–E concept was, at best, very limited in terms of its power to explain health-related behaviours. In particular, she emphasized the need for reinforcement value (in this case health value) to be measured in conjunction with I–E in order to increase its predictive power. Rotter (1975) had previously highlighted the value not just of the act of gaining control, but of perceived outcomes: 'without doubt, the most frequent conceptual problem on the part of a number of investigators is the failure to treat reinforcement value as a separate variable' (Rotter 1975: 59). It is self-evident that people are likely to make more effort to achieve a highly desired outcome. Health value is now widely recognized to be an important variable in studies that seek to link locus of control beliefs with health-related behaviour (see Norman and Bennett 1995).

Strickland (1978) observed methodological weaknesses in I–E health research, including the correlational nature of the research and lack of controls. She also argued that the proliferation of I–E measures had affected the interpretation and comparability of findings. Social desirability bias was thought to be problematic, particularly when used in clinical settings where patients are anxious to please, and variables such as socio-cultural background, race, gender and political ideology may also lead to social response bias. She noted that while internal orientation may generally lead to improved health practices, it is only appropriate where events are actually controllable, but not in situations which are uncontrollable and help-seeking beneficial. Nevertheless, Strickland (1978) noted the practical utility of I–E assessment for health personnel acting as change agents in order to assist in tailoring interventions, such as information-giving, to meet individual needs.

Dimensionality and locus of control

By the early 1970s, more researchers had begun to challenge the notion of locus of control as a unidimensional concept. Mirels (1970) identified two independent factors:

1 Beliefs that personally relevant outcomes are attributable to ability and hard work, as opposed to external forces.
2 Acceptance or rejection of the idea that the individual can influence political and world affairs.

It is important to note that the proportion of variance explained by the combination of these two factors was less than 20 per cent and would not appear, therefore, to represent a good fit to the data. There followed a series of studies challenging the unidimensional concept and proposing anything between two and five factors, based on factor analysis (see Table 3.3). Watson (1981: 320–1) reviewed the findings of studies that had examined the factor structure of the Rotter I–E scale from 1970 to 1977. The number of interpretable factors ranged from two to five. This favoured the abandonment of the Rotter scale in favour of situation-specific, multidimensional scales. Nevertheless, the Rotter I–E scale continued to be widely used.

The emergence of IPC (internal, powerful others, chance) scales

Hanna Levenson (1973a) reasoned that those who believe that the world is unordered (due to chance) behave differently from those who believe that the world is controlled by powerful others. The distinction was particularly relevant to social action. She tested a modified version of Rotter's (1966) scale that distinguished between three dimensions of control beliefs: internal, powerful others and chance (Levenson 1973a: 401). Her sample included psychiatric patients (those with schizophrenia, paranoia, depression and neurotic disorders) as well as normal individuals. Factor analysis yielded eight factors that accounted for 61 per cent of the variance. The first two reflected powerful others and chance and the third included four items related to personal ability/effort in obtaining desired outcomes. Levenson opted for the three-factor solution. As predicted, schizophrenics demonstrated highest chance scores, while paranoids and schizophrenics scored highest on powerful others. Her findings demonstrated increases in internality as a result of hospitalization among the psychiatric group, but little difference in scores on powerful others or chance.

Levenson (1973b) confirmed the existence of gender differences. Males, but not females, who were helped and taught by their mothers had higher internal scores. Girls who perceived that their mothers did not worry about them had higher internal scores than those whose mothers were protective. Lack of parental nurturance was related to beliefs in powerful others and chance, but not internality, suggesting that an absence of supportive behaviours is related to beliefs in an unordered and oppressive world. Parental demanding, affective and physical punishment and controlling behaviours were all related to beliefs in powerful others. Unpredictability of standards was related to chance but not to powerful others. Deprivation of privileges was related, in males, to chance control.

Levenson (1974) presented a revised three-dimensional IPC locus of control measure, each scale consisting of eight items involving a person-ideological stance, measured using a six-point Likert format (Levenson 1974: 381–2). She reported low correlations with social desirability, moderately high internal consistency and test–retest reliability. Items were formulated and included on ideological grounds. Factor analysis identified seven possible factors, based on eigenvalues greater than one, of which the first three represented I, P and C. These three factors were represented by 17 of the 24 items and jointly accounted for 32 per cent of the total variance. No attempt was made to refine the measure any further.

Despite these developments, Rotter (1975: 57) continued to support locus of control as a unidimensional concept:

> When a reinforcement is perceived by the subject as following some action of his own but not being entirely contingent upon his action, then, in our culture, it is typically perceived as the result of luck, chance, fate, as under the control of powerful others, or as unpredictable because of the great complexity of the forces surrounding him.

He asserted that Levenson's scales were not independent since they demonstrated relatively high intercorrelation.

In 1981, Levenson presented an overview of data collected from a wide range of groups (e.g. students, adults, elderly, psychiatric, disabled and pain patients, prisoners, alcoholics), using the original or situation-specific IPC scales between 1972 and 1979 (Levenson 1981: 19–21). She raised an important point with respect to the powerful other dimension which, she observed, was viewed by most groups as referring to those who thwarted attempts at mastery and control, rather than those who were facilitative or benevolent. This distinction is an important one when considering patients' views of powerful figures in health care.

Locus of control as personality trait or belief set

Phares (1976) argued that much I–E research had been limited because it was carried out with little regard to its relationship to other variables. He reviewed evidence that externals may be more susceptible to conformance to social influence, more anxious, less well adjusted and more likely to be depressed, though locus of control may change over time in response to situational change. Phares held that:

> Belief in personal control (or lack of it), is both a general disposition that influences individuals' behaviour across a wide range of situations and a rather specific belief that may apply to a limited number of

situations. For example, while people may generally subscribe to the notion that they have only restricted control over their lives, they nevertheless may feel that in some specific situations they can exert much control.

(Phares 1976: 25)

Lefcourt (1982) did not accept locus of control as a fixed personality trait and reviewed evidence in favour of responsiveness to change in the face of naturally occurring events, highlighting the importance of action-oriented therapeutic interventions. Of particular relevance, he cited studies indicating that the acquisition of social and work-related skills leads to measurable increases in internality and identified the need for further studies into the long-term effects, if any, of such interventions. Lefcourt argued in favour of locus of control as a mediating variable in the ways individuals view themselves as having some causal role in determining *specified events*, and one of many interacting variables that are likely to influence behaviour. According to Lefcourt, people should not be classified as internal or external, but may be said to 'hold internal and external control expectancies about different aspects of their lives' (Lefcourt 1982: 187). These debates supported the development of situation-specific locus of control measures.

It is noticeable from applications of locus of control in health care that measures have gradually become more specific (see Table 3.3). General measures have been adapted as measures of health locus of control, which have in turn been adapted to address specific conditions or disorders. As discussed in Chapter 2, health interventions are frequently aimed at per-suading people to take more responsibility for their own health. While expectancies of control over a specific situation or task may fairly easily be changed (see Chapter 4), it might be expected that the success or failure of a health promotion or education strategy will be more dependent on the extent of generalized expectancies of control. Those with generalized external control expectancies are less likely to desire or assume personal control. This has important implications for changing the health-related behaviour of those from disadvantaged socio-economic groups.

Multidimensional health locus of control

The late 1970s saw the development of the first health-specific locus of control measures by Barbara and Ken Wallston.[2] Wallston *et al.* (1976a) published their unidimensional health locus of control (HLC) scale and used it to confirm the hypothesis, based on Rotter's social learning theory, that health-related information-seeking is a joint function of a person's locus of control beliefs and the value placed by the individual on health (Wallston *et al.* 1976b). In 1978, Wallston *et al.* published the development of their multidimensional health locus of control (MHLC) scales, based on Levenson's (1974) IPC scale, which, they argued, offered far greater potential usefulness than the original unidimensional scale. Nevertheless, they emphasized that:

> in utilizing the MHLC scales it is important to keep in mind the theoretical and empirical underpinnings of health locus of control. As a health-specific indicator of generalized expectancy of locus of control or reinforcements, based on Rotter's social learning theory, there is no reason to expect that the MHLC scale scores alone should explain much of the obtained variance in health behaviours. Only in interaction with one, or preferably more, of a multitude of contributing factors will beliefs in the locus of control of health play a significant role in the explanation of health behaviour. Examples of other contributing factors are perceived severity and susceptibility; health motivation; social supports; previous behaviour; attitudes toward health professionals; perceived costs and benefits or specific actions; demographic factors such as race and social class and most importantly, the value of health as a reinforcement.
>
> (Wallston *et al.* 1978: 168)

The Wallstons reported on published and unpublished normative data that used the unidimensional (HLC) and multidimensional (MHLC) scales collected from a range of groups between 1976 and 1980 (Wallston and Wallston 1981: 201–3). They identified a range of implications for future research, including the recommendation that the MHLC scale be used in preference to the HLC. While it was felt that the internal and chance dimensions could be combined to approximate to the HLC, the powerful other dimension promised interesting independent results in the field of health. Wallston and Wallston (1981: 236–8) recommended:

- the continued development of situation-specific scales;
- more attention to treatment programmes tailored to locus of control beliefs;
- studies to measure the relationship between locus of control and health behaviour;
- attention to analytical procedures appropriate to multidimensional scales.

They observed that LOC scales had been more successful in predicting behaviour in chronic patient populations than preventive health behaviours and questioned whether health locus of control was an adequate concept in the context of health, rather than illness, behaviour. They observed that research into health locus of control had failed totally to take into account the controllability of the situation and noted that internal control may not be a positive attribute in uncontrollable situations. Therefore, they urged that environmental contingencies be taken into account when judgements are being made about the desirability of different types of control belief.

Wallston and Wallston (1982: 70) distinguished between eight possible different patterns of health locus of control expectancies:

pure internal	high I	low P	low C
pure powerful others external	low I	high P	low C
pure chance external	low I	low P	high C
double external	low I	high P	high C
believer in control	high I	high P	low C
yea-sayer	high I	high P	high C
nay-sayer	low I	low P	low C
untitled (type VI)	high I	low P	high C

They suggested that belief in control is adaptive, since it expresses the belief that health is controllable, by either self or other, and is not a matter of fate, luck or chance. This, they felt, would be most adaptive in coping with chronic disease or illness in which patients take responsibility for self-care in accordance with the advice and prescriptions of the doctor. Yea-sayers and nay-sayers may reflect response bias, though the latter might also represent the views of those who believe that God controls health and illness. The Wallstons took the view that type VI probably did not exist, though a more recent study by Bradley *et al.* (1990) identified just such a subgroup of diabetic patients. They proposed that this profile might reflect self-serving bias in attributing positive outcomes to internal factors and negative outcomes to chance factors.

In their review of health locus of control research, Wallston and Wallston (1982) explored its utility in the areas of health information-seeking, preventive health behaviours, reactions to physical conditions, disability and symptoms, and adherence to medical regimens. In each of these areas, beliefs in internal and powerful others control appear to be adaptive in terms of their association with appropriate health behaviours, while high scores on chance are associated with inaction. In considering responses to health care interventions, the Wallstons distinguished between health locus of control as dependent variable (beliefs that change as a result of an intervention) and independent variable (a belief set that influences response to an intervention). The Wallstons reported on evidence that drop-outs from health intervention programmes were more likely to be external, and observed that more work was needed to test the efficacy of tailoring treatments to suit different locus of control expectancies. In conclusion, they identified the need for greater consideration of situational variables that influence the potential for control and for exploration of the expectancies of health professionals. Following on from this, Wallston *et al.* (1983b) reported studies that suggested a distinction between expectancies of control and desire for control, and pointed out that the MHLC is not actually a measure of 'desire for control'. This important point is particularly relevant in health care settings where patients may have low expectations of control even though their desire for control is high.

In 1992, Ken Wallston presented a critical review of the construct of health locus of control, in which he asserted that locus of control is less significant in predicting health-directed behaviour than health value or self-efficacy (Wallston 1992). He observed that beliefs that powerful others influence one's health almost never correlate significantly with health behaviours in healthy people, while beliefs in luck, fate or chance are more appropriately conceived of as indicators of lack of perceived control than an external LOC dimension. He therefore argued that internal LOC (the belief that one's health is affected by one's own behaviour) is the most relevant consideration.

Wallston (1992) identified additional problems, including the multiplicative effect of health locus of control and health value and the need for measures of behaviourally specific expectancies for behaviours such as smoking or exercise. He pointed out that most of the reported studies had been based on small convenience samples, but identified three large-scale studies in which MHLC scores accounted for no more than 6 per cent of the variance of self-reported health behaviour, thus challenging the predictive validity of the MHLC. He admitted that he no longer advocated the use of the MHLC, favouring instead newly developed measures of 'perceived competence' (a generalized indicator of self-efficacy) and 'health hardiness', which included a component labelled 'perceived control of health'. Wallston concluded that an internal HLC orientation is a necessary but not a sufficient condition for engaging in healthy behaviour. In so doing, he put forward a modified social learning theory that substitutes perceived control for locus of control and provides a bridge between the social learning theory of Rotter and that of Bandura (1977a).

Locus of control measurement

Table 3.3 indicates a vast range of locus of control measures, starting with I–E measures, followed by general IPC measures and more recently condition-specific measures. Joe (1971) offered a comprehensive review of the I–E control construct, including the Rotter I–E scale. Test–retest reliability was found to be consistently in the region of 0.7 and discriminant validity in relation to other ideologies good, though there was some evidence that the I–E scale was not free of social desirability. Joe (1972) investigated the relationship between social desirability and the I–E scale and found that internal statements were rated as more desirable than external statements, possibly due to cultural expectations (see Hjelle 1971). Joe (1971) identified some concerns raised by previous authors that the I–E scale favoured items dealing with social and political events as opposed to personal habits or goals and may not therefore reflect all aspects of personal control.

The 1980s saw a proliferation of condition-specific locus of control measures. Table 3.3 gives the reader information about the type of scale,

Table 3.3 Locus of control measures

Type/title of measure	Abbreviated title	Date	Dimensions	Author(s)	Complete measure given?	Overview: number of items, style of presentation, factor structure, key points
Control over outcomes						
Internal–external	I–E	1966	1	Rotter	Yes (see also Phares 1976)	23-item I–E Scale plus 6 filler items. Forced-choice 'a' or 'b' (internal or external) for each item. Some evidence of social desirability bias using Marlowe–Crowne Social Desirability Scale.
		1970	2	Mirels	Yes	Factor analysis of 23-item Rotter I–E Scale identified a two-factor solution: 'personal control' and 'sociopolitical control'.
		1973	2	Reid and Ware	Yes	Factor analysis of Rotter I–E Scale revealed 2 factors: fatalism and social system control (cf. Mirels 1970).
		1974	2	Valecha and Ostrom	Yes	11-item abbreviated form of Rotter I–E with 2-factor solution 'ideological' and 'personal' control beliefs (as in Mirels 1970).
		1974	4	Collins	Yes	4-factor solution to Rotter I–E Scale: (1) difficult–easy world (inc. skills/chance); (2) just–unjust world (inc. ability); (3) predictable–unpredictable world (inc. luck); (4) politically responsive–unresponsive world (cf. Mirels's second factor). Subsequently modified to 38-item forced-choice I–E Scale.

	Author	Year	Factors	Description	
	Reid and Ware	1974	3	40-item forced choice questionnaire revealed 3 factors: self-control, fatalism and Social System Control.	Yes
ANS–IE	Nowicki and Strickland	1973	2	Adult Nowicki–Strickland I–E Scale. 40 items with yes/no responses.	
	Dixon et al.	1976	Review	Reviews Rotter I–E, James I–E and Adult Nowicki–Strickland I–E Scales. Further analyses fail to support a unidimensional concept.	
	Lange and Tiggemann	1981	2	2-factor structure of 23-item Scale similar to Mirels (1970). Supports stability of 2-dimensional Rotter I–E over time.	
	Watson	1981	2, 4, 5	Provided 2, 4 and 5 factor solutions to Rotter I–E Scale with goodness-of-fit.	Yes
	Lumpkin	1986	1	6-item brief I–E Scale taken from Rotter I–E, using 5-point Likert Scale format.	Yes
IPC Internal, powerful other, chance	Levenson	1974 1981	3	Describes development of 24-item 6-point Likert Scale IPC (internal, powerful other, chance) locus of control Scale with details of factor analysis. 3 factors account for 32% of the variance.	Yes Yes
		1981	3	Describes construction, scoring and interpretation, validation and group norms for 24-item 6-point Likert Scale.	Yes
	Walkey	1979	3	Comparison of Rotter I–E with Levenson's IPC and Crowne–Marlowe SD Scale. Levenson's I and C Scales represent Rotter I–E Scale. Maximum correlation with social desirability is −0.2 (powerful other).	

Table 3.3 *cont'd*

Type/title of measure	Abbreviated title	Date	Dimensions	Author(s)	Complete measure given?	Overview: number of items, style of presentation, factor structure, key points
		1996	Review	Mirowsky and Ross		Covariance analyses and structural equations used to support the view that instrumentalism and fatalism are opposite ends of the same pole, as originally proposed by Rotter.
Children						
Children's LOC scale		1961	1	Bialer	No	Description/validation unclear
		1973	1	Nowicki and Strickland	Yes	40-item yes/no response format, with abbreviated version for primary school children.
Stanford preschool I–E	SPIES	1974	1	Mischel *et al.*	Yes	Validation of 14 forced-choice item questionnaire for pre-school children.
		1991	Review	LaMontagne and Hepworth		Review of children's LOC scales.
Children and health						
Children's health	CHLC	1978	3	Parcel and Meyer	Yes	For children aged 7–12. 20 items (17 external, 3 internal), scored yes/no (agree/disagree).

Fetal health	FHLC	1986	3	Labs and Wurtele	Yes	18-item scale using 9-point graphic rating scale (strongly disagree to strongly agree); IPC subscales.
Parent health	PHLOC	1993	6	DeVellis et al.	Yes	30-item 6-point Likert scale format concerning parent beliefs about their child's health. Subscales: professional, parent, child, media, fate, divine intervention.
Parent/ parent–child						
Perceived parenting		1971		MacDonald	Yes	21 items reflecting 9 parent practice variables 5-point frequency response scale for completion by children.
Marital	MMLOC (Miller marital)	1983	1	Miller et al.	Yes	44-item 6-point Likert scale format. 2-factor solution (internal and external) interpretable. Scoring as a single dimension recommended.
Parents: Children's Improvement	CILC	1985	5	DeVellis et al.	Yes	Child Improvement Locus of Control scale to tap beliefs of parents about sick child recovery/ adjustment. 27 items, 6-point Likert scale format with 5-factor solution: (1) professional influence; (2) divine influence; (3) parental influence; (4) child's own efforts; (5) chance.
Parental	PLOC	1986	5	Campis et al.	Yes	47-item 5-point Likert scale format. Subscales: parental efficacy, parental responsibility, child control of parent's life, parental belief in fate/ chance, parental control of child's behaviour.
Parenting	PLOC	1992	1	Koeske and Koeske	Yes	14-item 5-point Likert scale format, measuring parents' beliefs about their ability to control their children's behaviour and development.

Table 3.3 *cont'd*

Type/title of measure	Abbreviated title	Date	Dimensions	Author(s)	Complete measure given?	Overview: number of items, style of presentation, factor structure, key points
Health-specific						
	HLC	1976a	1	Wallston et al.	Yes	6-point Likert scale format measure.
	MHLC	1978	3	Wallston et al.	Yes	18-item 6-point Likert scale format based on Levenson's 3-dimensional LOC. Two alternative sets of wording (forms A and B) are presented.
		1982		Winefield		Reliability and validity of MHLC tested. I subscale consistent and stable; predictive validity uncertain. C subscale inconsistent and unstable. P subscale subject to age and social status influences; predictive validity uncertain.
		1987	6	Rock et al.		Cluster analysis of MHLC form B. 6 clusters identified: pure internal, pure chance, double external, believer in control (internal plus powerful others), yea-sayer (yes to all), nay-sayer (no to all).
Desire for control in health care	DCON	1984		Smith et al.		14-item, 4-point Likert scale answered with reference to what the person would want as a patient in a specific health care situation. Includes desire for control (8 items), information (6 items).

HLQOC		1981	3	Lau and Ware	Lau (1982: 327)	20-item scale, measured using 7-point frequency responses (not at all to always), representing 4 subscales: efficacy of self-care; provider control over health; chance health outcomes; and general health threat.
		1996		MacLachlan et al.		Cross-cultural validation of HLOCQ in Malawi: findings failed to support it as a valid measure; HLOCQ appears to lack cultural relevance in this context.
Internal health control		1991	4	Marshall	Yes	15-item, 6-point Likert scale format, using existing and new items to measure internal control over health. Four factors – 'illness management; self-mastery; self-blame; illness prevention' – explain physical well-being and physical health problems.
Substance use Drink-related	DRIE	1978	2	Donovan and O'Leary	Yes, see also Ludtke and Schneider (1996: 366)	25 items using 5-point Likert scale format. 2 subscales: 'interpersonal' and 'intrapersonal'.
		1978	Review	Rohsenow and O'Leary		Presents overview of general and drinking control scales to that date, including validity, reliability and limitations, together with critical review of conceptual problems in relation to drinking.
Alcohol Responsibility Scale	ARS	1981	1	Worell and Tumily	Yes	32 item and 24 revised item forced-choice questionnaire described. Presented as measure of locus of control, but appears to represent perceived control (does not refer to control over outcomes).

Table 3.3 cont'd

Type/title of measure	Abbreviated title	Date	Dimensions	Author(s)	Complete measure given?	Overview: number of items, style of presentation, factor structure, key points
Smoking-specific		1991	1	Bunch and Schneider	Yes, see also Ludtke and Schneider (1996: 365)	25-item 4-point Likert scale format questionnaire modified from DRIE, Donovan and O'Leary (1978).
Smoking	SLC	1992	3	Georgiou and Bradley	Yes	11-item, 6-point Likert scale format representing internal–chance (2 items each); powerful other (3); significant other (4).
Cocaine abuse		1992	1	Oswald et al.	See DRIE	Modified DRIE consisting of 25 forced-choice paired-format items that substitute cocaine for alcohol, tested with 40 subjects. Test–retest reliability and internal consistency satisfactory, though low-order correlation with I–E scale which casts doubt on validity.
Mental health						
Mental Health Locus of Control/Origin	MHLC MHLO	1981	1 1	Hill and Bale	Yes	Reports on validation of two mental health scales: Mental Health Locus of Control Questionnaire (MHLC), 22-item (plus 6 filler items), 6-point Likert scale scored unidimensionally, and Mental Health Locus of Origin Questionnaire (MHLO), 20-item (plus 6 filler items) 6-point Likert scale scored unidimensionally.

Depression		1987	3	Whitman et al.	Yes	12-item, 6-point Likert scale format (4 items representing each of the IPC scales).

Medical condition-related

Heart disease		1985	3	O'Connell and Price	Yes	20-item, 6-point Likert scale format (7 internal, 8 chance, 5 powerful others).
Diabetes		1987	3	Ferraro et al.	Yes	18-item Likert scale format (6 items for each of the IP&C scales).
Diabetes		1990	3	Bradley et al.		35 items using 7-point scale. 3 main subscales: personal, medical and situational control.
Recovery from physical disability	RLOC	1989	2	Partridge and Johnson	Yes	9-item, 5-point Likert scale format (5 internal, 4 external).
Pain	BPCQ	1990	3	Skevington	Yes	15-item, 6-point Likert scale format pain locus of control scale. 3 dimensions: internal, powerful doctors and chance happenings, validated with chronic pain, cancer patients and students.
Pain	PLOC	1991	3	Toomey et al.	Copy available from authors	Adapted from MHLC: 36-item, 6-point Likert scale format, 12 items per subscale.
Headache	HSLC	1990	3	Martin et al.	Yes	33-item, 5-point Likert scale format representing internal (11); health care professionals (11) and chance (11).
Cancer		1992	3	Karpinski		Report of instrument designed to predict preventive behaviours associated with reduction of cancer risk. Includes IPC scales.

Table 3.3 cont'd

Type/title of measure	Abbreviated title	Date	Dimensions	Author(s)	Complete measure given?	Overview: number of items, style of presentation, factor structure, key points
Condition-specific	Form C MHLC	1994	4	Wallston et al.	Yes	18-item, 6-point Likert format (6 items each for internality and chance; 3 items each for doctors and other people). Validated for patients with pain, rheumatoid arthritis, diabetes and cancer.
Health-related behaviours						
Dental health	DHLC	1980	1	Beck	Yes	12-item, 7-point Likert scale format.
Physical fitness	FITLOC	1988	3	Whitehead and Corbin	Yes	11-item, 6-point Likert scale format.
Weight	WLOC	1982	1	Saltzer	Yes	Brief 4-item scale using 6-point Likert scale format for use in clinical practice.
Weight loss	DBS	1990	3	Stotland and Zuroff	Yes	16-item, 6-point scale (Dieting Beliefs Scale). Scaling and scoring not clearly delineated in this article.
Eating		1996	1	Ludtke and Schneider	Yes	20-item, 5-point Likert format, adapted from DRIE, Donovan and O'Leary (1978) and smoking-specific LOC (Bunch and Schneider 1991).

source and availability, and key features, including dimensionality.[3] It is clear that some authors appear to have used relatively small and selective samples to validate their scales. Where these are modifications of existing scales, this may not be a problem, provided the topic of interest is directly comparable (for example, substituting one form of substance misuse such as cigarette smoking for another such as marijuana taking). Some scales that purport to measure locus of control are not simply measures of control over outcomes. For example, Worell and Tumilty (1981) presented the Alcoholic Responsibility Scale (ARS) for use with alcoholics, which contains a combination of locus of causality (my drinking is a disease), locus of control (what happens to me as an alcoholic is up to me) and self-efficacy (if I make up my mind to quit drinking, I can do it).

During the 1990s, Wallston, apparently critical of the ability of multidimensional health locus of control measures to predict health behaviours, developed and reported a condition-specific version of the MHLC scales for use with people with any chronic illness or medical conditions (Wallston *et al.* 1994). This particular scale yielded four independent subscales: internality, chance, doctors and 'other powerful people'. It is evident that a number of tangible (as opposed to chance) external factors are likely to influence the lives of those suffering from long-term chronic conditions, though these are not always encapsulated in locus of control measures. They include hospital and community-based doctors, other health and social care professionals, formal and informal carers, benefits agencies and, where appropriate, legal services (for example, see Walker *et al.* 1999).

Applications in health care settings

By the early 1980s, researchers had begun to investigate applications of locus of control measurement in different types of health care setting. For example, Hill and Bale (1981) suggested that the Mental Health Locus of Control scale might be used to help to match clients to therapists as in matching passive clients with directive therapists and active clients with non-directive therapists. They speculated whether control beliefs might actually be part of the presenting problem. For example, how can people be expected to benefit from therapy if they believe their problems to be caused by some phenomenon beyond their control? Hence, changing control expectancies may reasonably be a goal of therapy. They postulated that mental health professionals might perpetuate, through an emphasis on medical aetiology, a passive stance in their patients.

Locus of control has been extensively used as an independent variable in health research. Some examples of research in relation to different aspects of health and illness are given in Table 3.4. This highlights the range of topics covered and types of measures used. It is evident that not

Table 3.4 Examples of studies of locus of control on health-related topics, with scales used

Topic	Authors	Scales used
Social class/ethnicity	Battle and Rotter (1963)	I–E
Childhood influences on LOC	Parish (1982)	Childhood LOC
Population norms and cross-cultural comparisons	Gorman et al. (1980) O'Brien and Kabanoff (1981)	I–E
Alcoholism	Oziel et al. (1972) O'Leary et al. (1975, 1976) Obitz and Oziel (1978)	I–E
Addiction	Berzins and Ross (1973) Dielman et al. (1987)	I–E
Age	Ryckman and Malikiosi (1975) Weisz and Stipek (1982) Lumpkin (1986)	IPC
Obesity/weight reduction	Balch and Ross (1975) Thomason (1983)	I–E
Health information-seeking	Wallston et al. (1976b)	HLC
Smoking	Kaplan and Cowles (1978)	HLC
Hardiness	Kobasa et al. (1982)	I–E
Involvement in health care	Wallston et al. (1983b)	MHLC
Health-related behaviours	Calnan (1989)	MHLC
Health screening attendance	Norman (1991)	MHLC
Diabetes	Lowery and DuCette (1976)	I–E
Diabetes	Schlenk and Hart (1984)	MHLC
Diabetes	Stenström et al. (1998)	DLOC

Occupational stress	Anderson (1977)	I–E
Elderly	Reid et al. (1977)	Locus of desired control
Elderly	Krause (1987b)	I–E
Work	O'Brien (1984)	I–E
Hypertension	Lewis et al. (1978)	HLC
Pain	Crisson and Keefe (1988) Johnson et al. (1989) Härkäpää et al. (1991)	MHLC
Pain	Toomey et al. (1991, 1993, 1995) Lipchik et al. (1993) Gorin et al. (1996)	PLOC
Counselling	Connolly (1980)	Patient expression
Faith	Tipton et al. (1980)	IPC
Depression/psycho-pathology	Evans (1981) Hutner and Locke (1984)	I–E
Chronic illness	Nagy and Wolfe (1983)	MHLC
Cancer	Burish et al. (1984) Marks et al. (1986)	MHLC
Cancer	Taylor et al. (1984)	Coded interview data
Heart disease	Strube (1985)	ASQ

Abbreviations:
I–E, Internal–External Locus of Control.
HLC, Health Locus of Control (unidimensional).
IPC, Internal, Powerful Other, Chance Locus of Control Scale.
PLOC, Pain Locus of Control (based on IPC).
MHLC, Multidimensional Locus of Control (based on IPC).
DLOC, Diabetic Locus of Control (Ferraro et al. 1987).
ASQ, Attributional Style Questionnaire (Peterson et al. 1982).

all researchers chose to abandon the unidimensional scale in favour of the multidimensional scale. Studies on the same topic are often quite difficult to compare because of the different measures used.

Locus of control is frequently included as a measure in correlational studies of health and health care. Yet the findings are often equivocal and difficult to interpret. Norman and Bennett (1995) presented evidence, based on a survey of nearly 12,000 people, that locus of control accounts for only 5 per cent of dietary behaviour and less in relation to other health-related behaviours such as smoking. The only reasonably consistent finding is that fatalistic beliefs (external chance locus of control) are associated with poor outcomes. In preventive health, fatalism tends to be associated with lack of initiative to engage in behaviour change. In chronic illness or conditions, it tends to be associated with poor compliance with medical instructions, increased depression and poor functional status. Where longitudinal or before–after measurement studies are proposed, locus of control is not nearly as useful as the measurement self-efficacy, particularly in relation to inter-vention studies. In clinical practice, I have found it useful to assess control beliefs by listening to what patients say. It is then possible to pick up nuances that do not emerge from measurement. People may say 'I like to do things myself', 'it is up to them (the doctors)' or 'there is nothing anyone can do'. But, most often, they express a mixture of beliefs that need to be attended to so that it is possible to correct fatalistic views and negotiate what they can do for themselves and what we can do for them. I have addressed these issues again in Chapter 8.

Predictive power of locus of control

This chapter has identified a number of theoretical and measurement issues that may limit the predictive power of locus of control. Below are some contextual reasons why locus of control might have poor explanatory and predictive power in relation to health-related behaviour. Some of these are linked with issues identified in Chapter 2 on perceived control.

Health maintenance is largely beyond personal control

Locus of control refers to expectations of control over outcomes. It is implicit in this assumption that outcomes are controllable. In reality, many health outcomes are not controllable. Even if I do not smoke, drink alcohol within specified limits, eat plenty of fresh fruit and vegetables and take regular exercise, there is no guarantee that I will remain healthy. For example, we as individuals are unable to control the level of potentially carcinogenic emissions into our environment; nor are we yet able to control our genetic response to these. The belief that my health is dependent on a combination of my own actions, the actions of others and chance would, in fact, appear to be the most realistic and logical belief set among those who are currently healthy.

Health outcomes are unpredictable

Health is an ill-defined, general concept that holds different meanings for different people. A number of authors have drawn attention to the fact that people will strive to achieve an outcome if it has value for them. However, it is not only the value of the outcome that influences the likelihood of behaviour, but its immediacy and certainty. Health outcomes, no matter how desirable, are neither immediate nor certain. In contrast, the pleasurable though potentially unhealthy outcomes of such activities as smoking a cigarette with a cup of coffee, drinking alcohol in congenial company, taking illegal substances or having unsafe sex are both immediate and certain (Walker 1993). It appears to be a truism that people only value their health once they have lost it or are under serious threat of losing it. This may help to explain why locus of control appears to have more explanatory power in relation to chronic illness than in the field of preventive medicine. Only when illness strikes does the impetus for engaging in behaviours to restore health exceed that of other more immediate and certain pleasures of life.

Health value competes with other values

Health is just one outcome of health-related behaviours. Most healthy people do not engage in a range of daily activities for the sole purpose of remaining healthy. Ask any group of smokers why they smoke and you will come up with a wide variety of perfectly logical reasons (see Marks 1993). They enjoy it; it relaxes them; keeps them alert; it gives them something to do with their hands; they do it automatically when undertaking certain other activities, such as drinking a cup of coffee; it is a social activity; it provides time out or escape from onerous activities and situations. Thus health might not be a primary motivator. A simple functional analysis of behaviour would reveal that even those who place high value on health might have stronger competing reinforcers for engaging in unhealthy behaviours.

Health-related behaviours are often 'mindless'

Health-related behaviours are generally treated as the same, regardless of whether they are deliberate (as in choosing to visit a screening clinic) or habitual (as in smoking). Most health-related behaviours are actually habitual and are therefore, to use Langer's term, 'mindless' (Piper and Langer 1986). As such these behaviours may be relatively impervious unless or until they can be brought under voluntary control or are in some way disrupted (see Hunt and Martin 1988; Walker 1993).

Personal control is not always best in times of illness

An individual stricken by illness or disability is faced with a number of possibilities: self-care, seek help or do nothing. The most appropriate course of action is determined entirely by the situation. For example, flu is best responded to by doing nothing. Simple back pain is best treated by self-care. A potentially malignant disease requires medical help. Strong stable generalized beliefs in personal control may in some situations militate against the most appropriate course of action. Thus researchers need to define the most adaptive course of action before designing and using locus of control questionnaires, while findings need to be interpreted with care. There are examples in the literature where medical guidelines have changed and patients who complied with medical advice were subsequently redefined as deviant for their failure to engage in self-care (see Fordyce 1996; Walker *et al.* 1999 on the issue of back pain). In most chronic illnesses or diseases, external locus of control is maladaptive since it is frequently associated with false hopes. Only in the case of a terminal illness that is entirely beyond medical control is a belief in luck, fate or chance likely to be adaptive.

Locus of control does not necessarily imply desire for control

As previously pointed out, beliefs about the controllability of a specific situation may modify the desire for control. Those with a strong desire to be in control of certain aspects of their lives may relinquish control in certain situations that they know they have no prospect of controlling. Alternatively, they may choose to exert control over others to get things done, rather than attempting to do it for themselves. The latter are often labelled 'control freaks'. For example, the person with a chronic illness or disability who 'manipulates' others into doing things for them may express the same desire for control and locus of control as someone who struggles to do most things for himself or herself. Whether or not each of these behaviours is adaptive is discussed further in Chapter 8.

Concluding comments

The concept of locus of control has immense intuitive appeal in health care. Perhaps this is partly a function of the emphasis on internal control by Western societies at the end of the twentieth century. The majority of research appears to confirm the benefits of internal locus of control over chance locus of control, though the advantages and disadvantages of beliefs in 'other' control remain relatively unexplored. On the other hand, cynics might suggest that it has been included in so much research because of the ready availability of measures and not because of its explanatory or predictive power. Overall, locus of control appears to have failed to fulfil its potential as a predictive measure of health-related behaviour. Some further reasons for this are explored in the next chapter, on self-efficacy.

Notes

1 See Chapter 8 for a theoretical explanation of this phenomenon.
2 Barbara Wallston died in the late 1980s.
3 I have not attempted to offer a critical review of each scale. Those wishing to use these or any other scales are urged to review their validity and reliability using the sources given.

Further reading

Conner, M. and Norman, P. (eds) (1995) *Predicting Health Behaviour*. Buckingham: Open University Press.
Lefcourt, H. M. (ed.) (1981) *Research with the Locus of Control Construct. Volume 1, Assessment Methods*. New York: Academic Press.
Lefcourt, H. M. (ed.) (1982) *Locus of Control: Current Trends in Theory and Research*, 2nd edn. Hillsdale, NJ: Lawrence Erlbaum Associates.
Wallston, K. A. (1992) Hocus-pocus, the focus isn't strictly on locus: Rotter's social learning theory modified for health. *Cognitive Therapy and Research*, 16(2): 183–99.
Wallston, K. A. and Wallston, B. S. (1982) Who is responsible for your health? The construct of health locus of control, in G. Sanders and J. Suls (eds) *Social Psychology of Health and Illness*. Hillsdale, NJ: Lawrence Erlbaum Associates, pp. 65–95.

Self-efficacy

Overview of contents

Self-efficacy theory

Self-efficacy theory is primarily a theory of human motivation. It is concerned with the ability to affect or change the environment. In 1959, Robert White published a review of theories of human motivation, including those derived from cognitive, psychoanalytic, gestalt, humanistic and social psychology, behaviourism, child development and personality theory. Quoting Freud, Maslow, Zimbardo, Skinner, Harlow, Piaget and Erikson, White (1959) identified how the concept of mastery over the environment was a central theme in all the main schools of psychology. White identified biological survival value in learning to interact effectively with the environment, the outcome of which he termed competence or effectance. He proposed that motivations towards achieving effectance produce a feeling of efficacy.[1]

Bandura (1997a) sought to distinguish White's theory of effectance from his own theory of self-efficacy. He argued that is difficult to verify a motivation for mastery because the motive is inferred from the very exploratory behaviour it supposedly causes. Although he identified considerable overlap between the two concepts, he argued that effectance theory focused on an innate drive towards exploratory behaviour. Thus efficacy reflects intrinsic pleasure derived from affecting the environment. In contrast, Bandura's self-efficacy theory has its origins in social learning theory. Efficacy, according to Bandura, is shaped by a combination of interaction with the environment, vicarious experiences, social evaluations by significant others and biofeedback from physiological states. Most important, it is amenable to self-regulation.

The concept (or construct) of 'self-efficacy' is inseparable from the name of Albert Bandura. Bandura was already well known and widely acknowledged for his work on observational learning in children when he published *Social Learning Theory* in 1977. This classic psychology text remains in print in its original form, perhaps due to its lucidity. Bandura uses simple language to define all psychological terms in ways that can be clearly and easily understood by a wide audience. In it, Bandura set out his scepticism of personality trait and psychodynamically oriented theories that seek to explain human behaviour in terms of internally driven motivations. Although this reflects his beginnings in the behaviourist school of psychology, Bandura was very critical of radical behaviourism for its assumption that all voluntary behaviour is externally regulated. He proceeded to study the importance of observation and vicarious processes in human learning, and social influences on the development of self-regulatory cognitive processes: 'Social learning theory approaches the explanation of human behaviour in terms of a continuous reciprocal interaction between cognitive, behavioural and environment determinants' (Bandura 1977a: vii).

Later in the same book, Bandura defined motivation as the activation and maintenance of behaviour. He identified the chief sources of motivation as: cognitive representations of future outcomes; goal setting, based on the evaluation of personal behaviour; and self-regulated reinforcement. He emphasized the role of personal autonomy: 'people function as active agents in their own self-regulation' (Bandura 1977a: 165). 'People may be considered partially free insofar as they can influence future conditions by managing their own behaviour' (Bandura 1997a: 205). Thus he rejected deterministic theories of behaviour that viewed people as entirely at the mercy of environmental conditions, in favour of a reciprocal determinism in which people seek actively to shape those conditions to suit their own purposes. He observed that some people are better at this than others because they have acquired skills that enable them to do so. This provided the foundation for his theory of self-efficacy.

In the same year, Bandura published another important piece of work in which he set out the framework for his theory of self-efficacy (Bandura 1977b). This was published at a time when radical (Skinnerian) behaviourism was being eroded by psychologists who were able to demonstrate through experimental laboratory studies that even such organisms as pigeons, rats and goldfish are able to predict the probability of future events, thus supporting a cognitive explanation for behaviour change. Bandura, whose work was concerned with humans in social settings, argued that although cognitive processes mediate behaviour change, these cognitive events are themselves 'induced and altered most readily by experience of mastery arising from effective performance' (Bandura 1977b: 191). This appears to represent an area of overlap with White's theory of effectance.

Bandura (1977b) identified four sources of information that contribute to efficacy learning (see also Ozer and Bandura 1990):

- Performance accomplishments – experiences of personal mastery.
- Vicarious experience – modelling effective coping strategies.
- Verbal or social persuasion.
- Emotional arousal – attribution of strength or vulnerability to changing physiological sensations. Borkovec (1978) claimed that, to Bandura, the importance of physiological states resides in their information value.

A useful and entertaining review of some of these processes, focused on organizational applications, is to be found in Bandura (1988). Bandura (1977b) noted that contextual cues function as important additional sources of information in determining action. Nevertheless, attribution errors do occur. Some people have a tendency to credit their personal achievements to external factors (and vice versa).

Bandura (1977b) pointed out that although others had viewed self-efficacy as analogous to Rotter's (1966) concept of locus of control, it is quite different. Locus of control is concerned with perceptions of action–outcome contingencies, whereas self-efficacy requires judgements about the availability of personal skills required to achieve a successful outcome. Lefcourt (1982: 187) observed: 'Perceived contingency is not identical to perceived efficacy. Yet, it is doubtful that the latter would exist without the former.' Bandura (1978, 1997b) claimed that self-efficacy theory was generalizable to Seligman's (1975) theory of learned helplessness. He suggested that people give up trying either because desired outcomes are unattainable or because they lack a sense of self-efficacy to believe that they could achieve an otherwise attainable outcome. The latter belief set appears to feature in many people suffering from depression and is central to cognitive-behavioural treatments of depression (see Beck 1976). Davis and Yates (1982) found support for the role of self-efficacy in learned helplessness in males but not females. In males, performance deficits and depressive affect were produced by a combination of low self-efficacy and high response–outcome expectancies. Lack of the same deficits in females was explained by a lowering of self-response expectancies in women. In fact, Gecas (1989) drew attention to developmental studies that had identified gender differences in personal agency in young children.

Bandura expanded his theory of self-efficacy in a subsequent paper (Bandura 1982), in which he emphasized the functional value of being able accurately to appraise one's capabilities. He identified a range of methodological problems to explain the weaker-than-predicted relationship between self-efficacy and action in research applications. These included:

- faulty self-knowledge;
- misjudgement of task requirements;
- unforeseen situational constraints (particularly in social situations);
- disincentives to act on one's self-percepts of efficacy;
- new experiences that prompted reappraisals of self-efficacy in the time between measurement and action;
- ill-defined global measures of perceived self-efficacy;
- inadequate assessment of performance.

He used the example of recovery from heart attack to illustrate some of these points, showing that psychological recovery lags behind physical recovery, leading patients (and spouses) to believe that they are unable to perform tasks that are quite within their capabilities.

Bandura and colleagues produced so many publications on the topic of self-efficacy that it is not possible, nor is it necessary, to refer to them all. Bandura personally led, or was involved in some way with, most of the research and theoretical development. Hence the concept of self-efficacy has remained consistent over the years and has not been exposed to the differences and changes in interpretation and conceptualization that are evident in most other control concepts. Review articles by researchers other than Bandura have generally added little to the overall understanding of the concept. In 1997, Bandura published a major review of the topic (Bandura 1997a). In it, he reviewed the theoretical background to self-efficacy, concept development and research, and applied research related to teaching and learning, health, clinical functioning, sport and research in organizational contexts. The final section moves on to consider the concept of collective efficacy. In this book, he offered the following clarification of terminology.

Self-efficacy

'Perceived self-efficacy refers to beliefs in one's capabilities to organize and execute the courses of action required to produce given attainments' (p. 3). He indicated that this may involve regulating motivation, thought processes, affective states or own actions, and/or it may involve changing environmental conditions. People contribute to their own functioning through the mechanism of personal agency even though they are not sole determinants of what happens to them. People are both producers and products of social systems, although actions can sometimes have unintended outcomes.

Agency

'Agency refers to acts done intentionally' (p. 3). This, of course, immediately raises doubts about the role of perceived efficacy in relation to habitual (overlearned) or addictive behaviours (I referred to this in Chapter 1).

Self-efficacy, self-concept and self-esteem

Self-efficacy, Bandura went on to suggest, is part of the self-concept, which leads to self-esteem. Although self-efficacy and self-esteem or self-worth are often used interchangeably, he argued that they are entirely different phenomena. He pointed out that people tend to develop their capabilities in activities that give them a sense of self-worth, but people need much more than high self-esteem to do well in given pursuits. Efficacy beliefs are likely to vary according to the demands of the task and the situation in which the task is performed.

Proxy control and collective efficacy

Bandura (1997a) referred to the concept of 'proxy control' (see also Bandura 1982). This describes situations in which people relinquish personal control and allow or persuade powerful others to take action on their behalf. This may be because they perceive themselves to be inefficacious, in which case it can lead to dependency, or it may be because they believe that others can perform a particular task better (I refer to this again in the analysis in Chapter 8). Bandura referred to the personal efficacy required to manipulate others into taking control on their behalf, though he did not mention the exchange of money or other types of reciprocal transaction. He (1997a: 157–9) recognized the importance of what he termed 'social self-efficacy' (the ability to recruit and retain social support) in coping with stress and protecting from depression. In a social milieu, efficacy is as likely to be gained from social skills as from practical skills, since those with good social skills are more likely to feel confident in their ability to gain help from others when they need it. These issues have obvious relevance to health care settings, where people are often unable, or believe that they are unable, to engage in self-care. This issue is referred to again in Chapter 6, on social support.

Bandura (1982) identified the importance of interdependency and the necessity for collective effort in bringing about change. He noted that in a rapidly changing world of new technologies, some people may be left behind, dependent on those with the necessary technical competence or under the control of official gatekeepers. Bandura (1997a) referred to self-efficacy in collectivist social systems and argued that group pursuits are no less demanding of personal efficacy than individual pursuits. Towards the end of the book (Bandura 1997a: 470), he returned to the issue of collectivist efficacy in the context of organizations. Here, he considered the need to share knowledge and know-how and how this can lead to creative outcomes. However, the issue of reciprocal control and reciprocal efficacy in interpersonal relationships appears to remain relatively unexplored.

Self-efficacy and behaviour change

The precise role of self-efficacy in the process of behaviour change remains unclear and the literature contains a number of confusions. Bandura conceptualized self-efficacy as a mediating variable, yet researchers often treat it as a dependent or outcome variable. Borkovec (1978) admitted to difficulty in understanding the distinction between efficacy expectations and outcome expectations when efficacy is defined in terms of the *successful* execution of a behaviour. How is success to be judged? Bandura (1978) responded that success merely refers to the execution of the behaviour pattern, not to its effects. Yet he later argued (Bandura 1984) that self-efficacy is not defined or measured in terms of motor components of an act. Bandura (1982) addressed the chicken and egg nature of the relationship between self-efficacy and behaviour, remaining firmly in favour of self-efficacy as a motivating force. Bandura (1982: 235) stated: 'how one behaves largely determines the outcomes one experiences'. He argued (p. 245) that 'partialling out past performance underestimates the relationship between perceived self-efficacy and future performance because such a procedure removes the self-efficacy contributor to past performance.'

Wilson (1979: 186) argued that perceived efficacy or control is therapeutic only to the extent that it is at least partly based on the experience of actual control over the situation in question. This is borne out by studies (see Table 4.1) that demonstrate that the acquisition of new self-management skills leads to an increase in perceived self-efficacy. Social learning theory predicts that self-efficacy beliefs may also be enhanced through symbolic modelling, systematic desensitization to manage and reduce physiological arousal, and persuasion. Studies such as that of Bandura *et al.* (1977) on snake phobia indicate that although vicarious modelling (watching others do it) has some impact, participant modelling (actually doing it; performance accomplishment) has the strongest effect on behaviour. Wilson (1979) discussed how self-efficacy in one important domain may generalize to other situations (see also Bandura *et al.* 1980). Bandura (1977b) attributed this to the mediating effect of self-efficacy. Brown (1979: 109) indicated that direct and vicarious experiences of loss of efficacy or 'helplessness' are mediated by similar processes. Bandura (1997a) considered a range of mediating processes through which efficacy beliefs produce their effects. He presented evidence from organizational research conducted with Wood in the late 1980s to support the view that self-efficacy affects the use of problem-solving strategies (see also Bandura 1988). Those with a stronger sense of efficacy are quicker to discard faulty cognitive strategies in search of better ones and are less inclined to reject good solutions prematurely. As self-efficacy improves, performance in a complex social context becomes less dependent on past performance (i.e. on ineffective ritualistic ways of operating).

Bandura relied on words rather than flow diagrams to represent his account of self-efficacy. This may account for Bandura's need to correct misunderstandings with lengthy responses (Bandura 1978, 1982), when these might have been more easily addressed through the use of a flow chart illustrating cause, effect and feedback relationships with other variables. These include situational factors, behaviour, outcomes, locus of control, helplessness, confidence, anxiety and self-esteem. I return to these issues in Chapter 8.

Applications of efficacy theory to health

Predicting behaviour change

Bandura (1997a: 10) located the value of self-efficacy theory in its explicit guidelines on how to enable people to exercise some influence over how they live their lives. Indeed, self-efficacy has increasingly assumed a central role in predicting health-related behaviour and behaviour change. An early detailed review of self-efficacy and health-related behaviour was conducted by O'Leary (1985). In it she focused on smoking cessation, pain experience, eating disorders, cardiac rehabilitation and adherence to medical regimens. Evidence was available at that time that self-efficacy is an important predictor of the maintenance of behaviour change (for example, see DiClemente *et al.* 1985). Strecher *et al.* (1986) reviewed studies of self-efficacy in relation to behaviour change, including smoking cessation, weight control, alcohol abuse and exercise. They identified efficacy enhancement as an important component of health behaviour change strategies in which the 'patient' is encouraged to take responsibility for change. Ajzen later modified the Theory of Reasoned Action by introducing the concept of perceived behavioural control to form the Theory of Planned Behaviour (Ajzen 1988, 1991). Strecher and Rosenstock (1997) subsequently identified self-efficacy as an important missing variable from the Health Belief Model and recommended its inclusion when attempting to predict personal behaviour change. Bandura (1984) argued that self-efficacy judgement is highly functional in the continued self-regulation of behaviour. However, peer pressure and other social influences, together with the availability of alternative coping strategies and social supports, need to be taken into account when considering reasons for relapse. As Bandura (1982: 252) observed, behaviour is multiply determined and any single factor leaves a fair amount of variance unaccounted for.

Conner and Norman (1995b) identified three types of expectancy, of which self-efficacy is one, the others being situation–outcome and action–outcome:

◆ Situation–outcome: there is a risk to my health that can have potentially damaging outcomes.
◆ Action–outcome: certain actions can prevent damaging outcomes.
◆ Self-efficacy–outcome: I am capable of undertaking the required action.

It may be necessary to measure each type of expectancy in order to predict behaviour change. Wallston (1997) drew attention to the need to distinguish between self-efficacy and locus of control in the prediction of health behaviours. He claimed: 'the construct of self-efficacy has proven to be a much more potent predictor of health behaviours than has locus of control' (Wallston 1997: 152).

Specificity

Wallston (1997) indicated that self-efficacy, as originally conceived by Bandura, was very behaviour- and situation-specific. He had earlier suggested broadening the concept to encompass the belief that one is able to *do whatever the situation requires* in order to achieve the desired outcome (Wallston 1992). Wallston highlighted the distinction between health locus of control, health value and self-efficacy thus: 'those who are motivated by health but do not believe that their health status is controlled by their own health behaviour are not likely to change their health behaviour *even if they are capable of doing so*' (paraphrasing Wallston 1997: 152).

This observation is supported by research that demonstrates that low self-efficacy results in little behavioural impact even under conditions where control is quite possible (e.g. Litt 1988). Hofstetter *et al.* (1990) concluded that 'self-efficacy is specific to selected behaviours and does not operate as a personality subtype' (Hofstetter *et al.* 1990: 1056). Bandura (1997a) denied that self-efficacy is concerned solely with 'specific behaviour in specific situations', identifying three levels of generality ranging from situation-specific performance to global beliefs in personal efficacy. Bandura (1997b), in summarizing the relationship between self-efficacy and health behaviour, identified two levels at which self-efficacy plays an influential role: 'At the more basic level, people's beliefs in their capability to cope with the stressors in their lives activate biological systems that mediate health and disease' (Bandura 1997b: 160). Bandura cited a growing body of evidence that supports a process of 'physiological toughening' as a result of successful coping. He continued: 'The second level is concerned with the exercise of direct control over the modifiable behavioural aspects of health and the rate of ageing' (Bandura 1997b: 160). He insisted that healthy behaviour is not achieved by an act of will. Improving health requires lifestyle change. This depends on self-regulatory capabilities as well as the functional value of the old and new behaviours. Bandura (1997b) identified self-efficacy as a key to primary and secondary prevention and drew attention to Holman and Lorig's prototypical model for the self-management of different types of chronic diseases (Holman and Lorig 1992).

Self-efficacy and self-care

From the discussion above, it would appear that self-efficacy is an important requisite for self-care. Self-care in relation to health may be defined as: 'those activities individuals undertake in promoting their own health, preventing their own disease, limiting their own illness and restoring their own health' (Levin and Idler 1983: 181). The concept of self-care emerged in the late 1970s to become central to the whole ethos of Western health care. While most of the research on self-care interventions was based on Bandura's concept of self-efficacy, self-care became a central theme in nursing through the self-care model of Dorothea Orem. The first edition of the book outlining her self-care theory of nursing was published in 1971 and it is currently in its fifth edition (Orem 1995). Orem (1995) described a series of presuppositions and propositions on which her theory of self-care is premised, including self-care requisites or needs, based on humanistic principles. Orem identified that the power of an individual to engage in activities essential for self-care may be limited by the behavioural repertoire, knowledge and abilities of the individual concerned (including the effects of illness, disease or disability), together with conditions and factors in the environment which allow or impede self-care action. Orem balanced the extent to which individuals are able to take care of themselves against the extent of care required from other agents (in her case the nurse or other carers). Although the acquisition of self-care skills is a central theme of her work, Orem's theory was worked out from first principles and has persisted in containing no reference at all to the concept of self-efficacy, Bandura, social learning theory or psychological research on self-management. This is perhaps one of the main reasons why it has failed to attract attention outside nursing or to stimulate research. Nevertheless, her work contains many relevant observations, albeit concealed in difficult jargon.

There have been several important reviews of self-care, including one by Hickey (1988) on self-care in older adults. Hickey observed that interest in self-care appeared to have increased in response to escalating health care costs, dissatisfaction with medical services and the positive physical, mental and emotional benefits derived from taking better care of themselves. The elderly, he noted, are at higher risk of illness and likely to be more experienced in treating their own illnesses. Research findings indicated that older people, when confronted with illness symptoms, tended either to self-treat or to ignore. Professional help was most likely to be sought for symptoms associated with pain and dysfunction. Kickbusch (1989) reviewed the concept of self-care in relation to health promotion. In it she identified that the power of the physician, with its emphasis on 'patient compliance', was increasingly giving way to self-help and self-care. She questioned whether we might actually be witnessing a paradigm shift from medicine to health, from cure to prevention, from medical care to self-care. She recognized the danger that self-care could lead to a culture of victim-blaming. Thus those who appear to choose unhealthy lifestyles as currently defined by health professionals are blamed when they become ill and have, in some instances, been refused treatment (for example, smokers refused heart surgery). Kickbusch (1989) pointed out that self-care actions do not take place in a political and social void, but that the new public health could provide a framework that enhances self-care action and research.

Measurement of self-efficacy

Table 4.1 identifies examples of self-efficacy measures applicable in a range of different situations. A number of authors have reviewed approaches to measurement. Hofstetter *et al.* (1990) reviewed domain-specific versus general self-efficacy measurement in relation to health-related behaviours such as eating and exercise. They identified that outcome expectancies were clearly differentiated from efficacy or agency expectancies. Knowledge, attitudes and media exposure items related to specific behaviours were most highly correlated with self-efficacy for those same behaviours. They concluded that their findings offered strong support for the original concept of self-efficacy; self-efficacy is specific to selected behaviours and does not represent a personality trait. Simple ratings of self-efficacy (e.g. I feel sure that I can *perform an activity*, even when family or social life takes a lot of my time) were found to produce robust and meaningful data.

O'Leary (1985) identified the need to measure self-efficacy in terms of three parameters:

- Level: the person's expected performance attainment.
- Strength: the confidence people have that they can attain each expected level of performance.
- Generality: the number of domains of functioning in which people judge themselves to be efficacious.

Maddux and Stanley (1986), in an overview of self-efficacy theory, drew attention to the need to distinguish between ability and willingness. Others have taken up these aspects of measurement. Lust *et al.* (1993) tested alternative ways of measuring self-efficacy. The first used Likert scales to measure three aspects of behaviour (anticipation of problems, availability of information, confidence), which were then averaged. This did not differentiate for task difficulty. The second required subjects to identify one of five items, ranked in terms of task difficulty, to reflect efficacy magnitude. Self-efficacy

Table 4.1 Examples of self-efficacy measurement scales

Type of measure	Date	Authors	Detail contained	Summary
General measures Self-Control Scale	1980	Rosenbaum	All 36 items given, with six-point Likert scale	SCS tested with different samples. Test–retest reliability showed high stability, internal consistency 0.78–0.84. Not a pure measure of self-efficacy. Includes coping strategies.
Self-Efficacy Scale (General and Social)	1982	Sherer *et al.*	All items given	General measure. 14-point Likert scale used (not given). Two factors identified. Tendency to social desirability influence.
General Self-Efficacy (GSE)	1984	Tipton and Worthington	General description of scale, no examples	35 *a priori* items reflecting perceived general competency and determination to succeed, plus 5 'faith in self' items: reduced to 27 items; 7-point Likert scale. Tested with 33 students. Test–retest reliability $r(30) = 0.37$. High GSE group showed greater sustained effort and habitual behaviour change.
Health promotion	1995	Maibach and Murphy	Examples given	Review of measurement construction, with exemplars. Useful guide to measurement of SE in context of health promotion.
Smoking Pre- and Post-Treatment Confidence Questionnaires (smoking cessation)	1981	Condiotte and Lichtenstein	Items described (taken from Best and Hakstian in 1978)	Items reflect variety of smoking situations. Tested in Oregon Smoking Control Program. Post-treatment self-efficacy was a good predictor of relapse.

Scale	Year	Author	Availability	Description
Smoking Self-Efficacy (SSEQ)	1985	Colletti and Supnick	Summary of item content (original available on request)	17 items retained, based on predictive validity. Scales reflected 'can do' and 'confidence', measured on 10–100 scale. Moderate reliability reported.
Smoking: Confidence Questionnaire	1986	Baer et al.	General description of scale, plus item example	Based on Condiotte and Lichtenstein's 1981 Confidence Questionnaire. 46 situations, measuring probability of resisting smoking on 11-point scale, e.g. 'the probability that you will be able to resist the urge to smoke . . .'
Contraceptive use				
Contraceptive Self-Efficacy (CSE)	1986	Levinson	Full scale given	15-item scale related to variety of sexual situations or encounters. 4 factors: (1) planning; (2) responsibility; (3) assertiveness; (4) sexual arousal.
Condom Self-Efficacy Scale (CUSES)	1991	Brafford and Beck	Full scale given	28 items. Test development described. Behavioural intentions used as predictor of behaviour.
Contraceptive Self-Efficacy	1995	Levinson	Full scale given	15 items relating to issues surrounding contraception negotiation and use.
Condom Use	1997	DiLorio et al.	Scale given	Adapted from HIV risk reduction SE. 27 items measured using 5-point certainty scale. Tested with STD patients. Modest reliability.
Medical conditions				
Asthma Self-Efficacy Scale	1987	Tobin et al.	Full scale given	80-item scale. Limited description of development, validity and reliability. High Cronbach alpha scores to be expected, given large number of items.
Arthritis Self-Efficacy Scale	1989	Lorig et al.	Full scale given	Excellent example of development, validity, reliability. 20 items relate to 3 subscales: pain, function and other symptoms. Predictive validity tested in intervention study.

Table 4.1 *cont'd*

Type of measure	Date	Authors	Detail contained	Summary
COPD Self-Efficacy Scale (CSES)	1991	Wigal *et al.*	Full scale given	34-item scale. Assesses confidence in dealing with a range of situations. Conclude that low self-efficacy is associated with over-generalization of aversive consequences. CSES facilitates assessment and intervention.
Review of health-related SE measures for oncology	1997	Lev	References given	Reviews SE related to screening procedures including self-examination. Relevance to SE-enhancing interventions considered.
Cardiac Self-Efficacy Questionnaire	1998	Sullivan *et al.*	Items and instructions given	16 items, two scales: controlling symptoms (CS) and maintaining function (MF). Validity needs to be confirmed.
Age Perceived Self-Efficacy in Children	1991	Cowen *et al.*	Items used are given and scale described	20 items describe self-efficacy in range of different situations. 3-factor solution related to types of situation or experience. 2 items excluded relate to speculative conditions.

strength was measured using an 11-point confidence rating. Magnitude/ strength was measured by combining this measure with a magnitude (yes/ no) measure. In pre- and post-exposure tests, the explanatory power of measures that included efficacy strength was found to be much greater. However, main effects were found for magnitude. The authors concluded that different measures could contribute to different interpretations. Furthermore, their study treated self-efficacy as an independent variable and there may be differences in studies that test the effects of training on self-efficacy. Lee and Bobko (1994) compared five measures of self-efficacy: magnitude (yes/no), strength (confidence 0 to 10), composites of these computed as raw scores or z scores and confidence in outcome. Composite measures and measure of strength correlated most highly with self-set goals. Outcome efficacy was most closely associated with affectivity and past performance. The weight of evidence from these studies is that composite scores derived from magnitude and strength have greater validity.

While self-efficacy measures need to be standardized for the purposes of research, there may be good reason in clinical settings to invite patients to identify the situations most likely to lead to 'relapse' or temptation, and to focus on the development of self-efficacy in relation to these. Even where there are commonalities of experience, there may be important individual differences in efficacy beliefs and expectations that influence self-care activities. Self-efficacy change as a result of the intervention may provide useful data against which to measure the effectiveness of the intervention and the likelihood of long-term outcome. Overall, it would appear that the most effective use of self-efficacy measurement in health research is to be gained from computing composite scores prior to, and after, efficacy-enhancing interventions, i.e. those that involve teaching new skills and strategies for dealing with difficult situations. The resulting change scores appear to be a useful measure of the effectiveness of the intervention and also appear to be relatively good predictors of long-term adherence.

Self-efficacy in applied research: the importance of self-help and self-care

The measurement of self-efficacy, though useful in identifying potential skills deficits, may not predict those likely to respond to information about, or teaching of, self-management techniques. Wallston (1989: 101) argued that self-efficacy beliefs only predict behaviour in those with internal locus of control. Externals may believe that others can do it better, or that it makes no difference to the outcome whether or not they engage in the behaviour. For this reason, Wallston recommended the use of a new 'perceived competence' scale that combines efficacy expectancy with outcome expectancy. Schwarzer and Fuchs (1995) maintained that both self-efficacy and outcome efficacy play a key role in the adoption of health-related behaviours, such as exercise, eliminating detrimental habits, such as smoking, and maintaining change. This is consistent with findings of Hofstetter *et al.* (1990) that outcome efficacy is quite distinct from self-efficacy. Schwarzer and Fuchs (1995) reviewed a range of research that, they claimed, indicates self-efficacy to be an important variable in health behaviour change. Yet, as with other researchers in this field (e.g. Ajzen 1988), the findings as presented are misleading. Impressive *r* (correlation) values are given, even though the r^2 value is more important in indicating the proportion of variance explained. Typically, self-efficacy, in conjunction with other variables including outcome expectancy, explains around 30 per cent of the variance of intention to engage in a lifestyle behaviour. When combined with intention, these variables account for around 20 per cent of the variance of behaviour (for example, see Schwarzer and Fuchs 1995: 184). Self-efficacy is shown to have a direct effect on predicting healthy eating behaviour, independent of intention (Schwarzer and Fuchs 1995: 185).

Overall, the performance of self-efficacy as a predictor of behaviour change in the field of primary prevention has been promising. However, it was only really intended to apply to volitional processes. Lack of predictive power may result from measuring the wrong thing. Sexual behaviour is a good illustration of this. For example, self-efficacy in relation to putting on a condom is far less important than self-efficacy in relation to negotiating condom use with a partner (see Schwarzer and Fuchs (1995: 166–7)). This illustrates how essential it is to ensure that any questionnaire based on self-efficacy theory includes all aspects of efficacy, including social efficacy, required to initiate and implement the proposed behaviour.

Self-efficacy and self-care in chronic illness

The area of behaviour where self-efficacy has had most impact is in the management of chronic disorders such as diabetes, asthma and rheumatoid arthritis, where self-care interventions based on patient education have been taken up by nurses with much enthusiasm. Connelly (1987) identified self-care as essential to the management of chronic illness in order to avoid progression and repeated exacerbation of symptoms. Self-care in this context may include such lifestyle changes as long-term use of appropriate drugs and diet, as well as exercising and not smoking.

Examples of research based on the concept of self-efficacy are given in Table 4.2. One of the earliest researchers to demonstrate the success of self-management programmes for chronic disease was Thomas Creer in the field of asthma. Creer's innovative work with asthmatic children extends back to the early 1970s. Creer (1987) linked self-management to the development of self-efficacy and shift in locus of control from external to internal. One negative consequence of this (Creer *et al.* 1992) was loss of parental role in asthma management and reduction of revenue for doctors, nurses and hospitals. This is possibly a small price to pay for increased

Table 4.2 Examples of applications of the concept of self-efficacy in health-related research

Topic	Date	Authors	Summary
Anxiety and phobias			
Snake phobia	1977	Bandura et al.	Participant modelling → vicarious modelling → controls in terms of reducing anticipatory fear, nightmares and coping self-efficacy.
Diving anxiety	1982	Feltz	Path analysis of learning new skill (back diving) using physiological and self-report measures of anxiety, diving efficacy and observed performance. Self-efficacy was best predictor of heart rate arousal at first attempt and first diving performance, with subsequent reciprocal cause–effect relationship between efficacy and performance.
Self-defence and personal threat	1990	Ozer and Bandura	Self-defence training found to increase coping and cognitive control self-efficacy and lower levels of anxiety. Anticipatory anxiety and avoidant behaviour found to be co-effects of perceived self-inefficacy.
Stress and coping			
Coping skills training	1989	Smith	Coping skills training led to increase in self-efficacy but no change in locus of control.
Stress and immune system	1990	Wiedenfeld et al.	Experiment with phobics using Perceived Coping Self-Efficacy (Bandura et al. 1977). Improved self-efficacy through mastery modelling was associated with enhanced immuno-competence.
Cardio-vascular reactivity	1995	Gerin et al.	Experimental challenge. Self-efficacy moderated the effect of control manipulation and must be regarded as situation-specific. Those with high self-efficacy benefit from availability of greater control over outcomes.
Pain			
Pain control in childbirth	1983	Manning and Wright	Longitudinal study of primiparous women. Self-efficacy negatively correlated with use of pain medication. Outcome expectancies not clearly differentiated from efficacy expectancies, possibly due to conditions of uncertainty.

Table 4.2 cont'd

Topic	Date	Authors	Summary
Pain tolerance	1986	Dolce *et al.*	Experimental study using cold pressor test. Higher self-efficacy ratings consistently associated with greater pain tolerance times. Results support: past successes and failures as primary determinant of self-efficacy; belief that the situation will not become overwhelming is central to successful coping. Coping skills must be learned and feedback on their effectiveness sustained.
Pain tolerance	1987	Bandura *et al.*	Pain tolerance tested under experimental conditions. Findings: interaction between placebo and self-efficacy. Perceived self-efficacy predicted how well subjects managed pain. Recommends: medication should be used to support coping strategies, but may undermine these if the patient attributes pain control to medication rather than their own capabilities. Coping shown to involve opioid mechanisms.
Pain tolerance	1988	Litt	Cold pressor test under high and low control and self-efficacy conditions. Self-efficacy predicted tolerance: high control high self-efficacy resulted in best performance, followed by high self-efficacy, low control.
Chronic pain	1990	Kores *et al.*	Higher self-efficacy scores after treatment were related to increased activity at follow-up.
Chronic pain	1991	Jensen *et al.*	Beliefs regarding capabilities strongly related to reported coping efforts. Beliefs about consequences of coping efforts only weakly related to coping.
Chronic disorders Chronic obstructive pulmonary disease (COPD)	1984	Kaplan *et al.*	RCT to improve exercise: behaviour modification, cognitive modification, cognitive behaviour modification, attention control. Self-efficacy related to lung function prior to commencement. Changes in walking self-efficacy during programme related to exercise compliance on follow-up.
COPD	1994	Kaplan *et al.*	Self-efficacy in relation to specific activities was closely related to indicators of disease severity and good predictor mortality. Patient self-reports are meaningful and may be as good as expensive medical tests.

Asthma	1987	Creer	Management principles, based on self-management.
Rheumatoid arthritis	1989	Lorig *et al.*	Tested effect of a cognitive-behavioural treatment. Perceived self-efficacy to manage pain and symptoms was enhanced by treatment. Increase in self-efficacy was associated with decrease in depression.
Arthritis	1994	Hirano *et al.*	Systematic review of arthritis patient education studies 1978–1991. Conclusions included need to focus on fatigue and life changes resulting from arthritis; need to examine what makes educational interventions effective and assess financial savings from patient education programmes; educate physicians about the need to understand patient needs.
Outcomes in fibromyalgia	1995	Buckelow *et al.*	RCT comparing biofeedback, relaxation, exercise and combination training with control. Scores on arthritis self-efficacy scale. Baseline self-efficacy and efficacy change predicted treatment outcome on a range of variables.
Rheumatoid arthritis	1997	Smarr *et al.*	Prospective, randomized stress-management study, followed over 15 months. Increase in self-efficacy was associated with decrease in depression, helplessness, pain and negative affect, but not disease activity.
Diabetes	1996	Coates and Boore	No relationship found between knowledge of the condition and diabetic control. Concluded that patients need more than knowledge to become autonomous self-managers of their condition. Practitioners must focus more on patient needs in relation to their contexts.
Diabetes mellitus	1996	Boland and Grey	Correlational study of relationship of self-care strategies to metabolic control. Cognitive strategies predicted coping strategies that account for 18% of the variance in metabolic control. Concluded self-care education and modelling required.
Chronic illness	1990	Braden	Correlational design examining the relationship between disease characteristics, dependency, uncertainty, enabling skill, self-help and well-being. Self-help (adult role performance) and uncertainty explained 49% of the variance of psychological well-being. Enabling skill (ability to manage adversity) was best predictor of self-help.

Table 4.2 *cont'd*

Topic	Date	Authors	Summary
Oncology	1997	Lev	Review of self-efficacy theory in relation to aspects of oncology, including smoking cessation, screening participation and quality of life issues. Self-efficacy-enhancing interventions found to be associated with better compliance, psychological adjustment and self-care.
Coronary heart disease	1998	Sullivan *et al.*	6-month prospective study. Self-efficacy for controlling symptoms and managing function demonstrated enduring effect over 6 months.
Health-related behaviours			
Stages of self-change of smoking	1985	DiClemente *et al.*	Compared long-term quitters, recent quitters, relapsers, contemplators and immotives. Self-efficacy scores higher in quitters. Efficacy expectations were related to ability to maintain smoking cessation and move through the stages of change over time for contemplators and recent quitters.
Longitudinal effect of a smoking cessation programme on self-efficacy	1986	Baer *et al.*	Questionnaire administered by phone at monthly intervals from the end of programme to 3 months, and by interview at 6-month follow-up, with verified smoking status. Tested three different models of the relationship between self-efficacy and changes in smoking status. Future smoking status was best predicted by current behaviour; neither efficacy nor change efficacy was predictive of future behaviour. Overall, there was little evidence in favour of self-efficacy.
Smoking cessation	1994	Stuart *et al.*	Self-efficacy measured using Condiotte and Lichtenstein's Confidence Questionnaire. Baseline self-efficacy was associated with cessation, while self-efficacy increased in those who attempted to stop.
Addictive behaviours	1986	DiClemente	Review of related research. Self-efficacy applicable in relation to smoking, alcohol consumption and eating behaviours. Self-efficacy covaries with the change process. Measurement items need to refer to specific circumstances.

Contraceptive use in teenage girls	1986	Levinson	Test of CSE. Planning related to contraceptive use; lack of responsibility and assertiveness, and sexual arousal were related to having unprotected sex. Importance of self-efficacy is based on assumption that girls should and can exercise responsibility and control for sexual and contraceptive behaviour.
Lifespan Age	1987	Woodward and Wallston	Survey based on self-report of desire for control of health care and self-efficacy using 5-item health care self-efficacy scale (HSE), SE with respect to desire for health-related information (KI-SE) and General SE. Those aged over 60 showed less desire for health-related control and showed lower self-efficacy related to health decisions and information. High control afforded no advantage for those with low perceived efficacy.
Children's cognitive performance	1990	Chapman *et al.*	Personal agency beliefs were most strongly and consistently correlated with cognitive performance, indicating that internal LOC may reflect agency expectancies, rather than outcome expectancies.
Children and adolescents	1990	Holden *et al.*	Report of meta-analysis of 25 articles testing relationship between SE and subsequent behaviour. Effect size declined with interval of greater than one day between measurement of SE and outcome.
Life-span: review	1993	Berry and West	Review of empirical studies from childhood to old age. Self-efficacy found to predict persistence, effort, goal-setting, strategy use and choice. Identified paucity of research into age-related changes.
Workplace Collective efficacy in the workplace	1994	Parker	Teacher self-efficacy and collective efficacy (school as a whole) in attaining basic skills passes. Collective efficacy, but not self-efficacy, related to socio-economic status, which was a strong predictor of academic achievement.

independence and reduction of the sick role on the part of the child. Sadly, however, he reported a lack of adequate progress in the implementation of self-management programmes for asthmatic children despite strong evidence in favour of this approach.

Another important area of research into self-management focused on osteo-arthritis and was initiated by Kate Lorig during the 1980s. Lorig *et al.* (1985) demonstrated that a 12-hour interactive patient education programme resulted in an increase in knowledge, practice of exercise and relaxation, and decrease in pain. Lorig and Holman (1989) showed that the Arthritis Self-Management Course (ASMC) remained effective in terms of decrease in pain, depression and visits to a physician, though not disability, after 20 months. Follow-up training at one year conferred no additional benefits. Lorig *et al.* (1993) subsequently conducted a four-year follow-up study and found that attendance on the Arthritis Self-Management Programme (ASMP) continued to confer benefits in reducing pain and use of medical services despite deterioration in physical abilities. Perceived self-efficacy appeared to increase with time and Lorig *et al.* suggested that this mediates the benefits of the programme. However, Hirano *et al.* (1994) conducted a review of arthritis patient education intervention studies conducted between 1987 and 1991 and concluded that the mechanisms for effective intervention are still not known. A useful review of self-efficacy and other approaches for the management of arthritis is provided by Gonzalez *et al.* (1990).

Interventions may need to be tailored to meet the needs of different age or cultural groups. For example, Hickey (1988) suggested that since pain and disability are among the most common reasons for seeking treatment, health promotion programmes for older people should focus directly on these issues. Older people may be helped to make appropriate decisions about medication and service use, identify effective strategies and learn useful self-care practices and behaviours. Miller (1992b) identified a series of coping tasks required for the chronically ill individual and which might therefore be regarded as self-care behaviours. These included: maintaining a sense of normalcy [*sic*]; modifying daily routine and adjusting lifestyle; obtaining knowledge and skill for continuing self-care; adjusting to altered social relationships; grieving over losses concomitant with chronic illness; dealing with role change; handling physical discomfort; complying with prescribed regimen; confronting the inevitability of one's death; dealing with social stigma of illness or disability; maintaining a feeling of being in control; maintaining hope despite an uncertain or downward course of health. The reader cannot fail to be impressed by the sheer enormity of these tasks for any individual to have to face without substantial social support from a variety of sources. Perhaps this helps to explain why Krantz *et al.* (1980) found that not all hospital patients expressed a preference for involvement in their own care. These individual differences led them to hypothesize that it might be better to match patient preferences to treatment approaches and physicians' attitudes to self-care (see Chapter 2).

Self-efficacy is of little relevance in predicting how people will cope under conditions of uncertainty, such as using newly acquired skills or applying practised skills in novel situations. Self-efficacy may have little relevance in situations that are beyond the control of the individual or seen as such. Instrumental skills, such as contraception use, cannot be separated from the social skills required to implement them, while habitual behaviour patterns and peer pressure may be an important source of unexplained variance in outcomes.

Concluding comments

Self-efficacy is a clearly defined and understood concept that has remained conceptually unchanged since its inception. Although there are a number of measures that are valid and reliable and easy to apply, these do not have particularly good predictive power as one-off measurements, especially in complex social situations. The main utility in the concept of self-efficacy lies in its role in informing interventions designed to help people to gain new and relevant skills, have the confidence to use them, believe that they can do them and that they will work. Thus patient education should involve much more than information-giving or one-off demonstrations. Measurable improvement in self-efficacy during a treatment programme is likely to indicate long-term sustainability.

Note

1 Lefcourt (1966a) attributed the development of the concept of mastery to Alfred Adler, and suggested that White's constructs of competence and effectance are similar to Adler's 'superiority striving' (becoming more effective in controlling one's personal world).

Further reading

Bandura, A. (1997) *Self-efficacy: The Exercise of Control*. New York: W. H. Freeman.
Conner, M. and Norman, P. (eds) (1995) *Predicting Health Behaviour*. Buckingham: Open University Press.

Learned helplessness

CHAPTER 5

Overview of contents

- Conceptual origins
- The original 'learned helplessness' experiment
- Concept testing
- Analysis of the original concept of learned helplessness
- Reviews of learned helplessness
- Attribution reformulation of learned helplessness
- Critique of the reformulated model of learned helplessness
- Applications of reformulated helplessness theory
- Helplessness versus reactance
- Learned helplessness and common conceptual confusions
- From helplessness to hopelessness
- Hopelessness and pessimism
- Measures of helplessness and hopelessness
- Applications of learned helplessness in health care
- Concluding comments
- Further reading
- Note.

Conceptual origins

The concept of learned helplessness is associated in everyone's mind with Martin Seligman, an academic psychologist who established his reputation through his early work on animal learning. He was also a practising clinical psychologist recognized for his contribution to our understanding of human depression. However, interest in a concept of helplessness was present in the literature long before Seligman coined the term 'learned helplessness'. The phenomenon of 'experimental neurosis' was well known to those conducting Pavlovian animal conditioning experiments earlier in the twentieth century. The term was used to describe animals that started to shake with fear and become incapable of responding in experimental situations. Some time later psychologists started to draw analogies between this type of reaction and human emotional responses of fear and anxiety. Mowrer and Viek introduced the concept of helplessness as early as the 1940s, observing that 'A painful stimulus never seems so objectional if one knows how to terminate it as it does if one has no control over it' (Mowrer and Viek 1948: 193). Similarly, Champion (1950) demonstrated that human subjects were less disturbed when they believed they could turn off (control) an electric shock. Champion attributed this to differences in 'attitude'. Perhaps closest to articulating the concept of helplessness was Seeman on alienation. Seeman's definition of powerlessness is remarkably similar to later definitions of learned helplessness: 'the expectancy or probability, held by the individual, that his own behaviour cannot determine the occurrence of the outcomes, or reinforcement, he seeks' (Seeman 1959: 784).

Experiments to investigate responses to aversive stimuli proliferated during the 1950s and 1960s, most of which (unlike research into perceived control) focused on escape/avoidance in animals. In 1967, Overmier and Seligman, then a postdoctoral research fellow, published an important experimental paper describing the effects of inescapable shock on subsequent escape and avoidance behaviour in dogs. They used a yoked apparatus similar to that used by Brady *et al.* (1958) in the executive money experiment (see Chapter 2). Rather than explaining the animals' lack of response in terms of conditioned fear response, they suggested the source of interference as 'learned helplessness' in which all instrumental responses are learned to be of no avail in eliminating or reducing trauma (Overmier and Seligman 1967). Seligman and Maier (1967) and Seligman *et al.* (1968) subsequently published a systematic investigation of what they termed 'learned helplessness' (see also Dweck and Goetz 1978).

The original 'learned helplessness' experiment

The experiment typically involved two stages: a training stage and a testing stage, as illustrated below.

Seligman and Maier (1967)
♦ *Stage one* (training session). Two dogs were placed side-by-side in a harness and wired up using a 'yoke' to receive identical levels, intervals and duration of electric shock. The only difference was that one of the dogs could, on pressing a panel beside its muzzle, turn off the shock once delivered.

♦ *Stage two* (test session). Both dogs were removed from the harness and placed in a 'shuttle box'. Here, electric shocks were administered through the floor but the dogs could easily escape by jumping over a low barrier.

The findings demonstrated that the dog that had no control in the first stage, failed to make any attempt to escape the shocks in the second stage experiment. It just passively accepted the shocks (Seligman *et al.* 1968).

Seligman *et al.* (1968) found that the effects of 'learned helplessness' could be reversed by forcibly exposing the helpless animals to conditions in which they gained instrumental control (they were pulled away from the area in which the shock was being delivered). They noted similarities between the behaviour of the dogs that had been deprived of all control and Bettelheim's description of prisoners in Nazi concentration camps. They also noted an important link with Lefcourt's (1966b) observations that perceptions of control over events are an important determinant of human behaviour.

Concept testing

The concept of learned helplessness quickly captured the imagination of the psychological scientific community, leading to numerous experiments with human 'volunteers'. One of the advantages of human subjects is that they are able to report their reasons for not responding to potentially controllable stimuli in the second stage of the experiment (the transfer task). A few examples of early experimental studies on human subjects using the original conceptualization of learned helplessness are given in Table 5.1.

Numerous experiments followed to test the application of learned helplessness to human depression and to test for an increased tendency to helplessness among 'depressives'. Much of this experimental work focused on samples of university students, comparing those with higher scores on depression inventories (the BDI) to those with lower scores, rather than to those meeting the criteria for clinical depression. This is offered as a reason why findings did not always support the predictions of learned helplessness (Miller *et al.* 1975). A number of critical reviews ensued, arguing against the adoption of learned helplessness as an analogue for human depression (see Buchwald 1978; Costello 1978; Depue and Monroe 1978). Depue and Monroe (1978) criticized the use of self-report measures with depressed 'normal' individuals, claiming that research with such samples failed to provide an adequate analogy for clinical depression. Costello (1978: 30) expressed even greater reservations, stating: 'the experimental paradigms proposed are far too general and loose . . . the conceptual problems of the theory are horrendous.' Nevertheless, by the time Seligman published his book on learned helplessness (Seligman 1975) he was able to state that it had been ten years in the making, based on an array of similar laboratory experiments as well as observations in clinical practice.

Table 5.1 Early human experiments using the original concept of learned helplessness

Author(s)	Date	Findings
Thornton and Jacobs	1971	60% perceived no control during the transfer task[a] (so why bother?), while another 35 per cent just abandoned the idea of escaping.
Thornton and Powell	1974	Noted individual differences in responses to a transfer task[b] and postulated that, in humans, personality differences may account for the propensity of some, but not others, to succumb to helplessness.
Hiroto	1974	Identified a close relationship between external (chance) locus of control beliefs and helplessness. He postulated that these might reflect a single process.
Hiroto and Seligman	1975	Used inescapable noise and insoluble anagrams to induce a state of helplessness and concluded: 'learned helplessness may involve a trait-like system of expectancies that responding is futile' (p. 327).
Miller et al. Miller and Seligman	1975 1975	Tested the prediction that depressed students manifested responses similar to induced learned helpless in non-depressed students when confronted with tests of skill. Findings supported the claim that beliefs in response independence are a feature of human depression.
Klein et al.	1976	When depressed students attributed task failure to task difficulty rather than to their own incompetence, their performance improved substantially. Failure alone did not produce helplessness.
Klein and Seligman	1976	Non-depressed students were exposed to inescapable noise; depressed students not exposed to noise. Subsequent experience with controllable skill task reversed perceptions of response-independence and performance deficits in both groups.

Notes
[a] Transfer task refers to the experimental task conducted after exposure to helplessness.
[b] Champion (1950) had previously noted this.

Analysis of the original concept of learned helplessness

It is helpful for those using the term 'learned helplessness' to understand the concept as it was originally presented, since the use of the term in health care is often different from that originally proposed by Seligman.

Seligman was a learning theorist from the behaviourist tradition in psychology. He defined learned helplessness in terms of 'response independence' (otherwise termed response irrelevance) which, in terms of human thinking, means 'it makes no difference whether I do something or do nothing, the outcome will be the same.' If an outcome depends on the action of the organism, the organism has control and the event is controllable. It the outcome does not depend on any action of the organism, the event is uncontrollable and the organism 'helpless'. Seligman presented this in the form of a 'contingency space', which is illustrated in Figure 5.1.

Response independence (uncontrollability) is seen in Figure 5.1 to apply whether the outcome is positive or negative. Yet it is a common assumption that depression is associated with perceived lack of control over aversive events or negative outcomes. There are several reasons for this. First, it is difficult to conceive a causal link between positive outcomes and depression. Second, experimental work focused predominantly on the escape/avoidance responses to aversive events, so responses to positive events were not tested. Finally, it is difficult to detect non-contingency when one is winning (Abramson *et al.* 1978). Nevertheless, it is important to note that Seligman failed to distinguish between the impact of positive and negative outcomes, and his original theory is ostensibly applicable to both.

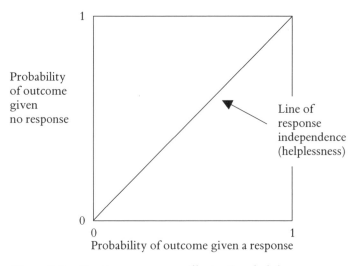

Figure 5.1 Contingency space illustrating helplessness
Source: after Seligman (1975: 17)

Seligman (1975: 47) asserted that information about contingent relation-ships between response and outcome is learned, leading to beliefs and expectations that affect future behaviour. He identified three deficits or disturbances associated with learned helplessness in experimental dogs which are also observed in depressed humans:

♦ a motivational disturbance (the organism gives up trying);
♦ a cognitive disturbance (the organism learns to predict an independent relationship between its actions and outcomes);
♦ an emotional disturbance which he identified as immediate fear and, in the longer term, depression.

Seligman (1975: 106) listed the similarities, in terms of symptoms, causes and cures, between learned helplessness and depression. Similarities of symptom included passivity, negative belief sets, weight and appetite loss, social and sexual deficits, and norepinephrine depletion. He claimed that both learned helplessness and depression were amenable to cure through direct exposure to successful responding, electroconvulsive therapy, time and norepinephrine stimulant drugs.

In addition to depression, Seligman addressed the relationship between anxiety and unpredictability, arguing in favour of the 'safety signal' hypothesis (cues to danger may cause fear, but prepare organisms for action; lack of danger cues mean that organisms are constantly on what might be termed tenterhooks). He argued that controllability implies that the outcomes of one's actions are predictable, though there is likely to be more to controll-ability than just predictability. Maier and Seligman (1976) reviewed the experimental evidence and presented experimental data in favour of the learned helplessness model, refuting alternative accounts and noting some theoretical confusion on the part of other investigators. Nevertheless, they agreed that the conditional boundaries within which learned helplessness applied were still vague, not least the apparent difference between subject-ive perceptions and objective conditions. They invited further experimental work to test the theory and emphasized the need to view learned helplessness within a cognitive framework.

Reviews of learned helplessness

Seligman and Weiss published a lengthy review of coping behaviour and learned helplessness, based on the transcript of a symposium held in 1976. In it, Seligman and his colleagues (1980) sought to distinguish between the conditioned physiological response (norepinephrine depletion) explanation favoured by Weiss, and Seligman's preferred cognitive explanation of learned helplessness. In addition to presenting empirical data to support the latter, Seligman favoured the cognitive explanation for its transferability to human depression. Weiss countered with his own interpretation of the empirical data, claiming that learned helplessness was 'a difficult concept to pin down scientifically' (Seligman *et al.* 1980: 480). Weiss concluded with the challenge: 'Is learned helplessness observable, falsifiable and testable?' (Seligman *et al.* 1980: 503), to which Seligman responded that indeed it was.

Klosterhalfen and Klosterhalfen (1983) subsequently published a review of 92 animal experiments, published in 49 papers, conducted between 1960 and 1980 (plus one in 1939), which had been cited in support of learned helplessness. In addition to exposing a variety of experimental flaws and ambiguous interpretations of findings, they identified that an important source of confusion lies in ambiguity in defining the term 'controllability'. They concluded that the majority of experimental findings were open to more parsimonious explanations (i.e. the effects of shock *per se*, or generalization effects). They acknowledged experimental evidence in favour of motivational deficits but found limited experimental support for associative (cognitive) and emotional deficits. This is important in view of the centrality placed on associative deficits in the formulation of the learned helplessness model and the central role of cognitive deficits in subsequent human research.

At this point, it is worth pausing to consider the changes that were taking place within psychology during the period in which the learned helplessness phenomenon was under study. Until the 1960s, psychologists tended to draw theoretical accounts from two main traditions, behaviourism and psychoanalysis. These were based on completely different sets of assumptions which, though some psychologists were brave enough to apply psychoanalytic explanations to behavioural phenomena, were fundamentally incompatible with each other. Seligman emerged from the behaviourist tradition and was one of the first psychologists to relate behavioural learning to cognitive processes based on probability learning, as exemplified in the use of the contingency space (Seligman 1975). However during the post-war period, social psychologists led by Heider (1958) developed attribution theory to explain human perceptions of events in a social context (i.e. whether they believed that they were responsible for outcomes, or if outcomes were caused by external agents). Indeed, Heider (1944) had already linked emotions to causal attributions, crediting Spinoza for the development of this understanding.

> In general it may be said that success or failure is experienced only when the source of the achievement (or, in the case of failure, the source of the inability to achieve a goal) is located in the own person. One of the devices used to lift morale is to restructure the field in such a way that a defeat is not attributed to one's own inferiority.
>
> (Heider 1944: 368)

It was only a matter of time before probability learning and attribution theory were linked together and one of the first theorists to do this appears to have been Carol Dweck (1975). In 1978, Dweck and Goetz published a review of the role of attributions in learned helplessness in children, based on a series of classroom experiments. They noted gender differences in susceptibility to helplessness. Girls, they noted, were generally more successful than boys in elementary school, yet they showed greater evidence of helplessness than boys following failure feedback from adults. Girls were more likely to attribute feedback on failure from a teacher to lack of ability, whereas boys tended to attribute this to lack of effort. Observation in the classroom led them to explain this in terms of the more frequent feedback received by boys for non-intellectual behaviours. In contrast, girls tended to receive little negative feedback, which was mainly directed at intellectual aspects of their work. Overall, attributions differentiated between helpless and mastery-oriented children. The latter regarded the experience of failure as a challenge, while failure had a very detrimental effect on children identified as 'helpless'. It was on the basis of Dweck's work that Miller and Norman (1979) published a review of learned helplessness and proposed a model based on attribution theory. This was prepared at the same time as the better known Abramson attribution reformulation (see below), and the two models were remarkably similar.

Attribution reformulation of learned helplessness

In 1978, Abramson *et al.* published a critical review of the literature on learned helplessness and reformulated the theory in terms of attribution theory. A number of inadequacies of the existing theory were identified, including the distinction made by Bandura between efficacy and outcome expectations. This resulted in the distinction between personal helplessness (my own inability to achieve the desired outcome) and universal helplessness (the inability of self or others to achieve the desired outcome), which they believed addressed this anomaly. This is illustrated in Table 5.2. Note that cells a and b were not considered relevant since individuals do not believe themselves to be helpless (Abramson *et al.* 1989: 11).

Table 5.2   Internal and external attributions of helplessness

Person expects	Outcome contingent on own response	Outcome not contingent on own response
Outcome contingent on response of other	(a) Not relevant	(c) Personal helplessness (internal attribution)
Outcome not contingent on response of other	(b) Not relevant (internal attribution)	(d) Universal helplessness (external attribution)

Source: after Abramson *et al.* (1978: 53).

The attribution reformulation remained problematic, possibly because locus of control had been conceptualized as unidimensional (internal–external). Had Abramson *et al.* (1978) drawn on the reconceptualization of locus of control offered by Levenson (1974), it might have become apparent that universal helplessness is associated with external (chance) attributions, though not necessarily with external (other) attributions (I analyse this distinction in Chapter 8). Another problem with the model as presented in Table 5.2 is that it fails to account for uncertainty. There are many situations where individuals living in a complex world are likely to be uncertain about their ability or the ability of others to deal with events that arise. To present the picture in black and white would appear to be unhelpful. Indeed, Abramson *et al.* (1989) acknowledged that these axes were supposed to represent continua.

An important inadequacy of the original helplessness model was identified by Abramson *et al.* (1978) as the failure to differentiate between beliefs related to specific situations and global beliefs; and stable versus unstable attributions. Their reanalysis led them to propose that chronic depression is associated with internal (it's me), global (in all situations) and stable (always) expectations of inability to achieve outcomes. They expressed the belief that this explanation accounts for the omnipresence of low self-esteem in depressives and explains the generality and chronicity of depression. This led them to include lack of self-esteem as the fourth deficit associated with learned helplessness, along with the previously recognized motivational, cognitive and affective deficits. Abramson *et al.* recognized that people rarely appear to become depressed when presented with positive outcomes over which they have no control, but postulated that such lack of control may contribute to increased vulnerability to depression in the face of subsequent failure.

Abramson *et al.* (1978: 69) presented a table of treatment strategies implied by both the original and the reformulated learned helplessness models. Some key principles included:

◆ support the individual to reduce the likelihood of aversive events and increase the likelihood of desired events;
◆ reduce the desirability of highly desired outcomes to avoid disappointment;
◆ provide skills training to increase the range of events that are demonstrably within their control;
◆ change attributions for failure towards external, unstable and specific, and for success to internal, stable and general.

Critique of the reformulated model of learned helplessness

Wortman and Dintzer (1978) were quick to offer a critique of the reformulated learned helplessness phenomenon, posing a series of questions:

♦ 'Do people make attributions?' (p. 76). They argued that this assumption cannot be taken at face value.
♦ 'Is there a relation between attributions of causality and subsequent behaviour?' (p. 77). They cited studies indicating that the link between attributions and behaviour is not straightforward and one of the reasons for this is the uncertainty usually associated with making causal attributions.
♦ 'What kinds of attributions are important?' (p. 78). They identified the need to distinguish among attributions for immediate causality, background or prior causal factors, and ability to manage outcomes. Using the example of cancer, they proposed that attributions of causality might not be nearly as important as attributions of one's ability to cope with the outcome.
♦ 'Is the reformulated account consistent with the experimental evidence?' (p. 79). They noted some inconsistencies in the findings of experimental studies, though this might have been accounted for by the contrived nature of the situations and samples used. In considering the findings of some of Wortman's own previous research, they noted that the best predictors of poor coping with chronic injury were: attributions of blame to others; perceived avoidability of the accident; lack of self-blame. Those who fell victim while pursuing an activity of their own free choice and who accepted the blame (made internal, stable attributions) coped best. Those who perceived themselves to be the innocent victims of others (external, unstable attributions) coped worst. These findings contradict the learned helplessness model as reformulated.

Wortman and Dintzer (1978) then considered issues not taken into account in the reformulated model. These included:

♦ 'Was the outcome foreseeable at the time of the original event?' (p. 81). For example, was the individual aware at the time that his or her behaviour might jeopardize future health?
♦ 'Was the outcome expected?' (p. 82). They cited evidence that it is easier to come to terms with the expected, than with the unexpected, death of a spouse.
♦ 'Is it possible to attribute meaning to the outcome?' (p. 83). Setting up a charitable trust in memory of the individual may help to give meaning to their death;
♦ 'Is the outcome likely to recur in the future?' (p. 84). Attribution to one's own shortcomings allows the individual to take action to avoid future recurrence.

Wortman and Dintzer went on to argue that the reformulated model did not predict when people were likely to respond to lack of control by becoming helpless and when, as reported in some experiments, they responded by enhancing their performance. However, it is very unlikely that the subjects of these experiments, university students, would accept personal responsibility for failure in such experimental situations and respond to a short period of helplessness training with generalized negative attributions for the outcomes of their subsequent actions. In terms of future research, they recommended longitudinal studies directed towards understanding what constitutes a maladaptive response to life crises, and ways in which these may be changed.

Applications of reformulated helplessness theory

In 1980, an important publication (Garber and Seligman 1980) appeared in which a number of well known authors addressed theory and applications related to helplessness in humans:

◆ Abramson *et al.* (pp. 3–34) reproduced their attributional reformulation of learned helplessness, together with some additional analyses of available evidence.

◆ Weiner and Litman Adizes (pp. 35–57) presented an analysis of attributions for learned helplessness based on Weiner's previous work on achievement motivation.

◆ Alloy and Abramson (pp. 59–70) presented a critical analysis of the cognitive component of helplessness and depression, identifying a lack of research on clinical populations.

◆ Miller (pp. 71–95) examined the willingness of individuals to endure aversive stimuli over which they have control, introducing the Minimax hypothesis as an alternative to internality. Here, individuals will endure the stimulus provided they can impose an upper limit to their suffering[1] but will choose to relinquish control to others when they believe it is in their power to minimize maximum danger.

◆ Chanowitz and Langer (pp. 97–129) explored anomalies in perceptions of control. In contrasting conscious (mindful) with unconscious (mindless) control, they suggested that mindless involvement can lead to misattributions of responsibility. They used the example of the car driver to illustrate how it is possible to maintain mindless control (in the absence of total conscious awareness of all that is occurring).

◆ Garber *et al.* (pp. 131–69) examined the important distinctions in affect, behaviour, somatic symptoms and cognitions between anxiety and depression in relation to perceived control, certainty and the probability of outcomes. They sought to clarify the relationship between controllability and certainty, using a contingency space that distinguished between different levels of probability of a bad outcome (this is illustrated in Figure 8.6d, where it is contrasted with other interpretations).

Garber and Seligman (1980) included a series of studies and reviews of helplessness theory applied to various topics, including depression (Hollon and Garber), intellectual achievement (Dweck and Licht), coronary-prone personality (Glass and Carver), locus of control (Lefcourt), ageing (Schultz) and coping with undesirable life events (Silver and Wortman). This book remains one of the most important texts on human helplessness. There followed a plethora of laboratory and field research into different aspects of the attribution model of learned helplessness, examples of which are summarized in Table 5.3.

One of the key issues to emerge was the issue of attributional style in depression. Sweeney *et al.* (1986) reviewed the available attributional studies in relation to both the Abramson *et al.* (1978) and Miller and Norman (1979) attribution models. Both models suggest that the relation between perceived loss of control and depression is mediated by causal attributions for uncontrollability. Internal attributions for loss of control would account for loss of self-esteem. Stable attributions account for the chronicity of depression. Global attributions account for generalization of perceived uncontrollability. Accordingly, Abramson *et al.* (1978) had proposed that internal, stable and global attributions for failure, but not success, are associated with depression. A meta-analysis of studies based on the use of the ASQ (Attributional Style Questionnaire: Peterson *et al.* 1982) was conducted by Sweeney *et al.* (1986). They identified that effect sizes were generally modest, though commensurate with other personality variables in psychology. Evidence in favour of a causal link between attributional style and depression was 'promising'. Overall, they concluded that attributions were found to relate to depression in the predicted manner.

Helplessness versus reactance

Much of the criticism by Wortman and Dintzer (1978) was based on earlier work by Wortman and Brehm (1975), which had studied responses to uncontrollable outcomes, comparing learned helplessness with Brehm's reactance theory. Reactance refers to the motivation to restore control once it has been removed. Wortman and Brehm predicted that the two theories might be complementary. Reactance should only occur when the individual expects to have control over outcomes, and then only to the extent that the outcome is important. Reactance is accompanied by feelings of arousal and anger. This may be superseded by a state of helplessness once expectations of control have gone. Wortman and Brehm thus proposed an integrative model that combined expectations of control with motivation to exert control. The integrative model was reviewed by Taylor (1979), who found evidence to support it in terms of patient behaviour in hospital. She proposed that 'good' patients (those who are compliant and passive) are in a state of helplessness, whereas 'bad' patients (those who are angry, make demands and complain) are in a state of reactance. Her paper makes an important contribution to our understanding of patient needs for a participative role in their own care.

Table 5.3 Studies of learned helplessness, based on the attribution formulation

Author	Year	Type	Main findings/observations
Seligman *et al.*	1979	Experiment with college students	Depressed students more likely to attribute bad outcomes to internal, stable and global causes, as measured by attributional style scale.
Dohrenwend and Martin	1979	Community-based study of reported stressful life events	Situational contingencies (negative life events) appeared more likely to affect perceptions of control than dispositional factors.
Burger and Arkin	1980	Experiment with college students	Perceptions of control or predictability appeared to be functionally equivalent. Highlights analogy between learned helplessness and Glass and Singer's (1972) 'urban stress' paradigm.
Garber and Hollon	1980	Experiment with college students	Depressed individuals attributed failure in skilled task to their own incompetence (personal helplessness), rather than response independence (universal helplessness).
Zuroff	1980	Review	Individual difference variables in helplessness are: generalized expectancies for reinforcement, perceived locus of control and problem-solving strategies. Situational variables are: valence of outcome and locus of control. Further studies of these in naturalistic settings required.
Baum and Gatchel	1981	Experiment with college students, part naturalistic	Attributing loss of control to environmental conditions was associated with mood and behaviour deficits. Attributions to personal factors may reflect initial reactance. Responses in laboratory settings may be different from 'real world'.
Peterson *et al.*	1981	Female undergraduates	Self-blame covaried with negative life events, but was found not to be a predisposing factor for depression.

Author	Year	Study	Findings
Alloy and Abramson	1982	Experiment with male and female college students	Non-depressed students exposed to uncontrollable noise showed illusions of control when subsequently faced with non-contingent problems offering the apparent possibility of winning. Depressed students judged control accurately in the same circumstances.
Raps et al.	1982	Comparison of attributional style of depressed patients with others	Attributional style questionnaire (ASQ) used to compare depressives, schizophrenics, medical/surgical patients. Depressives more likely to attribute bad events to internal, stable and global causes and more evenhanded in explaining success and failure in similar ways.
Seligman et al.	1984	Tested children's attributional style for good and bad events	Applied ASQ. As predicted, children with depressive symptoms were more likely to endorse internal stable and global explanations for bad events and vice versa for good events.
Peterson and Seligman	1984	Review plus series of cross-sectional, longitudinal and experimental studies of attributional style	Internal, stable, global attributional style results in depression once bad events encountered. Therefore, future investigations should treat attributional style as a dependent variable, to identify responsiveness to events and review its plasticity.
Seligman et al.	1984	Survey of 8–13 year old boys and girls	Children with depressive symptoms more likely to endorse internal, stable and global explanations for bad events, with opposite style for good events. Child's attributional style correlated with mother's but not father's. Gender differences not explored.
Peterson et al.	1985	Correlational study of college students	Attribution of recent end of a serious romance to internal, stable and global causes was not associated with depression, rather the reverse. Those depressed were more likely to be angry than helpless.
Nolen-Hoeksema et al.	1986	Longitudinal study of children	Children who associated bad events with internal, stable and global causes, and good events with external, unstable and specific causes, reported more depression.

Table 5.3 *cont'd*

Author	Year	Type	Main findings/observations
Metalsky *et al.*	1987	Reactions of students to examination	Findings supported a diathesis–stress model of depression in which individuals confronted with negative life events are more likely to become depressed if they make internal, stable, global attributions for failure. However, the diathesis × stress effect accounted for only 4–7% of the variance in residual changes in BDI scores and failed to predict anxiety.
Follette and Jacobson	1987	Longitudinal study of students	No relationship found between attributional style and depressed mood following examination failure in contradiction of Metalsky *et al.* (1987). Internal attributions related to lack of ability might be more likely to lead to depression than internal attributions related to lack of effort.
Peterson *et al.*	1988	35-year longitudinal study of risk for physical illness	Men who explained bad events with stable, global, internal causes at age 25 were less healthy later in life than men who made unstable, specific, external explanations. Mechanisms debated.
Brown and Siegel	1988	Prospective study of effects of negative events	Internal, stable, global attributions were associated with depression where events were attributed to uncontrollable factors. Perceived controllability explains inconsistencies in previous findings.

Learned helplessness and common conceptual confusions

The concept of learned helplessness has long held intuitive appeal for researchers working in the field of health care, regardless of its formulation. Most of us can identify with the concept at a very fundamental level. Perhaps one of the main reasons for this is that, by signalling that depressive beliefs are learned, they can be unlearned or even avoided in the first place. This enables the health professional to empower (or hand back control to) patients or clients. Very few health professionals appear to be familiar with the different formulations of the concept and even fewer are aware of the controversies surrounding the concept that have been fuelled by conflicting experimental findings. Evidence from the literature suggests that the concept is generally applied in a pragmatic way. Common usage is typified in a quotation from Ken Wallston:

> The antithesis of perceiving control is to feel helpless. Learned helplessness theory (Abramson *et al*. 1978) states that, when a person comes to believe that his or her outcomes are not contingent on his or her behaviour, there are significant motivational, emotional and behavioural consequences. Feeling helpless is similar to feeling incompetent, non-self-efficacious, and to having a chance locus of control orientation. People who feel helpless either do not engage in 'positive' health behaviours or abandon those behaviours before they can have a 'positive' effect on health status.
>
> (Wallston 1997: 153)

This quotation makes no mention of stable and global attributions and reference is made to chance, rather than internal, locus of control beliefs as emphasized in the concept of learned helplessness.

Learned helplessness is typically used by health professionals to explain lack of motivation, dependency and low mood, rather than clinical depression. For example, White and Janson (1986) used helplessness to explain passivity, dependency and powerlessness in older people, while Baltes and Baltes (1986) linked learned helplessness to dependency in their index. Yet nowhere is dependency identified as a component of learned helplessness in the theoretical literature. Helplessness has also been linked to powerlessness. For example, Mirowsky and Ross (1989) describe how learned helplessness, lack of personal control, fatalism and powerlessness are roughly interchangeable in a wide range of instances. Health professional conceptualizations of learned helplessness appear to be encapsulated in the sociological definition of powerlessness offered by Mirowsky and Ross:

> An individual learns through social interaction and personal experience that his or her choices and efforts are usually likely or unlikely to affect the outcome of a situation. Failure in the face of effort leads to a sense

of powerlessness, fatalism or belief in external control, which can in turn increase the passivity and the likelihood of giving up.

(Mirowsky and Ross 1989: 133)

Miller commented: 'constructs such as helplessness, learned helplessness, external locus of control and powerlessness all connote that individuals believe that outcomes of events are not contingent upon their own behaviours' (Miller 1992c: 51). This would appear to imply that events are seen as external to the self. However, as Gilbert (1992) pointed out, the attribution model was reformulated to conform to Beck's theory of depression, in which individuals are seen to blame themselves (internal attribution). The prospective study of Brown and Siegel (1988) indicates that depression results from a combination of internal attributions and uncontrollable outcomes (people blame themselves for negative outcomes that were beyond their control). These findings are in keeping with Wortman and Brehm's (1975) predictions. Overall, there remained theoretical confusion about the relationship between helplessness and locus of control.

From helplessness to hopelessness

Confusions of the type referred to above (see Phares 1990: 474–6 for a brief and succinct review) led, during the mid-1980s, to a further revision of the concept of learned helplessness. In 1988, Lyn Abramson, together with Lauren Alloy and Gerald Metalsky, first published their 'hopelessness' theory of depression (Alloy et al. 1988; Abramson et al. 1989). In fact, this was the reformulated theory of human helplessness (Abramson et al. 1978) under another name. Alloy et al. (1988) described how they reached the disturbing conclusion that conflicting findings resulted from the use of inadequate research strategies to test the theory. Previous strategies had failed to recognize the heterogeneity of depressive disorders (the presence of different subtypes), while causal relationships were inadequately defined. In this paper, they sought to distinguish between the necessary, sufficient and contributory causes of depressive symptoms: 'whereas helplessness is a necessary component of hopelessness, it is not sufficient to produce hopelessness (i.e. hopelessness is a subset of helplessness; Garber et al. 1980)' (Abramson et al. 1989: 359). Necessary refers to factors that must be present for helplessness to occur. Sufficient refers to a factor that, once present, assures the onset of depression. 'Contributory factors' refer to factors that increase the probability of depressive symptomatology. The authors also distinguished between distal and proximal causes. Distal causes refer to early aetiological risk factors, while proximal causes refer to precipitant risk factors.

According to hopelessness theory, a proximal sufficient cause of depression is an expectation that highly desired outcomes are unlikely to occur, or that highly aversive outcomes are likely to occur and that no response in one's repertoire will change the likelihood of occurrence of these outcomes.

(Alloy *et al.* 1988: 7; Abramson *et al.* 1989: 359)

Alloy *et al.* (1988) illustrated a causal chain of events likely to lead to depression, summarized below:

Negative life events (stress) + depressogenic attributional style (the diathesis)
↓
Stable and global attributions
+
Attachment of high importance to the event
↓
Expectations of hopelessness
↓
Symptoms of depression

According to this model, lowered self-esteem results from internal stable and global attributions. Other contributory factors, such as lack of social support, may also impact on expectations of hopelessness. Expectations of hopelessness are predicted to influence the continuance of the depressive episode (its chronicity) and future relapse. Alloy *et al.* (1988) proposed that an adequate test of hopelessness theory should contain the following components:

1 A test of the aetiological chain hypothesized to lead to hopelessness depression.
2 An examination of the depressive symptoms hypothesized.
3 A test of theoretical predictions about course, relapse and recurrence of hopelessness depressive symptoms.
4 A test of theoretical predictions about the cure and prevention of hopelessness depression.
5 Delineation between hopelessness and other subtypes of depression.

They went on to elaborate on the likely nature of the aetiological chain and the protocols for measuring attributional styles.

Abramson *et al.* (1989) published a more detailed elaboration of the hopelessness theory in which they envisaged revisions in the light of future research. Among the key issues to be resolved, they identified: the temporal development of helplessness depression; the stability of cognitive diatheses; the accessibility of attributions; the construct of 'negative life events' (including episodic events, chronic stressors and daily hassles); and the nature of feedback loops within the theory.

Metalsky and Joiner (1992) tested a causal model of hopelessness in which contributory factors included:

◆ depressogenic inferential style about causes, consequences and self (the diatheses);

- negative life events (the stress);
- situational cues (consensus, consistency, distinctiveness, information).

Leading to:

- stable, global attribution for negative life events;
- and/or inferred negative consequences of negative life events;
- and/or inferred negative characteristics of self.

Leading to:

- hopelessness depression (included retarded personal action, sad affect, apathy, sleep disturbance, difficulty in concentration, negative thoughts and, if attribution is internal, lowered self-esteem).

Other possible contributory factors were identified as lack of social support. Metalsky and Joiner reported evidence in favour of the diathesis–stress and causal mediation components of the hopelessness theory of depression in a prospective study of students; this despite the finding that the diathesis × stress effect accounted for only 4–7 per cent of the variance in residual changes in BDI scores and failed to predict anxiety. They concluded that the hopelessness theory offered a promising causal model. It certainly helps to address the complexity of the social situations in which most people live.

Abramson *et al.* (1989) described hopelessness depression as 'a theory-based subtype of depression'. Beck had previously identified hopelessness as one of the core characteristics of depression (Beck *et al.* 1974). In identifying the hopelessness theory as a 'new' theory, Abramson *et al.* (1989) distinguished it from other cognitive theories (notably those of Beck, and Brown and Harris) in a number of ways, the most salient of which is its emphasis on environmental causes in addition to cognitive, explanatory or attributional style. Nevertheless, much of the subsequent research appears to have emphasized cognitive style.

Hopelessness and pessimism

The literature supports a recent renewal of interest in optimistic and pessimistic cognitive style. Schulman *et al.* (1993) investigated heritability of optimism, administering the Attributional Style Questionnaire (ASQ) to monozygotic and dizygotic twins, reared together, recruited at a twins fair. They found evidence of concordance among monozygotic but not dizygotic twins, favouring an inherited tendency to optimism. This explanation is in keeping with the hopelessness theory in predicting an interaction between beliefs and experience. These authors elected not to use the Hopelessness Scale developed by Beck *et al.* (1974), which directly measures pessimism/optimism. Wallston (1994) signalled scepticism about the use of such scales. He favoured a distinction between cautious optimists (those in touch with reality) and what he referred to as 'cockeyed' optimists (those who have illusions of positive outcomes and delusions of control over outcomes). Cockeyed optimists are likely to hold chance locus of control beliefs, believing that things will turn out OK. They may therefore be unlikely to take direct action to avert bad outcomes, even if they could. There is no reason to suppose that a similar analysis would not apply to pessimism. Some pessimists do nothing to try to avert bad outcomes – indeed some may actually set out to support their negative predictions – while others are labelled pessimists because they routinely weigh up the possibility of bad outcomes but then do their best to avert or avoid them.

Measures of helplessness and hopelessness

Examples of measures used in research into helplessness/hopelessness are given in Table 5.4. These largely reflect either hopelessness or attributional style (pessimism versus optimism). Many studies that make reference to learned helplessness are actually based on measures of locus of control or depression, neither of which measures helplessness. While the affective and motivational deficits associated with hopelessness are reflected in measures of depression, the cognitive deficit associated with helplessness is often overlooked. Studies in institutional settings have provided good examples of research into the phenomenon of helplessness, though confounding between helplessness and dependence remains a problem. The measurement of helplessness is most usefully incorporated into longitudinal studies, where it is possible to establish whether helplessness is increasing or decreasing over time. This at least facilitates an investigation into causal factors. One of the main attractions of the concept of learned helplessness was that it directed attention to situational factors. The measurement of optimistic or pessimistic attributional style would appear to be a rather retrograde step in health care. It focuses attention back to the patient, rather than their circumstances. This can precipitate fundamental attribution error and lead to victim-blaming. We can do nothing about personalities, but we can change situations.

Applications of learned helplessness in health care

A summary of studies that have applied learned helplessness in the field of health care is given in Table 5.5. It can be seen that the range of topics is far less than those studied in relation to the concepts previously reviewed. One reason may be the absence of valid and reliable measures and the reluctance on the part of many researchers to use objective tests of cognitive deficits in addition to using self-report measures. Another problem, as identified in the study by Raps *et al.*, is the difficulty in distinguishing between helplessness, hopelessness and dependence.

Table 5.4 Measures of helplessness and hopelessness

Title	Date	Authors	Availability	Summary of measure used
General measures				
Hopelessness Scale	1974	Beck *et al.*	All items given	20 true–false items developed for use with depressed psychiatric patients. Three factors identified reflecting affect, motivation and cognition.
Subjective Helplessness Measure (H25)	1979	Donovan *et al.* (originated by Glass in 1977)		Based on future-oriented motivational deficits in relation to pleasurable events that, when engaged in provide a source of response-contingent reinforcement. Tested with alcoholics. Findings indicate that H25 is a valid measure of helplessness depression.
Attributional Style Questionnaire (ASQ)	1982	Peterson *et al.*	Example item given	Rather complex. Based on 6 good and 6 bad hypothetical events related to interpersonal or achievement-related situations. Subjects asked to write down cause, together with ratings of internality, stability, globality and importance. Resistance to social response bias demonstrated by Schulman *et al.* (1987).
Extended Attributional Style Questionnaire (EASQ)	1987 1992	Metalsky *et al.* Metalsky and Joiner		Similar to the ASQ. Includes a generality subscale (stability + globality).

Learned Helplessness Scale (LHS)	1988	Quinless and Nelson	No details given	20-item scale developed as part of doctoral research. 5 factors elicited: internality–externality, globality, stability, ability and choice.
Specific measures				
Arthritis Helplessness Index (AHI)	1985	Nicassio *et al.*	All items given with scoring system	15 items with 4-point Likert scale for use with rheumatoid arthritis. Internal consistency 0.69. Authors suggest the scale may reflect predictability and helplessness. Strong correlation with internal LOC (–ve), self-esteem (–ve), anxiety and depression.
Rheumatology Attitudes Index (RAI)	1988	Callahan *et al.*	All items given with scoring system	15 items with 5-point Likert scale that substitutes 'condition' for 'arthritis'. For use with rheumatology patients.
Arthritis Helplessness Subscale	1988	Stein *et al.*	All items given with scoring system	5 items with 6-point Likert scale (includes one positive item). Patients classified into high, normal and low helplessness using cut-off scores. Suggest this may be a simple and useful clinical screening tool. Good correlation with AHI and predictive validity confirmed by DeVellis and Callahan (1993).

Table 5.5 Applied health-related research using learned helplessness

Topic	Date	Authors	Overview
Epilepsy	1980	DeVellis *et al.*	Sample with epilepsy was less internal and more inclined that their health was a matter of chance or fate, and were more depressed than normative populations. Findings accounted by unpredictability/uncontrollability and severity of the seizures.
Patient behaviour in hospital	1982	Raps *et al.*	Tested helplessness and reactance theory (after Taylor 1979). Data supported prediction that helplessness is engendered by hospitalization. Increased stay associated with decrease in problem-solving ability and depressive symptoms.
Comment on Raps *et al.*	1983	Baltes and Skinner	Suggested that the cognitive deficits found are not due to non-contingency but as reinforcement of passive, dependent behaviours or role change.
Comment on Baltes and Skinner	1984	Peterson and Raps	Agreed with methodological criticism. Helplessness proposes sufficient conditions for performance deficits, not necessary conditions.
Chronic pain	1983	Skevington	Depression associated with higher external (chance) LOC and lower internal LOC scores, but not self-blame. The findings support the presence of universal helplessness, but not personal helplessness in back pain patients attending a self-help group.
Attempted suicide	1983	Petrie and Chamberlain	Hopelessness, rather than depression, explained suicidal intent.
Psychiatry	1984	Valine and Phillips	Tested if helpless beliefs militated against outcomes in group therapy. No significant differences found and methodology acknowledged as problematic.

Topic	Year	Author	Findings
Prediction of illness	1987	Peterson and Seligman	Stability + globality, but not internality, was associated with subsequent infections, illness and visits to the doctor. Various explanations offered.
Predictors of long term health	1988	Peterson *et al.*	Long-term study of explanatory style and physical health using CAVE (content analysis of verbatim explanations) technique. Men who explained bad events with stable global and internal causes at age 25 were less healthy later in life.
Rheumatoid arthritis	1990	Smith *et al.*	Helplessness accounted for association between disease severity and depression. Cognitive distortion (hopelessness) and helplessness are unique predictors of depression, controlling for disease severity.
Burnout in nurses	1993	Glass *et al.*	Structural modelling indicates that lack of perceived job control leads to burnout that leads to depression. Those scoring high on burnout were more accurate in their perceptions of job control, supporting the 'depressive realism' effect.
Cocaine dependence	1996	Sterling *et al.*	Compared LHS (Quinless and Nelson) scores between completers and non-completers on treatment programme and relationship to negative urine tests. Findings support the use of the LHS for clinical purposes, over and above measures of depression.
Multiple Sclerosis	1996	McGuiness	Correlational study. Learned helplessness measured using LHS (Quinless and Nelson), disease impact using specific measures. Scores on learned helplessness associated with functional and social incapacity, employment but not disease status. Causal links not established. Attributional retraining recommended.
Cocaine dependence	1996	Sterling *et al.*	Helplessness was related to more distress, but not to cocaine at start of treatment. Higher LHS scores were related to premature treatment termination.

In the field of mental health, Gilbert (1992: 178) maintained that learned helplessness theory has become one of the most important theories of depression for a number of reasons:

♦ it predicts a relationship between control and psychobiological change;
♦ its effects have been noted in many species;
♦ the effects of loss of control on exploratory behaviour, vegetative and appetitive processes are consistent.

It seems ironic that while psychologists have moved away from the original conceptualization of learned helplessness, those working in the field of sociobiology and sociology have clung on to its original tenets. Learned helplessness remains one of the most important concepts in the field of health care and one with which most professionals can easily identify. However, common usage usually seems to be closer to the original formulation than with subsequent reformulations, leading to much confusion. I address some of these confusions and indicate how I believe they may be resolved in Chapter 8.

Concluding comments

Learned helplessness has tremendous intuitive appeal. It has entered the common language used by health professionals, where it is often confused with dependence. In reality, the concept appears to have failed to live up to its promises as a theory of human depression, and neither has it proved productive in terms of generating much in the way of research or predictive findings in real-life settings. In Chapter 8, I offer a new analysis of learned helplessness that, I hope, will lead to a resurgence of interest among academics and researchers.

Note

1 An important factor in patient-controlled analgesia.

Further reading

Garber, J. and Seligman, M. E. P. (eds) (1980) *Human Helplessness: Theory and Applications*. Orlando, FL: Academic Press.
Gilbert, P. (1992) *Depression: The Evolution of Powerlessness*. Hove: Lawrence Erlbaum Associates.
Peterson, C., Maier, S. F. and Seligman, M. E. P. (1993) *Learned Helplessness: A Theory for the Age of Personal Control*. New York: Oxford University Press.
Seligman, M. E. P. (1975) *Helplessness: On Depression, Development and Death*. New York: W. H. Freeman.

Social support

Overview of contents

- Rationale for the inclusion of social support
- Defining social support
- Types of social support
- Social support and stress: the buffer hypothesis
- Negative aspects of social support
- Reciprocity, equity and social exchange
- Help-giving and help-seeking
- Social skills, personality and social relationships
- Self-help and social support
- Social support and health
- Variables that interact with social support
- Measurement of social support
- Concluding comments
- Further reading
- Note.

Rationale for the inclusion of social support

Social support is fundamental to any discussion of control for reasons that will become apparent in this chapter and in Chapter 8. The previous chapters have focused almost exclusively on individuals and their perceptions of their own abilities or inabilities to control events or achieve certain outcomes. Although it was recognized by Bandura, the main reference to the role of 'others' in control has been in relation to the concept of external locus of control, in particular the role of 'powerful others'. 'Powerful others' in the context of health care are commonly interpreted as 'powerful doctors'. This ignores the important role of family and friends, on whom most of us depend during the course of our lives, and the support agencies on which many sick or disabled people must depend in order to survive. The fact is that human beings live in a social world in which they are unable to exist or keep things 'under control' without the support of others.

The inclusion of this chapter is based on the premise that the way in which we interact with others, and they interact with us, not only provides us with a direct source of control, but can also have a profound impact on our beliefs about the nature and extent of our own control over various aspects of our lives. This includes our beliefs about our responsibilities in health and sickness, our health-related behaviours and our responses to illness, disease or disability.

Defining social support

Veiel and Baumann (1992b) traced the philosophical origins of social support theory to John Bowlby's theory of attachment as a fundamental requirement for healthy development. Much of the early research was based on the notion of support as a moderator of stress (Sarason *et al.* 1996). By the 1990s, Veiel and Baumann (1992b) noted the proliferation of definitions of social support and the need for conceptual clarification. Stewart (1993) presented eleven different definitions of social support put forward by key theorists between 1974 and 1990. Thoits (1982: 147) based her definition on that of Kaplan:

> the degree to which a person's basic social needs are gratified through interaction with others. Basic social needs include affection, esteem or approval, belonging, identity and security. These may be met by either the provision of socioemotional aid (e.g. affection, sympathy and understanding; acceptance, and esteem from significant other) or the provision of instrumental aid (e.g. advice, information, help with family or work responsibilities, financial aid).

This definition identifies the importance of emotional support in meeting higher level needs, such as belonging, security and esteem (see Maslow 1970), as well as assistance with the meeting of other basic needs. This is also evident in the more parsimonious definition of social support given by Stevan Hobfoll:

> those social interactions or relationships that provide individuals with actual assistance or that embed individuals within a social system believed to provide love, caring, or a sense of attachment to a valued social group or dyad.
>
> (Hobfoll 1988: 121)

Hobfoll encompasses the key attributes of social support to emerge from the literature: attachment, practical help and reciprocity. Both definitions identify social support as important in helping people to meet basic and higher order needs.

Types of social support

Possibly the earliest attempt to categorize different types of social support was that of Weiss (1974: 18). He based this on a phenomenological study of families who had recently moved to a new location and identified six categories of relational provisions. His work is still among the most relevant and persuasive in the literature on social support. He identified:

◆ Attachment – relationships that provide security and feeling 'at home'.
◆ Social integration – based on shared experience, companionship and social activity.
◆ Opportunity for nurturance – being needed and taking responsibility for the well-being of another.
◆ Reassurance of worth.
◆ Sense of reliable alliance – having someone on whom one can rely (usually kin).
◆ Obtaining of guidance.

Most of these aspects of social support are contained within subsequent definitions and theories, and received further support from an interview survey of single mothers conducted by Gottlieb (1978). Gottlieb's findings revealed two main categories of helping behaviours:

1 Emotionally sustaining behaviours that accounted for 75 per cent of all responses and included providing reassurance, encouragement, listening and understanding, trust, respect and companionship.
2 Problem-solving behaviours that included focused talking, suggesting and directing, sheltering the individual from the problem, material aid and distraction.

Two smaller categories reflected 'being available if needed' and 'direct intervention to diminish the source of stress'. These studies serve to illustrate the possibility that the types of social support identified may vary according to the nature of sample and context in which support is given and received. Nevertheless, commonalities soon emerged. Barer and Ainlay (1983) reviewed typologies of social support used in the literature and identified six categories, some of which were found to overlap in previous conceptualizations:

◆ Material aid (also referred to as concrete aid, instrumental support or tangible assistance): the provision of help in the form of money or other physical objects.

- ◆ Behavioural assistance (also referred to as practical service, active support, tangible or instrumental support): the sharing of tasks through physical labour or 'doing for'.
- ◆ Intimate interaction (also referred to as emotional or affective support): listening, caring, understanding.
- ◆ Guidance (also referred to as problem-solving, advice and instrumental support).
- ◆ Feedback (also referred to as reassurance of worth): giving feedback to individuals on their behaviour, thoughts or feelings.
- ◆ Positive social interaction (also referred to as socializing, social integration): social engagement for fun and relaxation.

Forty items reflecting the above categories were formulated to make up the Inventory of Socially Supportive Behaviours (ISSB). The resulting factor analysis revealed four factors:

1 Guidance and feedback accounted for 76 per cent of the variance.
2 Non-directive support (this included activities typical of non-directive counselling) accounted for 11.6 per cent of the variance.
3 Positive social interaction (sharing jokes, interests and diversionary activities) accounted for 7 per cent of the variance.
4 Tangible assistance (sharing tasks and providing shelter, money or physical objectives of value) accounted for 5 per cent of the variance.

It is unlikely that these factors are orthogonal (completely independent of each other), and the first factor to be extracted inevitably contains most of the shared or common variance. Therefore, this analysis appears to indicate the presence of a single phenomenon entitled 'social support', with four distinct subcategories. These analyses were originally based on the responses of introductory psychology students, which may affect generalization. More importantly, the ISSB required individuals to identify frequency of occurrence. Subsequent studies have emphasized the importance of perceived availability of social support (rather than its actual occurrence), which requires a different approach to measurement.

Schwarzer and Leppin (1988) distinguished between five types of support:

- ◆ Emotional support – including esteem support and belonging.
- ◆ Tangible support – instrumental support including material aid.
- ◆ Informational support – including advice-giving.
- ◆ Appraisal support (problem-solving support) – discussing problems and giving feedback.
- ◆ Social companionship – sharing leisure time.

To this list, Hobfoll (1988) added what he termed 'social prodding'. By this he referred to the type of nagging or direct intervention that leads individuals to seek or obtain medical attention or help, or modify their health-related behaviours.

In addition to types of support, Wallston *et al.* (1983a) proposed two primary dimensions of social support:

◆ quantity (amount) versus quality (goodness of fit);
◆ instrumental versus expressive.

They also identified source of support (kin versus friends) as another important component. More recently, Langford *et al.* (1997) presented a conceptual analysis of social support that distinguished between its theoretical foundations (social comparison theory, social exchange theory and social or relational competence), attributes or types of support (emotional, instrumental, informational and appraisal) and antecedents (social network, social embeddedness and social climate).

Overall, the impact of social support on health and well-being has been shown to be at best modest (Schwarzer and Leppin 1989), and one reason may be the failure to discriminate between different types of support. Type and direction of impact of different types of social support are likely to vary according to different types of situation or demand.

Social support and stress: the buffer hypothesis

House (1981) was among the first to differentiate between main effects of social support on health and buffering effects on the relationship between stress and health. Main effects include the provision of practical help or of assurance or care during illness. Buffering effects of social support impact on health only under situations of high stress in which demands exceed personal ability to respond. Cohen and Wills (1985) conducted a 'systematic review' of the literature that indicated strong support for the buffer hypothesis when instruments measured perceived availability of support. Schwarzer and Leppin (1988) also highlighted the need to distinguish between received and perceived support, suggesting that emotional well-being depends on *feeling* supported. They recognized the need to distinguish between sources of support. For example, they cited evidence that close family is in the best position to offer emotional support, while information support may be most beneficial when received from a health professional.

Cohen and Wills (1985) reported that instruments that provided measures of social network or past support were not found to demonstrate any buffering effect. Buffering, it was argued, occurs through enhancing coping resources, and includes esteem and informational support functions. Social integration and social network were shown to have a direct effect on well-being, though not as a buffer against stress. Cohen and Wills noted the consistent positive relationship between social networks and well-being. Conflict may be a significant factor in a relationship at an individual level but, they argued, is not an important phenomenon in personal relationships overall. Furthermore, reciprocity may be accounted for within most measures of social support, since 'perceived availability of support' is generally interpreted to refer to relationships with those who participate in the 'give-and-take' of daily life. What was not clear was whether buffering and main effects of social support derive primarily from one or a few close relationships. Among the methodological problems considered by Thoits (1982) was the fact that those who report close supportive relationships are less likely to have recently experienced negative life events such as divorce or widowhood. Therefore, evidence in favour of the buffering effects of social support on stressful life events needs to be interpreted with extreme caution. Lazarus and Folkman (1984) highlighted the fact that the ability to draw on social support is a coping skill in its own right. Furthermore, social support may be confounded by earlier illness status. Thus those with poor social skills and poor physical health may be those least likely to recruit good social support.

Negative aspects of social support

Your life isn't your own, it's controlled by other people.
(Patient with chronic pain, in Walker *et al.* 1999)

As Jean Paul Sartre observed ('hell is other people'), not all interpersonal encounters or their effects are positive. Suls (1982) challenged the blanket assumption that social support is necessarily associated with positive health outcomes. He outlined a range of negative effects of social support on health, including:

◆ creating uncertainty and worry;
◆ setting a bad example;
◆ negative labelling;
◆ giving misleading information;
◆ discouraging compliance;
◆ negative social comparisons;
◆ creating dependence.

Social support, according to Shinn *et al.* (1984), is not an exogenous variable but a reciprocal process. Drawing on previous studies, they noted that although positive social interaction normally tends to outweigh negative interactions in terms of frequency, negative interactions can have greater impact on well-being. Shinn *et al.* provided a detailed review of all aspects of social support to date, arguing that any effort to promote health and well-being by increasing social support should begin with an assessment of individual needs and constraints, including the costs and benefits to all concerned in a supportive transaction. Wortman and Dunkel-Schetter (1979) noted the vulnerability of caring professionals to 'burnout', in which repeated contact with those who are suffering can lead to detachment and deper-sonalization. Wallston *et al.* (1983a) noted that giving social support can place an intolerable burden on family and friends. Furthermore, receiving help can create dependency and have a negative impact on self-esteem.

Pearlin and Turner (1987) expressed some surprise that more attention had not been given in the literature to the social origins of stress, including loss of family function due to job loss, premature death or disablement of a family member, dissolution of marital ties and the chronic strains of the dysfunctional family, right through to the routine stresses and strains asso-ciated with family life. They identified several dimensions of interpersonal conflict between husband and wife (or partners), including:

- ◆ lack of reciprocity and perceived equity with the relationship;
- ◆ lack of affective exchange;
- ◆ failure of authentication of the self (which can be an alienating experience);
- ◆ frustration of role expectations (for example around the division of labour).

They presented similar analyses for extended family members. They also highlighted that stresses outside the home (notably job stress) can cause problems within the home; for example, through emotional distress or competing or incompatible demands. They concluded by indicating that it is too simplistic to refer to 'the family' in relation to the stress process. Each family may be host to a range of unique stressors or buffers, while the stress process can be strikingly different for men and women. Some of these latter issues are central to issues discussed by Mirowsky and Ross (1989), who highlighted the trade-off between social support and social demands within relationships, presenting data that illustrate depression as a function of marital power. Overall, it is evident that social support can have a negat-ive impact on both giver and recipient. However, this is often difficult to identify, since, as Hobfoll (1988) concluded, positive and negative social inputs are often provided within the same relationship.

Reciprocity, equity and social exchange

Equity or social exchange theory suggests that people are likely to reject offers of help if they incur feelings of indebtedness due to insufficient opportunities or resources to reciprocate. Gottlieb (1983) reviewed the com-plexities of social support in community-based research that emphasized the importance of equity in social exchange in the maintenance and stability of social networks. He was particularly critical of available social support measures that take no account of social exchange processes (Gottlieb 1983, 1985).

Social exchange theory, attributed to Homans in 1958 and Blau in 1964, indicates that helpers may gain intrinsic satisfaction from helping, but inability to reciprocate may reduce future help-seeking among recipients or induce dependency and reduce self-esteem. Close personal relationships may give rise to a variety of negative social interactions that increase distress or dependency. The timing of support may not always be appropriate. For example, help is not always available at the right time following bereavement. The source of advice, information or support may also be important. Gottlieb (1985) urged a transactional approach to social support, arguing that measures of social support failed to reflect the social processes that underpin support. He recognized the need for more research into processes of socially mediated coping and suggested that people often receive or extend support while failing to recognize or report it as such. He gave examples of informal experience swapping and modelling of adaptive responses.

Help-giving and help-seeking

The roles and behaviour of help-giver and help-receiver, and the relationships between the two, are important issues, particularly for those working in the caring services or professions. Batson (1975) reviewed research into attribution processes that explained helping behaviour. In particular, he drew attention to Jones and Nisbett's suggestion that there are two main sources of attributional bias: the different perspectives of the observer and actor and the different information available. Discrepancies can lead the person seeking help to attribute the cause of the problem to different sources and/or its solution to different sets of action. Batson highlighted a number of researchers, including Goffman (1961), whose studies indicated that professional helpers tend to see the person in need, rather than the situation, as the locus of the problem. This is possibly because the helper is directly exposed to the individual but not their social environment. The tendency to underestimate the impact of situational factors and overestimate the role of dispositional factors is typical of the fundamental attribution error (Hewstone 1989) and a phenomenon commonly associated with the medical model (Goffman 1961). From these observations, Batson developed five hypotheses:

- A helper's attribution of the locus of the problem significantly affects his or her helping response. If a helper infers that the problem lies with the person seeking help, he or she is more likely to offer help oriented to changing the person rather than his or her social situation.
- If a helper identifies with a professional helping role, he or she is more likely to attribute problems to and direct help towards changing the person in need rather than the social situation, even if the needy person is clearly seeking the opposite.
- A helper's attribution of the locus of the problems and thereby his or her helping response is more likely to be focused on the person in need when the helper has diagnostic information cast in the medical model than

when he or she does not. This effect may be limited to situations in which the diagnosis suggests a personal mental problem rather than a social problem.

♦ A helper's attribution of the locus of the problem and thereby his or her helping response is more likely to be focused on the person in need when the helper perceives the client as a low-credibility source of information about the situation.

♦ A helper's attribution of the locus of the problem serves a mediating role in determining his or her helping response. The effects of role orientation as well as diagnostic and credibility information on helping are a result of their effect on this attribution.

Brickman *et al.* (1982) referred to what they termed the 'dilemma of helping', in which helpers take responsibility for solving a problem, rather than those asking for help. They also address the problem of welfare dependency, which provides a disincentive for people to solve their own problems. One of the important questions raised by Brickman and colleagues is whether some helping models (those which encourage self-management or care) are better than others, or whether different models are best for different clients and types of problem. Support is not the prerogative of professional carers or families. For example, Cowen (1982) examined help obtained from informal sources, such as hairdressers and bartenders. Cowen identified that these are important sources of sympathy and encouragement, with women more often adopting the role of confidante than men.

Hobfoll (1988) presented a very practical analysis of why helpers help:

♦ they value the relationship and are empathic with the needs of the other;
♦ they fear the consequences of not helping (such as anger or even divorce);
♦ they have a sense of role obligation (as contained in marriage vows).

In explaining why others may decide not to help, he cited the work of Wortman and Lehman in proposing:

♦ confronting another's problems or distress engenders feelings of help-lessness or resentment because one feels obligated to help (this again places those in greatest need for social support among those least likely to receive it);
♦ perceived lack of expertise and fear of making the wrong move;
♦ misconceptions about how people should react in a crisis.

Social skills, personality and social relationships

Argyle (1992) reviewed various aspects of supportive relationships, referring to research that indicated gender differences in coping. Women, he noted, tend to talk to a friend and cry when they feel depressed, whereas men tend to avoid thinking about it and engage in vigorous exercise. He argued, controversially, that the talking strategies used by women tend to increase depression, while men's coping strategies increase feelings of control. Some evidence in support of this was obtained by Ross and Mirowsky (1989), who found that although social support acted as a buffer against depression, the use of talking to others was associated with increased depression. Argyle argued that instrumental support can reduce individual autonomy and leave the recipient feeling inadequate, particularly where they are unable to reciprocate. Argyle (1992) suggested that friends make us cheerful because we do enjoyable things together and gain mutual satisfaction from each other's company. Extraverts may be happier because they find it easier to recruit this type of social support. Moreover, people find the company of friends rewarding and seek it out.

Argyle also highlighted the importance of the implicit skills of conversational synchrony and of obeying informal social rules. In considering the development of social skills and competence, Gottlieb (1983) focused on empathy and the ability to take the perspective of others. He reasoned that the development of such skills in children might have important implications for their ability to make and maintain social relationships and networks in later life. Those who are lonely frequently have poor social skills and lack of social or relational skills is a major factor in mental disorders. Hobfoll (1988: 139) pointed out:

> those who lack relational competence may also lack the skills necessary to create and maintain effective support systems. This may result in a social environment that fails to provide them with help when they need it and that leaves them with a chronic sense of social isolation. Consequently, their psychological health suffers both because they are exposed to stress without the buffering support of close ties and because lacking such ties is itself a major source of stress. Their physical health may also suffer because prolonged stress produces negative health consequences and because they are not privy to the social prodding toward health maintenance that close associates provide.

Characteristics of those who lack social skills include lack of self-esteem and assertiveness. These happen to be characteristics of many people with mental health problems, including anxiety and depression. It would thus appear that those most in need of social support are among those least likely to receive it. This links closely with Lewinsohn's theory of depression (see Chapter 7). Lewinsohn et al. (1980) investigated the link between social competence and depression in comparing patients receiving treatment for depression with psychiatric and normal controls using observation measures. They found that depressed patients perceived themselves to be less socially skilled. Discrepancies between self-assessment and observer assessment of sociability indicated that illusions of sociability were significantly less in the depressed subjects than in control group subjects. Social skills apply equally to helpers and to the potential recipients of help. Veiel and Baumann (1992b) drew attention to the fact that within every interaction, the most trivial gesture or utterance potentially has supportive (or unsupportive) value.

Self-help and social support

Self-help appears to imply personal control. Indeed, the self-help group consists of a group of people with similar problems who support each other to find explanations and ways of dealing with them. In other words, they support each other to gain personal control. Theories used in support of self-help groups in the literature include affiliation, attribution, change, coping, deviance, empowerment, equity/social exchange, group, loneliness, self-esteem, social comparison and social movement theories (Stewart 1990). The importance of social comparisons in psychological adjustment was highlighted by Taylor *et al.* (1983). They found that the victims of disease or disaster tended to make comparisons with those less fortunate than themselves. This included maintaining that the negative impact of the event was small or non-existent, highlighting hidden gains or maintaining that they were coping well with the situation. The reasons for selective evaluation remain unclear, although it appears to serve an adaptive function. Self-help groups can have unintended and unfortunate outcomes, particularly for those who draw negative social comparisons in relation to other group members. This phenomenon is often beyond the control of those setting and running such groups. Nevertheless, the self-help group emerges as an important tool in health care, providing a created social support network which performs a number of support functions: information about causes, solutions and coping strategies; companionship; role models; and reciprocal opportunities to help others and be helped.

Social support and health

Interest in the concept of social support focused initially on issues related to mental health. Cobb (1976), drawing on an already rich literature, summed up the view of the time by defining social support in terms of information that an individual is cared for and loved, esteemed and valued, and belongs to a network of communication and mutual obligation. He reviewed research evidence to suggest that this protects against the potential health consequences of life stress, including low birth weight, premature death, recovery from illness, arthritis, tuberculosis, mental health problems including depression and alcoholism, and social breakdown (Cobb 1976). Norbeck (1981) linked social support to the concept of attachment. Her review of the literature identified the importance of supportive relationships that enable people to cope better with the stresses of the environment, enhance feelings of mastery and reduce feelings of vulnerability and helplessness. Norbeck identified the need to provide social support as part of nursing practice. There is a need for high intensity support in times of acute stress or illness, moderate support in times of life change, rehabilitation or chronic stressors and low support for day-to-day living. She also noted the potential importance of self-help groups and establishing contact with others who had had similar experiences.

By the late 1970s and early 1980s, theories and measures of social support were proliferating and support groups were becoming institutionalized. The importance of social networks and kinship to health and their consequences in illness were recognized. Concerns were being expressed that the decline of the extended family in the Western world might have a significant impact on health in Western societies (Pilisuk and Froland 1978). Kaplan *et al.* (1977) addressed: the role of social support as an independent variable in health and well-being; the mechanisms in the social environment that provide or remove support from individuals; the multidimensional nature of social support; and the implications for medical care policy. They identified that health and disease embrace the social and psychological, as well as the biological, arenas of human life; therefore prevention and treatment should likewise embrace these.

By the late 1980s, Ganster and Victor (1988) described the literature on social support as so voluminous, including hundreds of empirical studies of its effects on physical and mental health, as to require several volumes to effect a systematic review. In summarizing the research-based literature, they concluded that several fundamental issues surrounding the relationship between social support and health remained unresolved, notably its influence on physical well-being. These observations were supported by a meta-analysis on social support and health conducted by Schwarzer and Leppin (1989). Their findings are summarized as follows:

- Empirical evidence of a linear relationship between social support and health.
- Wide variations in the degree and direction of the relationship. The overall strength of the relationship was small.
- A growing trend away from global measures of social support in favour of asking more precise questions about how different kinds of support affect specific outcomes in different populations.
- Correlations of between −0.43 and +0.23 between social support and health and well-being, with most values close to zero.
- Social support might be more health-relevant with increasing age, though the results were not entirely reliable.
- Spouse support was more closely related to depression than friend, boss or co-worker support. The effects for all groups were significant but the results subject to sampling error.
- Support for the buffer hypothesis (that social stress is related to health in stressful situations), with results indicating the impact of social support

on health status, symptoms, physiological reactivity (blood pressure and heart rate) and mortality (mostly in men).

◆ Consistent evidence that social support is more closely related to health for women than men.

They concluded:

> there is no doubt that social support and health are related in a way that ill health is more pronounced for those who lack support. However, the degree of association depends on the circumstances, the population and the concepts and measures of support and health employed. On the average, social support and health are more closely associated for women than for men. These findings thus provide some empirical evidence for the specificity model of social support as it has been put forward by Cohen and Wills (1985) and Wills (1985).
>
> (Schwarzer and Leppin 1989: 11)

Lakey and Drew (1997) reviewed the theoretical changes that had taken place over the past two decades. It was originally believed that individuals with high support had better mental health because they received more or better enacted support. This enhanced the individuals' coping efforts and reduced vulnerability to stress. However, research findings indicate that in contrast to perceived support, enacted support is rarely associated with psychological symptoms and has even been found to have a negative effect. Furthermore, received support appears to be only weakly related to perceived support. The authors advocated a social cognition analysis of social support and more research to understand how perceived support judgements are made and how low perceived support leads to emotional distress. I address this issue directly in Chapter 8.

Bartholomew et al. (1997) proposed a model of social support in which the causal link between enacted and perceived support is modified by attachment pattern and relationship security. Thus some individuals are less accepting of support when offered or given. Situational characteristics likely to influence this relationship include the extent to which instrumental support allows the recipient to retain a sense of personal control, individual achievement and autonomous help-seeking and does not induce a sense of dependence. Collins and di Paula (1997) identified that perceived emotional support is more consistently beneficial than other types of support, though different types of support may be helpful in different types of situation. They presented an analysis based on caring, which they defined as including feelings of empathy, concern, affection and love.

Planning health care interventions

Wallston et al. (1983a) identified the need to avoid the creation of dependency. They concluded from their review of the literature on social support and health outcomes that social support may influence health by immunizing against a state of learned helplessness. Thus supportive actions might include:

- providing assistance when asked;
- providing information that helps the individual to anticipate sensations or events and feel a greater sense of predictability;
- helping the individual to interpret events so as to reduce perceptions of personal non-control;
- forcing or cajoling adaptive responding that produces desirable outcomes and heightens the individual's sense of control.

Stewart (1989) claimed that five theories of social support allow health professionals to plan intervention strategies that are more likely to be effective in practice (see Table 6.1). Stewart's discussion of attribution theory is worthy of extended consideration in view of the links with previous chapters in this book. She drew on Brickman's 'just world' hypothesis, which proposes that people are seen to get what they deserve and deserve what they get (Brickman *et al.* 1982). Attributions of cause to the client (for example, that the client's smoking led to the health problem, or that the patient's personality has somehow contributed to their current difficulties) can lead to victim-blaming on the part of potential helpers. This can lead to avoidance of offers of help or to uncaring and unhelpful behaviour. Clients who hold internal attributions for causality may be less likely to seek help when they really need it, out of guilt and from fear of reprimand or reprisal. Thus external attributions of causality are healthier for clients and carers, since they are more likely to lead to sympathy and help-giving. Attributions for solutions appear to deserve rather more attention than Stewart gives to them. First, and for reasons already given, attributions for solutions to health problems really need to be entirely separated from attributions for causality in the minds of clients and carers if the proposed solution is to be effective. Second, it cannot be assumed (as Stewart's original proposition was framed) that a solution will be effective just because the client seeks help, help is recognized to be needed and is given. It has to be the right type and amount of help at the right time. Too much help, even if gladly accepted by the client, can engender dependence and lead, in the long term, to the breakdown of support networks through physical fatigue or compassion fatigue.

Support in the workplace

House (1981) was particularly interested in reducing the effects of work stress and provided a useful overview of the differential roles of supervisor, co-worker and home support. He identified two major determinants of socially supportive outputs: the ability and motivation of providers to give support, and the degree to which the larger interpersonal and social context

Table 6.1 Conceptual framework for social support with particular reference to the role of the health professional

Theory	Implications for health care
Attribution	1* Help is likely to be forthcoming *if* there are external attributions for the causes of the health problem and health professionals/support network hold internal attributions for the solutions. 2 If the attributions for causes and solutions to health problems by clients, health professionals and support network are congruent, that help is more likely to be effective.
Coping	Social support networks (natural or created) can facilitate client coping with stress and prevent health problems (the buffer hypothesis).
Loneliness	1 Clients who lack a support network or lose their network support through bereavement, divorce or other loss are likely to be lonely and are more susceptible to health problems through decreased immunocompetence. Furthermore, health problems may instigate loss of support network, particularly where client/network attributions are incongruent. 2 The health professional may mitigate or prevent such problems by mobilizing created networks, enhancing natural networks or temporarily supplementing support.
Social comparison	* Downward comparisons with those worse off raises self-esteem and prevents demoralization. Health professional should encourage upward comparisons with role models who demonstrate good coping.
Social exchange	Health professionals can promote reciprocal exchange of support between their clients and the social network, thereby increasing their clients' self-esteem and effectiveness of helping.

Note
* In relation to these points, I have changed or added to the content and may slightly have altered Stewart's original meaning.
Source: adapted from Stewart (1989: 1280).

warrants such efforts. He observed that the instrumental and competitive orientation of Western societies might militate against support, but that within the workplace much depended on the attitudes of higher management (House 1981: 110).

In a study of high stress executives, Kobasa and Puccetti (1983) sought to distinguish between different types of social support, including family and boss support. They found that hardiness combined with boss support reduced illness symptoms in the face of adverse life events. Those scoring high on hardiness showed no effects of family support, but those low on hardiness demonstrated higher illness scores when they reported higher family support. They suggested that the families of executives low in hardiness might foster inappropriate coping in the face of stressful life events. This early study is important in highlighting potentially negative consequences of social support.

The Whitehall study (Rael *et al.* 1995; Stansfield *et al.* 1997) provided an opportunity for one of the most comprehensive reviews of the effects of social support in the workplace. However, the findings are not particularly strong, perhaps owing to problems of measurement. These studies have found that high levels of emotional support at home might actually encourage people to stay at home when they are sick, while negative aspects of close personal relationships might also lead to increased sickness absence. Support from colleagues and supervisors at work was found to be related to less risk of short spells of psychiatric sickness absence, particularly among those with less emotional support at home.

Variables that interact with social support

Social support and age

It is fairly obvious that the social support networks for the young, middle-aged and old are likely to be totally different. Oleson *et al.* (1991) found that psychological well-being in a large Danish sample was influenced in the younger group (under 30) by family and friends; in the middle age group (30–59), it was spouse, family and children; and in the group aged 60 + it related to the number (but not quality) of friends. These data may not generalize to other populations, but they highlight the importance of taking into consideration the life cycle. Oleson *et al.* (1991) also concluded that summed scales of social network as currently applied are inappropriate for studying the impact of various sources and aspects of social networks on different age groups. Instead, it is important to have a proper conceptualization of social support in relation to the target group before operationalizing and measuring it. It is of interest, in comparing the findings of Oleson *et al.* (1991) with those of the study of older adults by Mancini and Blieszner (1992), to note that morale in the latter study was significantly related to opportunities for nurturance as well as friend contact. It may well be that as certain people grow older their need for support from others diminishes, though they may derive benefit from giving support to others. This would mean that older people who are physically disabled and require a substantial amount of instrumental help for daily living are able to reciprocate by offering emotional, appraisal and/or informational support in return.

Social support and gender

A sufficient number of studies (for example, see Mirowsky and Ross 1989; Stansfield *et al.* 1997) have demonstrated gender differences to justify studying males and females as separate population groups. The support needs of men and women appear to be qualitatively and quantitatively different, while the types of support given by men to women are often quite different from those given by women to men. In research terms, this has obvious implications for sampling procedures, types of measurement used, statistical analysis and the interpretation of the data. In clinical practice it means that assumptions applicable to one sex may not apply to the other. This has implications for health care professionals caring for patients of the opposite gender. It would appear that more research might be needed to examine the support needs of different genders in relation to different types of illness or situation.

Social support, locus of control and self-efficacy

There is growing evidence of interaction between social support and locus of control. Cummins (1988) found that internal locus of control combined with received social support had a buffering effect on well-being in a healthy population. Perceived locus of control moderated the effects of perceived social support on psychological distress. Feelings of emotional closeness and belongingness were found to be important to well-being regardless of locus of control. However, reassurance of self-worth appeared to have a negative effect for internals. Stewart (1989) provided epidemiological evidence in favour of psychoneuroimmunological effects of social support. Though little evidence is currently available to support the impact of self-help groups on immunocompetence, social learning theory provides a basis for such links by facilitating an increase in personal efficacy and control. Ross and Mirowsky (1989) conducted a large-scale telephone study of support, control and psychological distress in a general population. They concluded that 'support and control are alternative ways of dealing with threat. Each decreases depression: each substitutes functionally if the other is absent' (Ross and Mirowsky 1989: 216).

Buschmann and Hollinger (1994), in a study of institutionalized elderly people, found that social support (based on touch) and control were alternative ways to reduce depression such that each may substitute in the absence of the other. They suggested that an individual in control of his or her life relies less on supportive relationships with others to maintain well-being. On the other hand, an individual who feels a great deal of social support from others is not as dependent upon the need to control the environment. Reich and Zautra (1995) found startling interactions in the effects of locus of control and self-control encouragement by husband on psychological distress in rheumatoid arthritis, according to age and health status. Those with external locus of control were more sensitive to encouragement by their husband to take control than internals. The data suggest that people respond favourably to being encouraged to rely on other people when they do not believe that they have control, when they are older and when they are in poorer health. The same type of spousal behaviours tended to have the opposite effects on younger and healthier people. Krause (1997) examined the effects of social support on feelings of personal control in older adults, drawing on the earlier prediction of Sandler and Lakey (1982) that control affects support such that individuals with a strong sense of control may utilize their support networks more effectively. They regarded feelings of personal control as a dimension of personality, though they acknowledge that this may be modifiable and suggest that the relationship between perceived personal control and social support may be reciprocal. These observations all lend support to the analysis offered in Chapter 8.

Measurement of social support

A number of issues have become evident during the preparation of this book. First, most textbooks that review health measurements make no mention at all of measures of personal control, locus of control, self-efficacy or helplessness, yet devote considerable attention to the measurement of social support. Second, there is an enormous number of measures of social support that appear extremely diverse in terms of theoretical framework, content, presentation, number of items, time to complete, scoring system and application. These issues render any general interpretation and comparison of findings problematic. Finally, a cursory look at the available literature indicates no evidence of any consistency at all in the measures and approaches used. The most commonly used measures, together with available reviews, are presented in Table 6.2.

Schwarzer and Leppin (1989) argued against global measures of social support in favour of differentiating between structural versus functional support, perceived versus actually received support, and emotional versus instrumental support, each to be considered according to source (spouse, friend, boss etc.). Studies by well known research teams have used items on seeking informational and emotional support from the Folkman *et al.* Ways of Coping Questionnaire Scale (e.g. Dunkel-Schetter *et al.* 1987; Cormier-Daigle and Stewart 1997; Stewart *et al.* 1997) and the staff support subscale of the Moos Work Environment Scale (Kobasa *et al.* 1985). Some studies report the use of purposefully designed scales. Indeed, one of the most important studies of stress in recent years, the Whitehall study (Roberts *et al.* 1995; Stansfield *et al.* 1997) falls into this category. For their purposes, the research team designed the Close Person Questionnaire (Stansfield *et al.* 1997), which reflects three types of support (confiding/emotional support, practical support and negative aspects of support) from the person or persons nominated as closest.

Table 6.2 Examples of measures of social support

Measure	Reviewer	Date	Content	No. of items	Observations of reviewers
UCLA Loneliness Scale [Russell et al. 1978; revised 1980 to include positive items]	Bowling (examples p. 146)	1991	Loneliness Satisfaction with relationships	20	Described as the most extensively tested of all loneliness scales (mainly on student groups), results encouraging.
Rand Social Activities Questionnaire [Donald et al. 1978]	Wilkin et al. (full scale given p. 114)	1992	Social contacts Group participation Social activities Subjective evaluation of quality of relationships	11	Mixes types of support, interpretation difficult.
Social Support Scale	Lin et al.	1979 1981	Involvement with members of social network	9	Developed for use with schizophrenia.
Interview Schedule for Social Interaction (ISSI) [Henderson et al. 1980]	Bowling (examples p. 134)	1991	Availability of attachment; Perceived adequacy of attachment Availability of social integration Perceived adequacy of social integration	52	Structured interview, takes 30–60 minutes to complete. Promising scale requiring further testing.
Arizona Social Support Interview Schedule (ASSIS) [Barrera, 1980, 1981]	Kasl and Cooper Bowling (examples pp. 128–9); Stewart	1987 1991 1993	Received support: confiding (private feelings); material aid; advice; positive feedback; physical assistance; social participation		Takes 15–20 minutes to complete. Ratings on a 3-point scale. Further testing of reliability and validity required (validity modest). Allows evaluation of network size; conflicted network size; unconflicted network size; support satisfaction; support need.

Table 6.2 *cont'd*

Measure	Reviewer	Date	Content	No. of items	Observations of reviewers
Inventory of Socially Supportive Behaviours (ISSB) [Barrera 1981; Barrera and Ainlay 1983, all items given pp. 138–9]	Kasl and Cooper; Sarason *et al.*; Bowling (examples p. 126); Stewart	1987 1987 1991 1993	Received support: emotional; instrumental; information appraisal; socializing (frequency of receipt and enactment)	40 items using 5-point scale	Attention drawn to the problem that statements may or may not relate to real events in people's immediate lives. Problems with interpretation. More work needed to test reliability and validity.
Social Support Scale (SSS) [Dean *et al.* 1981]	Pearson (p. 393)	1986	Confidant Family Community Instrumental	43	Validity and reliability supported.
Social Relationship Scale (SRS) [McFarlane *et al.* 1981]	Kasl and Cooper McDowell and Newell (p. 160) Wilkin *et al.* (p. 120)	1987 1987 1992	Addresses 6 areas of life stress: work; money and finances; home and family; personal and social; personal health; society in general	Depends on number in support network	Most items are concerned with emotional support. Scoring system combines number of support persons and satisfaction with support given. Intended for self-completion, but interviewer expected to be present to answer queries. Limited in scope; no information about nature of support provided; more evidence of validity and reliability required; not likely to be useful in clinical practice.

Measure	Source	Year	Description	Format	Comments
Family Relationship Index (FRI) [Moos 1981; Billings and Moos 1982]	Bowling	1991	Perceived/available support Family support (e.g. cohesion, expressiveness, conflict)	9-item (cohesion scale) yes/no format	No clear conceptual base. Validity largely unknown. Manual available.
Norbeck Social Support Questionnaire (NSSQ) (Norbeck et al. 1981, scale given on p. 265; 1983)	Wilkin et al. (scale given on p. 127) Stewart	1992 1993	Received support: affect; affirmation; aid; for each personal in social network	9 questions per person identified	Multidimensional measure. Convenient to use, clear conceptual basis, encouraging evidence of reliability and validity. Particularly used for measuring support from different sources.
Perceived Social Support from Family and Friends (PSSFA-FR) [Procidano and Heller 1983]	Bowling (examples p. 131)	1991	Provision/receipt of support Sources Content Availability Satisfaction	2 × 20 items yes/no/don't know format	Uses scenarios about work, home and family, personal and social, health and general social issues. Provides for positive and negative outcomes. Far more testing required.
Social Support Questionnaire (SSQ) (Sarason et al. 1983)	McDowell and Newell Bowling	1987 1991	Given in full (McDowell and Newell 1987: 164) Focuses mainly on emotional support	27	Self-report scale takes 15 minutes to complete. Each question has 2-part answer to include satisfaction with aspects of support on 6-point scale. Described as a viable measure.
Social Network Scale (SNS) [Stokes 1983]	Bowling	1991	Support network (quantity)		Scoring totals number of network members, relatives, confidantes. Interpretation problematic and more evidence of validity and reliability required.

Table 6.2 cont'd

Measure	Reviewer	Date	Content	No. of items	Observations of reviewers
Social Support Network Inventory (SSNI) (Flaherty et al. 1983)			Availability Reciprocity Practical support Emotional support Event-related support.	11	Measurement on 5-point scale of support. Factor analysis grouped availability, emotional support, practical support and reciprocity, casting doubt on validity.
Interpersonal Support Evaluation List (ISEL) [Cohen et al. 1985]	Bowling (examples p. 143)	1991	Perceived availability of support: emotional; tangible; informational; guidance	40	Tests buffer hypothesis. 20 positive and 20 negative statements. Evidence of validity and reliability given.
Personal Resource Questionnaire (PRQ) (Brandt and Weinert 1981; Weinert and Brandt 1987)	Stewart	1993	Received support: intimacy; social integration; nurturance; worth and assistance; plus self-help ideology scale	25	2 parts: part 1 descriptive, part 2, measurement on 7-point Likert scale.
Social Support Appraisals Scale (SS-A) and Social Support Behaviours Scale (SS-B) [Vaux et al. 1986, 1987]	Bowling (examples, pp. 140–2)	1991	SS-A. Relationships with family and friends SS-B. Supportive behaviours: emotional support; socializing; practical assistance; financial assistance; advice/guidance	SS-A: 23 SS-B: 45	SS-A: validity questionable, no data on reliability. SS-B: problems with assuming the value of activities such as going to a movie. Little tested for validity and reliability.

Instrument	Author	Year	Dimensions	No. of items	Comments
Cost and Reciprocity Index (CRI) [Tilden and Galyen 1987]	Weinert and Tilden	1990	Social support Reciprocity Conflict Includes negative aspects	38	Based on social exchange theory and equity theory.
Duke-UNC Functional Social Support Questionnaire (DUFSS) [Broadhead et al. 1988]	Wilkin et al. (scale given p. 124)	1992	Confidant Affective	8	Measures qualitative aspects of support; validity and reliability encouraging. Scope for developing additional dimensions of support.
Dartmouth Coop charts [Nelson et al. 1987, 1990]	Rowan (Full scale given pp. 69–76) Wilkin et al.	1994 1992	Interference with: social activities; social support	Single items	Each measured on 5-point combined verbal rating/pictorial/numerical scale. Social support refers to availability for support or practical help (though no reason why these should not be separated out). Verbal scales signal adequacy, pictures signal number. Designed primarily for clinical practice. Test–retest reliability excellent; validity encouraging; sensitive to disease impact; user friendly.

Citations of authors given in square brackets [ ] are not referenced.

Winemiller *et al.* (1993) reviewed strategies used to measure social support, noting the substantial increase over the previous decade and a lack of consensus and clarity. The use of unstandardized, *ad hoc* instruments tailored to the idiosyncratic nature of the research question renders it difficult, if not impossible, to make comparisons with other findings. On the other hand, standardized measures often fail to account for the complex and multidimensional nature of social support and fail to allow the researcher to distinguish the effects of different types of support. One solution suggested is the use of multimethod approaches.[1] Winemiller *et al.* identified 262 empirical studies published between 1980 and 1987 in which social support was measured. They identified that 61 per cent used novel measures. Thirty-three per cent of studies used open-ended questions that render them unreplicable and difficult to compare. Sixty-eight per cent measured social support in a global or unspecified manner, while in 18 per cent of studies the method of measurement was described so poorly as to be indeterminate. The literature indicated a strong bias in favour of support perceived and received, with many studies focusing exclusively on close nuclear relationships. The most popular measures were the ISSB and the SSQ (see Table 6.2). A uniform conceptual model was not apparent in the literature and Winemiller *et al.* recommended that it is necessary to distinguish between functional, structural and perceptual aspects of support through separate measures.

Hupcey (1998) presented a systematic review of studies that had used social support measures. It makes for rather depressing reading, highlighting a general lack of attention to conceptual detail and clarity. Hupcey questioned many causal assumptions by asking:

> Does depression or the inability to cope cause a true lack of social support by sending potential supporters away? Does depression cause the perception of lack of social support? Is a provider actually providing adequate amounts of social support for a particular situation but the recipient is perceiving a deficit in support?
>
> (Hupcey 1998: 316)

Finally, Hupcey asked if it is relevant to know the size of the social network when the most important factor may be the marital or other close personal relationship. She concluded that despite the hundreds of studies undertaken, research into this concept had become stagnant.

Sarason *et al.* (1996) urged researchers to examine carefully the definitions and theoretical assumptions used by previous researchers to study similar issues. He suggested that much initial work on social support and health had been operationalized in a simplistic way, which may or may not be entirely appropriate. The measures used should reflect the situational, interpersonal and intrapersonal processes that are relevant to the research question (Sarason *et al.* 1996: 22). Among the issues that clinicians need to consider are those of length, interpretability and applicability. Review articles likely to be of relevance to those formulating research designs are given in Table 6.3.

Table 6.3 Review articles related to social support

Authors	Date	Key issues raised
Wortman and Dunkel-Schetter	1979	Comprehensive review and theoretical analysis of interpersonal relationships and cancer that provide the foundations for cancer care. Recommended that health care professionals should encourage open communication with patients and between patients and families about all aspects of the disease and treatment, including feelings and emotions.
Lin et al.	1981	Methodological notes in relation to schizophrenia. Good example of scale development, though actual measures not given.
Thoits	1982	Definitions and methodological issues – see text.
Barrera and Ainlay	1983	Conceptual review of different components of social support based on the 1970s literature.
Depner et al.	1984	Review of methodological issues in design and measurement. Measures must be purposively selected to suit context and theory. Confounding may exist between support, stress and strain, e.g. in bereavement. Timing of measurement may obscure or exaggerate effects. Longitudinal studies recommended in the literature, but repeated measurement may sensitize respondents. Important to control for age, sex, socio-economic status and relevant personal traits or coping strategies.
Rock et al.	1984	Psychometric review of social network scales.
Tardy	1985	Identifies 5 aspects of social support with conceptual model (see text). Reviews ASSI, ISSB, PSSF-F, SRS, SSNI and SSQ according to each of the five aspects. Identifies room for improvements noted.
Cohen and Wills	1985	See text.
Pearson	1986	Conceptual review and review of validity and reliability of SSS, NSSQ, PRQ, ISSB.

Table 6.3 *cont'd*

Authors	Date	Key issues raised
Orth-Gomer and Unden	1987	Review of most available instruments including time to completion, psychometric properties and social response bias. Functional measures found to be time-consuming and difficult to interpret. Structural measures easy to apply.
Sarason *et al.*	1987	Reports on studies which tested correlation between SSQ, ISSB, FES (FRI), ISEL, PSS, ISSI with student samples. Contributes to conceptual clarity and confirms or disconfirms the dimensions and sensitivity of each scale.
McDowell and Newell	1987	Offers a table reviewing range of measures (p. 157) including ratings of reliability and validity, time to administer, number of items and type of scale used.
Schwartzer and Leppin	1988	Meta-analysis – see text.
Stewart	1989	Models of social support – see text.
Veil and Baumann	1992b	Traced philosophical origins and conceptual developments – see text.
Hupcey	1998	Conceptual analysis. Lay use limited to emotional and tangible/material support; theoretical definition often ambiguous. Presents overview of systematic review of studies that have used social support (full reference list available from the author).

Table 6.4 Examples of studies of the impact of social support in different types of context and situation

Author(s)	Date	Focus	Overview/findings
Cohen and Hoberman	1983	Stress in the workplace	Appraisal and self-esteem support, but not instrumental support, were buffers against depression in stressful situations.
Dunkel-Schetter	1984	Support for medical patients	Medical care was reported by patients to be unhelpful unless accompanied by emotional and information support. Family and friends were valued for being there in times of need to listen and provide encouragement, but advice and information from these sources was seen as unhelpful.
Kobasa et al.	1985	Relationship between stress and illness	Combination of hardy personality, social support and exercise decreases likelihood of illness in the face of highly stressful conditions.
Parkes	1986	Stress in student nurses	Interaction found between direct coping, social support in the workplace and stressfulness of episode among student nurses. Trend for high social support to facilitate direct coping among extraverts but not among introverts.
Flor et al.	1987	Chronic pain	Having a solicitous spouse is related to reduced activity levels and increased depression.
Murphy	1987	Bereavement	Measured social support using Coppel's Index (quantity and perceived quality), self-efficacy and mental health using SCL-90-R to compare those who experienced bereavement or residential loss as a result of the St Helens volcanic eruption, with matched comparisons. Social support was not a significant predictor of mental distress, though self-efficacy was.
Coombs et al.	1989	Recovery from heart surgery	Emotional support was important in reducing the incidence of depression immediately following heart surgery.

Table 6.4 *cont'd*

Author(s)	Date	Focus	Overview/findings
Brown *et al.*	1989b	Rheumatoid arthritis	Emotional support was associated with less depression in rheumatoid arthritis patients, particularly where pain was more severe. But emotional support failed to demonstrate a buffering effect against depression over time. Authors suggested that the type of support given must help patients to mobilize their coping resources to engage in active pain-coping strategies.
Major *et al.*	1990	Psychological adjustment following abortion	No direct association found between social support (confiding) and adjustment. Path analysis showed that self-efficacy mediated between social support from each source (partner, friend, family) and psychological adjustment.
Oakley	1992	Women at risk of having low birth weight babies	Risk factors included unwillingness of the father to take emotional or physical responsibility, lack of money or decent housing, and social isolation. Intervention: three home visits from a midwife in the antenatal period during which the women were encouraged to discuss their needs and concerns and information was given. Psychological variables showed significant improvements and birth weight demonstrated a trend in the expected direction. Helpful discussion of the methodological problems.
Linn *et al.*	1993	HIV	Those with more confidants reported higher self-esteem and lower anxiety. Realistic information about what to expect, tempered with optimism and the belief that their situation was under control encouraged positive adaptation.

Author	Year	Topic	Findings
Walker et al.	1995	Maternity care	Qualitative study indicated that a balance of personal control and midwife support contributed to good experiences of childbirth.
Seale and Addington-Hall	1995	Hospice care	Hospice care, based on the principles outlined by Wortman and Dunkel-Schetter (1979), was associated with an increased desire to die earlier. They suggested that 'good care' which involves encouraging patients and carers to voice their fears and assert control may encourage this.
Schultz and Decker	1995	Disability	Middle-age people disabled by spinal cord injury resulting from polio in earlier life demonstrated mean well-being scores only slightly below that of the normal population. Those who had high levels of social support were satisfied with their social contacts, and those with high levels of control reported high levels of well-being.
Paykel et al.	1996	Psychiatric patients	Longitudinal study of life events, social support and marital relationships, remission and relapse in psychiatric patients diagnosed as suffering from severe depression. No association between psychosocial stressors or social support and outcome were found. Severity of illness and predominance of inpatients in the sample may have accounted for negative findings.
Stansfield et al.	1997	Sickness absence from work	Confiding/emotional social support from spouse or close family is associated with increased sickness absence. Identified an interaction between direct coping, social support in the workplace and stressfulness of episode among student nurses.
Walker and Sofaer	1998	Chronic pain	Self-report of emotional support (using single-item measure) was associated with less psychological distress, practical help was associated with more distress.

The application of social support in health and health care

A small selection of studies of health and health care that have used measures of social support are given in Table 6.4. These are intended to provide examples of research on a range of topics related to primary and secondary prevention and tertiary care. It is important to note that studies in Table 6.4 appear to demonstrate that self-efficacy mediates between social support and depression. Supportive actions that increase self-efficacy promote well-being while those that decrease self-efficacy promote depression (see Chapter 8 for a possible explanation for this).

Concluding comments

It is evident from this brief review that social support and personal control are closely linked. Social support, depending on the type, has the facility to reduce personal control and induce dependence. Conversely, it has the possibility of enhancing personal control, sense of self-efficacy and self-esteem. Some types of support may enhance or damage health and well-being, depending on the needs of the individual, the demands and controllability of the situation and the personal resources of the individual, issues which are reconsidered from a theoretical perspective in Chapter 8. Meaningful measurement remains a significant challenge for researchers.

Note

1 Though some may feel that this poses ethical problems, particularly where it involves exposing those in vulnerable groups to a 'battery' of inventories and questionnaires.

Further reading

Ganster, D. C. and Victor, B. (1988) The impact of social support on mental and physical health. *Journal of Medical Psychology*, 61: 17–36.

Hobfoll, S. (1988) *The Ecology of Stress*. New York: Hemisphere.

Hupcey, J. E. (1998) Social support: assessing conceptual coherence. *Qualitative Health Research*, 8(3): 304–18.

Pierce, G. R., Lakey, B., Sarason, I. G. and Sarason, B. R. (eds) (1997) Sourcebook of social support and personality. New York: Plenum.

Schwarzer, R. and Leppin, A. (1989) Social support and health: a meta-analysis. *Psychology and Health*, 3: 1–15.

Winemiller, D. R., Mitchell, M. E., Sutcliff, J. and Cline, D. J. (1993) Measurement strategies in social support: a descriptive review of the literature. *Journal of Clinical Psychology*, 49(3): 639–47.

Emotional states

Overview of contents

- The nature of emotion
- Anxiety
- Depression
- Other emotional states associated with loss of control
- Measuring emotions
- Applications for measures of emotion
- Concluding comments
- Further reading.

The nature of emotion

The inclusion of this chapter was discussed in Chapter 1, and it should by now be apparent that emotional responses are central to theories of control. But emotions may be conceptualized in different ways and it is helpful to have some understanding of these issues. DeCharms (1968) addressed three fundamental philosophical dilemmas in relation to emotion. The first was mind–body dualism: how do mental events affect bodily actions? The second was causation: what is a cause and how do we come to recognize it as such? The third was hedonism: the notion that all human action results from the desire to gain pleasure and avoid pain. Within these questions, DeCharms identified a number of common assumptions. These include: mental events cause bodily actions, rather than vice versa; motivation is related to seeking pleasure and avoiding pain, as in Freud's pleasure principle.

Emotions are generally accepted to have affective (mood), physiological, cognitive and behavioural components, though the causal relationship between these has been the subject of much deliberation. Folkman and Lazarus

(1988) observed a division in the literature between animal and ego psychology models of emotion and coping. Animal models treat emotion as a drive, activation or arousal that motivates behavioural response. For example, fear motivates avoidance or escape, while anger motivates confrontation or attack. The expression of emotion serves to indicate the drive state of other animals and prime suitable responses. For example, anger indicates the likelihood of attack while grief generates sympathy and help. Psychoanalytic models of emotion stress the ego-defensive signalling role of emotions. Thus, Folkman and Lazarus (1988) pointed out, animal models of emotion focus predominantly on behavioural responses, while ego psychology focuses on cognitive responses. Behavioural coping involves direct action to deal with a situation. Cognitive coping enables the individual to reinterpret a perceived threat as a perceived challenge, thereby enabling him or her to gain mastery over the situation. According to Folkman and Lazarus, both cognitive and behavioural models conceptualize emotions as independent variables that are causally related to cognition and behaviour. An opposing view was taken by Heider (1958), who argued that emotions occur in response to attributions. Thus a pain may elicit feelings of aggression, misfortune or a stupid mistake, depending on the perceived locus of causality. Likewise, thwarted achievement may lead to feelings of frustration or anger, depending on whether the cause is attributed to self or other.

The attribution model of emotion was supported by Schachter and Singer (1962). Their classic experiment in support of this involved the administration of an arousing drug (adrenalin) under different environmental conditions. This demonstrated that the same physiological state of arousal might be labelled in terms of different emotions, depending on the environmental or contextual information available. The resulting 'Schachter and Singer' theory of emotion is widely quoted in the literature on control. It states that physiological arousal and cognition are both necessary conditions for an emotional state. Physiological arousal determines the intensity of the emotion, while cognition determines the nature of the emotion that will be experienced, such as joy, fury and jealousy (Schachter and Singer 1962: 398). A review of research to test this theory by Reisenzein (1983) found evidence to support the influence of arousal feedback on the intensity of emotion, and some evidence in support of the role of causal attributions in determining the nature of the emotional state. Reisenzein concluded that the arousal–emotion relationship was mediated, in part, by causal attributions regarding the source of the arousal. This is illustrated below:

Event → arousal → attribution → emotion

It is questionable whether emotion leads to behavioural action, or behaviour and emotion occur concurrently. Most prominent theories of emotion link emotional response to perceived locus of causality (Schachter and Singer 1962; Lazarus 1966). On the other hand, Weiner (1985) and Graham and Weiner (1986) sought to identify a link between outcomes and emotions.

They viewed this in the context of successful and unsuccessful outcomes and controllable or uncontrollable circumstances, using attribution and expectancy-value theories. Success is generally associated with happiness and satisfaction, failure with sadness. Successful outcomes achieved through personal effort and ability are associated with pride, confidence, contentment and self-esteem. Successful outcomes achieved through the effort of others result in gratitude. Persistent failure is associated with hopelessness. Personal failure in the face of controllable outcomes leads to shame and guilt, while failure attributable to others in the face of controllable outcomes is associated with anger or pity. Thus each of these emotions can be linked to locus (source), controllability and outcomes (Weiner and Litman-Adizes 1980; Graham and Weiner 1986: 157). Weiner (1985: 560; see also Graham and Weiner 1986: 154) presented a simple model of cognition–emotion to account for this process, in which the dimensions of causal attribution are locus (of causality), controllability and stability:

$$\text{Outcome} \begin{cases} \nearrow \text{Outcome evaluation} \longrightarrow \text{General positive / negative emotions} \\ \searrow \text{Causal attribution and dimensions} \longrightarrow \text{Distinct emotions} \end{cases}$$

Weiner's model clearly identifies emotion as a response based on attributions of both outcome and causality. However, this does not fully explain the relationship of control to the states of anxiety and depression.

Anxiety

At a phenomenological level, anxiety is commonly experienced as a state of physiological arousal associated with unpleasant feelings, ranging from unease to panic. Strelau (1992), reviewing 30 years of research into anxiety, characterized it in terms of:

- affective symptoms (persistent feelings of tension);
- behavioural symptoms (behavioural agitation, repetitive behaviours);
- somatic symptoms (discomfort associated with increased sympathetic arousal);
- cognitive symptoms (lowered self-confidence and cognitive disorganization).

Other symptoms not specific to anxiety include crying, irritability, insomnia and restlessness, worry and self-doubt (Garber et al. 1980). Severe and persistent anxiety is associated with pathological states identified in DSM-IV (1994), but these are not within the remit of this book. Instead, the following review is concerned with theories that account for anxiety in terms of causation. The theories identified here include: evolutionary theory, psychoanalytic theories, trait and state theories, stress and perceived threat, and theories related to control and helplessness.

Evolutionary theory and anxiety

According to evolutionary theory, anxiety is associated with symptoms of arousal caused by the fight/flight stress system. The fight/flight mechanism was conceptualized by Cannon in the 1940s as one that primes an organism to deal with situations of threat. Put quite simply, when faced with threat from an enemy, an animal has two choices: stand its ground and fight, or run away as fast as possible. A third alternative is to stay very still in the hope that its presence is not noticed; thus the mechanism is sometimes referred to as fight, flight or freeze. Awareness of a potential threat stimulates a state of sympathetic arousal in preparation, it is suggested, for the two main responses of fighting the enemy or fleeing. Simeons (1960) proposed that this response is redundant in modern man with the result that chronic states of arousal or anxiety are likely to occur.

The fight/flight theory of anxiety came under attack from Gray (1987), who maintained that the neurophysiological substrates of behavioural activation associated with fight or flight are quite separate from those associated with behavioural inhibition (freezing or passive avoidance). Whereas evolutionary theory generally links anxiety with fight and flight, Gray has argued that fear and anxiety are usually related to behavioural inhibition and not to escape or defensive aggression. Furthermore, although evolutionary theory explains anxiety in terms of a chronic state of arousal, thus linking it with stress, it does not identify what is meant by the term 'threat' in terms of human ecology, nor does it explain individual differences in perceptions of threat and hence susceptibility to anxiety. Nevertheless, these issues have been addressed by cognitive theorists and need not, in my view, detract from the contribution of evolutionary theory to our understanding of the physiological responses associated with anxiety.

Psychoanalytic theories of anxiety

Freud (1936) conceptualized anxiety as a primary motivating force, an unpleasant state of inner tension or undischarged energy that individuals are motivated to reduce. This also forms the basis of drive-reduction theory. Freud identified two main causes of anxiety: real environmental threat and threat to the ego (the part of the mind that attempts to cope with the demands of reality and mediate between internal drives or impulses and reality). Put simply, real environmental threat requires direct action, while ego-threat may be dealt with by one of a range of defence mechanisms. Defence mechanisms are unconscious strategies that serve to protect the individual from painful feelings, often caused by overwhelming internal impulses. In other words, they serve to reduce anxiety and other unpleasant emotional states. There appears to be little research evidence in favour of the details of Freud's theory. However, his ideas are important inasmuch as they have phenomenological appeal and have permeated much of the subsequent literature on anxiety within psychology and psychiatry, most notably theories of anxiety that distinguish between state and trait. They have also entered lay language and are central to theories of coping that view the reduction of anxiety as a primary drive or motivation.

Anxiety trait and state

Cattell was the first to distinguish between anxiety trait and anxiety state (Strelau 1992), though these concepts were subsequently elaborated by Charles Spielberger and incorporated into his widely used State Trait Anxiety Inventory. Trait anxiety refers to anxiety-proneness, while state anxiety refers to the unpleasant feeling of apprehension that occurs in situations of uncertainty or threat. Experimental evidence suggests that there is frequently a high correlation between the two, which may be explained by the mediation processes discussed below.

Whether anxiety trait is inherited or acquired as a result of childhood experiences remains a matter of some debate. Psychoanalytic theories, such as that of Bowlby, are likely to refer to poor ego strength and self-esteem resulting from lack of secure attachment relationships during childhood. Others have attributed anxiety-proneness to genetic predisposition:

> Anxiety is a monitor, forcing us to keep abreast of the new demands that will be made upon us by our environment and forcing us to develop the appropriate new patterns of behaviour. The mechanisms subserving this function appear to be firmly built into the gene pool of human beings. As one might expect, some individuals are born with too great an amount of this genetic disposition and then we get states of persistent, chronic anxiety with episodes of panic.
>
> (Costello 1976: 27)

Eysenck (1991) found experimental evidence in favour of selective bias among those scoring high on trait anxiety, such that they were more likely to attend to threat-related than neutral environmental stimuli. Eysenck observed that while cognitive bias is now well recognized, its mechanisms remained uncertain.

Spielberger's early conceptualization of anxiety drew heavily on the work of Lazarus (1966) and Lazarus and Averill (1972), as well as Freudian concepts. According to Spielberger (1972c: 43), appraisal of situational demands is influenced by a combination of thoughts, feelings, biological needs and trait anxiety. Appraisal determines state of apprehension (anxiety state). Appraisal and apprehension bring defence mechanisms into play and a combination of appraisal, anxiety state and defence mechanisms determine behavioural response. Spielberger (1972c) identified stress as an objective stimulus property of a situation – one that is dangerous or threatening. In other words, he equated stress with features of the stressor. He defined threat in terms of individual perception of the situation as psychologically or physically harmful or dangerous. State anxiety and other emotional reactions are evoked by perception of threat. He identified personality trait in terms of individual differences in frequency and intensity of emotional states over time. Individuals with high trait anxiety will perceive situations that involve failure or threat to self-esteem as more threatening than those with low trait anxiety, though there is no difference in relation to perceived physical danger. Thus Spielberger appeared to draw heavily on psychoanalytic explanations of anxiety and neurosis.

Gray (1987) equated neuroticism with high trait anxiety. Neuroticism refers to a state of chronic fear and anxiety that includes anxiety states, phobias and obsessive-compulsive behaviours. It also refers to a personality dimension. Based on the work of Hans Eysenck, neurotics are described as demonstrating strong emotional lability and are easily aroused, leading them to be moody and anxious. Thus trait anxiety may reflect individual differences in physiological as well as psychological response.

Anxiety and cognitive appraisal

Lazarus (1966) made a substantial advance in theories of stress and anxiety by associating emotional states with cognitive appraisal processes. Lazarus and Averill (1972: 243) proposed a three-stage model of appraisal consisting of:

- Primary cognitive appraisal of threat. (What is happening here? Does it constitute a threat to my physical or psychological integrity?)
- Secondary appraisal of coping alternatives. (What can I do about it?)
- Reappraisal. (Were my actions successful? What do I need to do next?)

Lazarus identified that all stages of the appraisal process are influenced by both situational and dispositional variables. Appraisal may lead to direct action, such as attack, avoidance, inaction, active striving towards goal and/or cognitive modes of conflict resolution, such as vigilance, psychological defence or reappraisal. Lazarus and his colleagues thus provided an important link between evolutionary and psychoanalytic theories of anxiety.

Lazarus et al. (1985) proposed that anxiety state is a consequence of the relationship between individuals' appraisal of environmental demands and their perceptions of their capabilities to meet, mitigate or alter these demands in the interests of their own well-being. This definition appears to link state anxiety to perceived lack of control. When Folkman and Lazarus (1991) reviewed the relationship between emotion and coping, they were critical of structural approaches that treat recurrent cognitive, behavioural and emotional patterns as stable characteristics. They claimed that this constitutes only a part of the total picture. They argued that appraisals of a situation are influenced by the individual's understanding of the situation and their mood state at the time. Appraisal determines the coping response, which in turn affects the person–environment relationship and emotional response. Thus emotional response mediates coping and emotion mediates coping. The relationship is both dynamic and mutually reciprocal.

Anxiety and control

The relationship between control and anxiety was set out by Mandler and Watson in 1966 (Mandler 1972). These authors predicted that an organism which has, or expects to have, some control over the onset and offset of potentially stressful stimuli experiences less anxiety or arousal. Watson (1967) upheld this prediction. Bowers (1968; see Table 2.1) subsequently demonstrated that predictions of control over aversive stimuli reduce anxiety and increase tolerance to the stimulus. Bowers (1968) also identified an important interaction between anxiety and locus of control, such that externals tended to be more anxious. Ray and Katahn (1968) also confirmed a positive relationship between anxiety and external locus of control suggestive that a feeling of lack of control over the environment and the outcome of one's actions is associated with anxiety. However, the causal mechanisms remained unclear.

Mandler drew on first principles to support his theoretical position:

> in a state of arousal, the organism who has no behaviour available to him, who continues to seek situationally or cognitively appropriate behaviour is 'helpless' and so may consider himself, in terms of the common language as being in a state of anxiety.
>
> (Mandler 1972: 369)

Mandler was very critical of other 'so-called' theories of anxiety, referring to most of them as 'reshufflings of classical psychoanalytic models or rather old-hat stimulus–response models'. He identified that theories had previously focused on anxiety as one of the following:

- produced by fear or terror;
- a protective device;
- related to activation;
- a conditioned response;
- an innate disposition;
- a drive.

In contrast, Mandler proposed anxiety as a state of helplessness. He suggested that arousal leads to helplessness when no appropriate cognitive or behavioural response is available, or when there is no escape from the situation as a means of terminating the state of arousal. This seems to be similar to Seligman's theory of learned helplessness, yet Mandler applied it to anxiety rather than depression. Mandler's theory of anxiety received support from Ray and Katahn (1968) and later from Bandura (1977b), who proposed that a state of high emotional arousal is maintained until effective coping behaviours are achieved. Mandler's theory is also concordant with that presented in Chapter 8.

Garber *et al.* (1980) presented a review of theories of anxiety in relation to controllability and helplessness. Seligman (1975) had proposed that anxiety occurs when the individual is uncertain about controllability, whereas depression occurs when the individual is convinced that the situation is uncontrollable. Garber *et al.* concluded that anxiety is likely to occur when the probability of achieving a desirable outcome is perceived to be uncertain. In contrast, depression is likely to occur when the probability of achieving desired outcomes is perceived to be unlikely (hopeless). Garber's explanation allows that an individual may feel anxious or depressed about one aspect of his or her life and not about others, or anxious and depressed simultaneously. Experimental research by Schultz and Schonpflug (1988) indicated that state anxiety could be reduced by achieving a satisfactory outcome and through verification of this by external feedback. Uncertainty about outcomes was found to lead to increased state anxiety likely to contribute, in the longer term, to tension, apprehension and neurotic behaviour.

Schultz *et al.* (1991) confirmed that positive and negative emotions had long been linked to control over the environment. An important question that remained unanswered was whether people are primarily motivated to act to reduce negative feelings (avoid feeling bad) and maximize positive feelings (aim to feel good), or whether the primary motivation is to act to gain and/or maintain control over the environment. Fowles (1992) expressed a preference for the latter, linking anxiety to perceptions of control. He based his argument on Mineka's theory that perceptions of lack of control associated with chronic anxiety in adulthood (trait anxiety) are linked to the failure to develop a sense of mastery and control within the social environment during childhood. This also supports an explanation of trait anxiety based on nurture in preference to nature. Nevertheless, as Gray (1987) pointed out, nurture and nature normally interact to produce responses that adapt to the environment. Pekrun (1992) addressed some of these issues in his review of anxiety in relation to expectancy-value theory. He proposed that expectancies might relate to situation–outcome, action–control (self-efficacy) or action–outcome. Thus the nature and strength of an outcome may be due to factors inherent in the event or situation, or be based on individuals' evaluation of the likely effectiveness of their actions (similar to external or internal locus of control). He proposed that anxiety formation might be linked to genetic predisposition and habitualized responses, as well as to cognitive mediation.

Fear versus anxiety

Psychiatric classifications, and many theorists, have failed to differentiate between fear and anxiety states, with the result that anxiety is often viewed as a generalized or chronic state of fear. Gray (1987) suggested that fear is a response to perceived threat, which may be innate, learned or conditioned. But he failed to make any clear distinction between fear and anxiety. Fear and anxiety have each been conceptualized as a response to threat. Fear is generally conceptualized as a response to a specific threat and therefore has a tangible object, while anxiety frequently has no tangible object. However, as Phares (1976) noted, not all anxiety is to be regarded as undesirable, since a degree of anxiety may act as a motivating force.

A control perspective on fear and anxiety

The distinction between fear and anxiety may lie in distinguishing between the state of physiological arousal and the attributions of causality or outcome associated with an eliciting event or situation. A state of arousal induced by a novel stimulus is sufficient to act as a motivating force, since the stimulus requires attention and possibly action. Fear is likely to result from appraisal of the stimulus as potentially harmful, and fear may persist until the threatening situation has resolved or suitable coping responses are found to deal with it. Fear thus reflects potential loss of control due to a tangible threat. In contrast, anxiety appears to be a state of physiological arousal that persists in the absence of knowing what the precise nature of the threat is or how to deal with it. Anxiety is thus associated with uncertainty (not knowing what is happening), unpredictability (not knowing what is likely to happen next) and uncontrollability (not knowing how to deal with it). Uncertainty and unpredictability are sufficient, though not necessary, conditions for loss of control. This explains anxiety as both a positive motivating force (to find ways of regaining control) and an unpleasant emotional state. It suggests that trait anxiety may be due to: an innate susceptibility to physiological arousal; an innate disposition to view the world as uncertain or unpredictable; prolonged early exposure to uncertainty or deprivation of control; poor problem-solving or life skills (including social skills); or any combination of these.

Anxiety, uncertainty and locus of control

A theory of anxiety based on uncertainty and lack of control would predict that those with internal locus of control would be less anxious than those with external locus of control. Early experimental findings tended to confirm this, though the association was not strong (e.g. Feather 1967; Watson 1967). Phares (1976) identified that most research suggested a linear relationship between externality and anxiety and adjustment, though he suggested that there might be theoretical reasons to propose an inverted U relationship in which both extreme externals and internals might be expected to be more maladjusted and anxious: externals because they are incapable of influencing events and internals because they are sensitive to failure. He argued that these extremes are unlikely to be picked up in college populations on which most research had been conducted. Furthermore, Phares's proposition needed to be reviewed in the light of the reformulation of locus of control and its measurement. A variety of chronic illnesses and conditions give rise to great uncertainty with respect to its course or outcome. For example, Wiener (1975) identified that rheumatoid arthritis patients suffered variable loss of control associated with unpredictable acute exacerbations. Sufferers never know from day to day how they are likely to feel or function. Studies have confirmed that poor coping in chronic pain patients tends to be associated with external (chance) locus of control (e.g. Toomey *et al*. 1993).

Overall, there has emerged strong support for a relationship between anxiety and control, though its precise nature remains somewhat unclear. Although it was originally conceptualized as a response to danger or threat, there is considerable support for viewing fear as the immediate response to danger, and anxiety as a response to the uncertainty that occurs during the period in which the nature of the threat is appraised and a suitable response sought. This may take a few seconds or pervade every aspect of life. In the social world, environmental threats are frequently of a social nature, including those that result in damage to confidence and self-esteem. Hence anxiety is frequently associated not with physical danger, but with so-called ego threats.

Depression

Depression is a state of general dysphoria. It is also classified as a psychiatric illness whose symptoms include two or more of: poor appetite or overeating; insomnia or hypersomnia; low energy or fatigue; low self-esteem; poor concentration or difficulty making decisions; feelings of hopelessness (DSM-IV 1994). It frequently includes self-deprecation, self-neglect, feelings of guilt and social withdrawal, and may include suicidal thoughts or intentions. While the affective components of depression are relatively invariant, the somatic, cognitive and behavioural elements are more susceptible to variation. Theories of depression include those based on psychoanalytic theory, behaviourism and cognition theory (Garber *et al*. 1980; Gilbert 1992). The cognitive and behavioural theories of Beck, Lewinsohn and Seligman feature most prominently in the current literature.

Psychodynamic theories

Psychodynamic theories of depression emphasize the role of childhood separation, loss and lack of secure attachment (Brown and Harris 1978). Thus individuals grow up with negative expectancies of themselves (and low self-esteem) and others. Depression is frequently associated with low self-esteem, but also with a sense of alienation and internalized hostility. Psychodynamic theories of depression may be seen as complementary to, rather than alternative to, other theories of depression. They are particularly helpful in emphasizing the potential impact of childhood experiences on adult beliefs, behaviour and emotional states.

Beck's cognitive theory

Beck's theory of depression (Beck 1974, 1976) was developed in the 1960s and is a cognitive theory that focused on cognitive distortions associated with the development of negative cognitive set or mental state of hopelessness. According to Beck, an adverse event, including loss and failure, leads traumatized people to reflect on what it tells them about themselves. Depression-prone people are likely to assign the cause of an adverse event to some shortcoming in themselves. Such causal attributions are very simplistic and may be quite erroneous. They lead to loss of self-esteem, self-blame and pessimism that, in a depressed person, permeate every specific wish and task undertaken. The snowballing of sadness and apathy is associated with complete loss of motivation and withdrawal. The state of hopelessness may be associated with suicidal intentions or actions. Thus, according to Beck, the ingredient for depression is a proneness to depression, which may be brought about by exposure to adverse life events or situations. Quite often there is also a precipitating event, such as loss of a job or unexpected disability.

Beck's approach to therapy is ostensibly aimed at reducing cognitive distortion; for example, by demonstrating to the depressed person that the negative predictions held about his or her capabilities are wrong. Therapy encourages positive self-talk. Beck's theory has since been contradicted (see Chapter 2), since depressed people have been shown to hold a more realistic view of their capabilities than non-depressed people, who tend to hold illusions of personal control.

Behavioural theories of depression

Ferster and Lewinsohn undertook a behaviourist analysis of depression during the 1960s. Ferster (1973) presented a functional analysis of depression that is in many ways similar to the better known theory of Lewinsohn. Ferster noted a high frequency of escape and avoidance behaviours in depressed people that leads to a reduction in exposure to positive as well as negative stimuli. Depression, according to Lewinsohn (1974), is an extinction phenomenon. Depressive symptoms such as dysphoria and fatigue are a conditioned response to a low rate of response-contingent positive reinforcement, while low rates of activity represent a prolonged phase of extinction. Reasons for the low rate of positive reinforcement include: individuals' personality (lack of outgoingness); the lack of availability of rewards in the environment due to social isolation or exclusion through, for example, loss or poverty; and a limited repertoire of behaviours that would enable them to achieve rewards (social skills). As the individual becomes more depressed, social avoidance leads to further reductions in exposure to positive reinforcement and the problem is compounded. Lewinsohn (1974) claimed that lack of self-esteem, central to Beck's model, is not an inevitable consequence of depression.

Therapy based on Lewinsohn's analysis focuses on strategies to increase the amount of positive reinforcement in the lives of depressed people through ensuring increased exposure to positive reinforcement. Since most positive reinforcement is available in interpersonal situations, social skills training is an important component of therapy to enable people to gain and sustain positive social reinforcement (social support) through the ability to establish reciprocal relationships with others.

Seligman's theory of learned helplessness

Seligman's theory is described in Chapter 4. It has undergone a gradual evolution from a behavioural theory of learned response-independence to an attributional theory of helplessness. This has since led Seligman's co-researchers to propose an attributional theory of hopelessness to explain a subset of depression. The latter theory appears to have little in common with the original theory of learned helplessness and more in common with Beck's theory, except that it does not make an assumption of cognitive distortion. It is probably the best recognized theory of depression outside of clinical psychology.

Commonalities among theories of depression

Most critiques of these models set out to contrast each with the others (for example, see Blaney 1977). However, for the purposes of this book, it is more productive to examine their similarities. Central to each of the theories, including psychodynamic models, is the concept of loss or lack of control over important outcomes in one's life (Blaney 1977), whether these relate to personal or social needs. According to psychodynamic models, loss refers to loss of a loved one or lack of social support at a time when the child is dependent on those who care for him or her. According to Beck's theory, individuals believe that they have no control over events in their lives and are of no use to others (see the importance of reciprocity in social support, Chapter 6). According to Lewinsohn, individuals are unable to obtain desired outcomes and by implication lack control, while Seligman's original model was based on the notion of personal loss of control.

If we accept that the main area of commonality is that of lack or loss of control over the events or situations in one's life, it appears that an important area of difference between these models lies in the centrality of the social milieu in which the individual lives. Lewinsohn's theory is predominantly an interpersonal theory of depression that requires an interpersonal solution.

Psychodynamic theories of depression focus on an intrapersonal model of depression that has social origins. Psychodynamic therapy, while encouraging an introspective view, is heavily dependent on the role of the therapist, who represents a temporary source of emotional social support as well as guidance. Beck's cognitive theory of depression, while taking account of situational factors, is predominantly an intrapersonal theory that requires intrapersonal changes in belief about the self. The role of the cognitive therapist is rather more directive than that of the psychodynamic therapist but is equally important as a source of informational and emotional support. Seligman's original model of learned helplessness was essentially an intrapsychic theory in which both causal model and therapeutic interventions failed to take adequate account of the social environment. I believe this to be a fundamental flaw in the theory of learned helplessness, and it is one that I take up again in the next chapter. The attribution reformulation was heavily influenced by Beck's model in taking account of loss of self-esteem, thereby focusing particularly on personal helplessness.

It appears that each model has the potential to be partially correct. Take the example given below (I have arbitrarily selected a male for the purpose of this illustration):

An innately introverted child grows up in an abusive environment in which he is constantly being told how stupid and inadequate he is. He is discouraged from bringing home friends and becomes socially ill at ease and isolated. He drops out of school early and takes a series of insecure, low-paid jobs. He suffers from periodic bouts of depression and makes an unsuccessful suicidal attempt. He eventually finds a mate who also experiences emotional difficulties and they have a child. Things look good for a while, but then he loses his job. The relationship breaks down, he loses his home, his wife and his child. He becomes clinically depressed.

Genetic theory accounts for a propensity to introversion. Psychodynamic theory accounts for the social origins of the problems in childhood. Lewinsohn's theory accounts for socially determined deficits in reinforcement throughout life, leading to depression. Beck's theory accounts for the state of hopelessness and Seligman's model accounts for the state of personal helplessness (nothing the individual does ever appears to work). Though each theory is capable of explaining depression, no one theory is capable of predicting depression. The fact is that not everyone born and brought up in these circumstances becomes depressed, while not everyone who loses everything in adulthood succumbs to depression.

Coyne and Gotlib (1983) reviewed studies designed to test competing cognitive and behavioural theories of depression. Overall, they found that the available evidence offered little support for either the Beck or the Seligman models of depression. What these models of depression fail to explain is the high rate of spontaneous remission. In fact, only Ferster's theory offers a possible explanation for this. Ferster (1973: 865) pointed out that sudden changes associated with loss could cause depression; for example, retirement. He neglected to mention the impact of many other changes that afford opportunities for positive lifestyle change. Lazarus (1968) referred to the 'truism' that time heals. The environment is constantly changing and we interact with it in a dynamic way. Anti-depressant drugs reduce negative thought and affect, enabling people to interact in a more positive way with the social environment. Equally, an improved social environment may make them feel more valued and lead to the same improvement.

Anisman and Zacharko (1982) studied the link between stress and depression and concluded that the pharmacological and biochemical evidence supported the need to conceptualize depressive illness according to a number of subtypes that share some common underlying features. Overall, it would appear that each theory of depression accounts for certain aspects of depression. No single theory appears to account for all aspects of depression, and it remains difficult, if not impossible, to predict who will become depressed, and who not, given the same set of events or circumstances.

Other emotional states associated with loss of control

Although anxiety and depression are most commonly identified as affective or emotional states associated with loss of control, other mood states may also be linked directly to sense of control, most notably in social contexts. These issues are central to the analyses presented in Chapter 8.

Anger, hostility and blame

Wortman and Brehm (1975) proposed that anger or hostility results when an individual expects to achieve an important outcome but fails to do so because of the perceived intervention of another. Beck (1976) highlighted the importance of distinguishing anger from frustration, noting that anger is a response to the deliberate or avoidable thwarting of a controllable outcome. Frustration, in contrast, is a response to an unavoidable uncontrollable situation. Anger is thus associated with attributions of fault or blame, and external control beliefs. Mirowsky and Ross (1989) pointed out that anger and depression are both reactions to situations over which the individual may have little control and which, applying equity theory, are felt to be unfair. Such situations may arise in close personal relationships such as marriage (Mirowsky and Ross 1989), the workplace (Greenglass 1996) or society (Gilbert 1992).

Anger was central to psychoanalytic theories of depression during the early part of the twentieth century, but has played little part in more recent cognitive and behavioural theories (Gilbert 1992). According to Gilbert (1992), suppressed anger and grievances about past events are common among those who are depressed, though Mook *et al.* (1990) found little evidence of trait anger among psychiatric patients. Mook *et al.* suggested that the suppression of anger in those with chronic anxiety might precipitate depression. This fits with stage models of reaction to undesirable life events (Wortman and Brehm 1975; Silver and Wortman 1980) in which anger gives way to depression. Recently, more attention has been given to the role of suppressed anger in the genesis of stress-related physiological disorders and diseases such as hypertension and coronary heart disease, earning the label 'the silent killer' (Spielberger *et al.* 1991a).

Personality and coping style factors (Spielberger *et al.* 1991a) and socio-biological reasons (see Gilbert 1992: 244–5) have been put forward to account for the suppression of anger, but social factors must play an important role. In highly organized but densely populated societies, situations likely to provoke angry responses abound, while the physical expression of anger is discouraged. Julkunen (1996) suggested that it is not clear how it is possible to express anger constructively, while at the same time avoiding an escalation of conflict. It is well recognized that, in a British context, those from the lower socio-economic groups have higher levels of morbidity and mortality (Marmot 1999). These groups also have far less control over their lives, being at the mercy of large and anonymous social systems (e.g. benefits and housing) designed ostensibly to support and protect them. Suppressed anger is common among patients with chronic pain (Fernandez and Turk 1995), and the findings of Walker *et al.* (1999) indicate that this might reflect feelings of helplessness in their encounters with medical, social and legal support agencies. Other researchers (e.g. DeGood and Kiernan 1996) have found an association between attributions of blame and psychological distress in chronic pain patients.

Culbertson and Spielberger (1996) identified the need to distinguish between angry responses to anger-provoking situations and anger as an emotional state. The STAXI (Spielberger *et al.* 1988; see Table 7.1) differentiated between three components of anger: overt expression (saying nasty things, losing one's temper), suppression (boiling inside but not showing it) and control of angry feelings (keeping one's cool, dealing with it calmly). The last appears to reflect an adaptive way of dealing with anger, while suppression is not. While anger is recognized to be a universal emotion, there are strong cultural differences in its expression. Tanzer *et al.* (1996) demonstrated that the expression of anger is socially unacceptable in Chinese cultures and the Chinese must learn to control overt expressions of anger and tolerate situations that might give rise to feelings of anger. Learning to deal with potentially anger-provoking situations in a tolerant way may prevent the negative health consequences associated with suppression.

Shame, guilt and low self-esteem

Gilbert (1992) identified shame with a sense of inferiority or losing out to others, and hence low self-esteem. Both shame and guilt are internally directed. However, shame is associated with a belief in an inferior self compared to able others. Wilkinson (1999) described how situations that induce shame lead to anger and overt hostility as people defend themselves against ridicule, or being treated as incompetent or inferior. Not always do people strike back at those who have exposed them to humiliation. For example, men may try to regain their sense of control by taking it out on those weaker then themselves, such as their wives. It is relatively common for people who are depressed to blame themselves for things that have gone wrong. Weiner and Litman-Adizes (1980) identified guilt and shame as resulting from perceived lack of personal effort in the event of failure. In contrast to shame, guilt is associated with a belief that the self is able and should, therefore, have been able to achieve a successful outcome for self or less able others, leading to feelings of having let others down (Gilbert 1992). Gilbert identified that shame is about power and dominance, whereas guilt is concerned with breaking internal moral codes, particularly where a personal act has resulted in harm to another.

Positive emotional responses

The majority of research based on the concept of control has focused on measures of negative emotions associated with loss or lack of control. As Mook et al. (1990) pointed out, the more frequently negative affect is experienced, generally the less frequently positive affect is experienced. Nevertheless, an absence of negative affect may or may not imply the presence of positive affect, and vice versa (Mook et al. 1990: 29). Both Bradburn (1969) and Radloff (1977), whose measures included a balance of positive and negative items, found that depressed and positive affect are independent of each other (though Mirowsky and Ross (1996) have suggested that this might be an artefact of factor analysis). This led Diener (1984) to support the argument that psychologists have focused too exclusively on negative emotional states. Interestingly, turn to any thesaurus and you will find that there are actually more words in the English language to describe negative emotions than there are to describe positive ones. Immediate responses to positive outcomes include happiness, pleasure, satisfaction, joy and delight. Responses to sustained positive outcomes include optimism and contentment. Some responses depend on attributions of responsibility for success. For example, attributions of personal responsibility for success include self-confidence, pride and sense of self-worth (associated with raised self-esteem). Attributions of responsibility for success to someone else, in situations over which individuals perceive themselves to have little or no personal control, are associated, in the short term, to gratitude and, in the longer term, to confidence, faith and trust.

Measuring emotions

A selection of measures of anxiety, depression, psychological well-being/distress and self-esteem are given in Table 7.1. Researchers using the concept of control are encouraged to identify measures that are theoretically appropriate as well as appropriate to administer to their population group. Many of the measures available arise from quite different theoretical bases and were designed for specific population groups (mostly psychiatric patients).

The choice of measurement instruments is inevitably selective and I omitted most of those that are not readily accessible and/or available. Some are included because they are widely recognized and used, and facilitate comparison of findings. For example, the Beck Depression Inventory is the most widely known and used instrument for measuring depression, even though, in the context of research into control and helplessness in a general population, the BDI may not be the first choice for a number of reasons. It was designed primarily for use with psychiatric patients to reflect symptoms of clinical depression and, although widely used for other population groups, the full version includes many aspects that do not specifically address the affective, cognitive and motivational deficits associated with loss of control. The most common measure of anxiety is undoubtedly the Spielberger State-Trait Anxiety Inventory. This is only available from the publishers but remains most widely used by most researchers. Mook *et al.* (1990: 28) noted the importance of using frequency scales to measure trait and intensity scales to measure state. Not all measures adhere to this, and their validity may therefore be open to challenge.

Some measures have been designed for particular age groups. Kazdin and Petti (1982) reviewed 13 different measures used to measure depression in children and adolescents, including adaptations of the long- and short-form Beck Depression Inventory, ranging from three to 66 items. They commented that more items are not necessarily better. Some studies indicated a poor correlation between the ratings of children and their mothers. Self-report in children may be limited by their awareness and willingness to report symptoms. Diener (1984) reviewed studies of well-being using a variety of single-item and multi-item measures. He concluded that most measures correlate moderately with each other and have adequate temporal reliability and internal consistency. Numerous published texts have included reviews of measures of psychological well-being, anxiety and depression (e.g. Bowling 1995), and these are referred to in Table 7.1. Researchers are invited to refer to these sources for details of validity and reliability.

Table 7.1 Measures of emotional response

Emotion	Measure	Reviews	Comment
Anxiety	Spielberger State–Trait Anxiety Inventory (STAI) [Y1, Spielberger et al. 1970; X1, Spielberger et al. 1983]	Bowling (1995: 84–5)[b]	Most widely used measure of anxiety in clinical and psychological research. 20 items with 4-point intensity scale used to assess transitory anxiety; 20 items with 4-point frequency scale used to assess stable anxiety. Positive and negative items included. Bowling (1995) reports on version available for children.
Anxiety	6-item shortened version of STAI (Marteau and Bekker 1992)		Consists of 3 positive and 3 negative items taken from STAI.
Depression	Beck Depression Inventory (Beck et al. 1961[a]) [Beck Depression Inventory – II: Beck et al. 1997]	Bowling (1991: 101–4)[b] Wilkin et al. (1992: 80–5)[b] Bowling (1995: 78–80)[b] Gilbert (1992: 550–1)[a]	21-item version has cut-off points for mild (11) and moderate (18) depression. 13-item short version usually used for non-psychiatric populations. No positive items: well-being inferred by absence of depression.
Depression	Self-Rating Depression Scale (Zung 1965: 65–6)	Bowling (1991: 95–6)[b] Wilkin et al. (1992: 75–80)[a] Bowling (1995: 82–4)[b]	Each item quantifies a known diagnostic symptom of depression on a 4-point scale. Includes positive items. Full scale and scoring system given.
Depression	The Hopelessness Scale (Beck et al. 1974: 862)		20 true/false items (10 positive, 10 negative) measuring negative expectations (pessimism). Reflects affective, motivational and cognitive aspects.

Topic	Scale	References	Description
Depression	Centre for Epidemiologic Studies' Depression Scale (CES-D) (Radloff 1977: 387)	Bowling (1995: 73–4)[b]	Responses on 4-point frequency scale. Includes positive and negative affect, somatic and retarded activity and interpersonal factors. Cut-off score for depression 16. Tested by Ross and Mirowsky (1984), some gender differences noted.
Depression in the elderly	Geriatric Depression Scale (GDS) [Yesavage et al. 1983]	Bowling (1995: 82–3)[b]	Longer version has 30 items, Short version 15 items (5 positive). Yes/no answers. Rather negatively biased.
Postnatal depression	Edinburgh Postnatal Depression Scale [Cox et al. 1987]		10-item scale used widely in research and midwifery/health visiting practice to detect postnatal depression.
Anxiety, depression	General Health Questionnaire Scale B (anxiety) and D (depression) (Goldberg and Hillier 1979[a])	McDowell and Newell (1987: 139–50)[a] Fallowfield (1990: 57)[b] Wilkin et al. (1992)[b] Bowling (1995: 76–8)[b]	7 items per scale measured on 4-point scale. Reported to screen for responses to acute rather than chronic conditions. Includes measures of anxiety and depression.
Anxiety and depression	Hospital Anxiety and Depression Scale (HADS) [Zigmund and Snaith 1983]	Fallowfield (1990)[a] Bowling (1991: 104–6)[b] Wilkin et al. (1992)[a] Bowling (1995: 76)[b]	7 anxiety and 7 depression items (6 positive), each measured on four point frequency scale. Designed to measure mood disorder in non-psychiatric patients. Particularly useful in clinical/primary health care. Excludes somatic symptoms.
Anxiety, depression, anger	Profile of Mood States Bipolar (POMS-BI) (Lorr and McNair 1984)	Fallowfield (1990)[b] Bowling (1995: 85–7)[b]	6 scales each with 6 positive and 6 negative items scored with 4-point intensity scale (elated–depressed; composed–anxious; confident–unsure; agreeable–hostile; energetic–tired; clearheaded–confused).

Table 7.1 *cont'd*

Emotion	Measure	Reviews	Comment
Anger	Spielberger State Trait Anger Scale (STAS) [Spielberger *et al.* 1983] Spielberger State–Trait Anger Expression Inventory (STAXI) [Spielberger *et al.* 1988]	Haseth (1996: 84)	STAS analogous to STAI. STAXI assesses how anger is expressed and controlled.
Well-being	Review of measures (Diener 1984)		Review of single-item and multi-item measures, with theoretical implications.
Psychological well-being	Affect Balance Scale [Bradburn 1969, revised version]	McDowell and Newell (1987: 120–5)[a]	10 items (5 positive, 5 negative), yes/no response. Widely used, though now rather outdated.
Psychological well-being/ distress (includes anxiety, depression)	General Well-Being Schedule (GWBS) [Dupuy 1977]	McDowell and Newell (1987: 125–33)[a] Bowling (1995: 106–8)[b]	Includes anxiety (4 items), depression (3 items) positive well-being (3 items), self-control (3 items), each measured on 6-point frequency scale or global 10-point semantic differential scale.
Well-being/ life satisfaction	Four single item indicators of well-being [Andrews 1976]	McDowell and Newell (1987: 213–18)[a] Wilkin *et al.* (1992: 276)[a] Bowling (1991: 161–3)[b] Bowling (1995)	Includes 7-point delighted–terrible scale, 7-point faces scale and 9-point ladder scale. Equivalent to numerical and visual analogue scales.

Notes
[a] Questionnaire or scale(s) given in full.
[b] Examples of items given.
Citations of authors given in square brackets [ ] are not referenced.

Applications for measures of emotion

Examples of research on the subject of control and emotion are given in previous chapters. In general terms, measures of anxiety and depression have been used in the following types of research:

♦ Responses to acute illness or pain: anxiety.
♦ Adjustment to chronic illness or disability: depression, anger (blame).
♦ Mental illness: anxiety, depression, guilt, shame, anger.

Emotion as independent or dependent variable

In the examples given, it appears that anxiety and depression are treated as dependent variables in stressful situations. Researchers need to determine the theoretical relationship between the variables in their study and decide whether mood or emotional state should be treated as a dependent or an independent variable. This is particularly important if the intention is to use multiple regression or path analyses, which are highly dependent on a theoretical model. Some of the possible models of response to events are given in Figure 7.1. Within these, emotional response is given varying degrees of primacy in determining the outcome and perceived outcome.

Each of the models in Figure 7.1 takes place in a dynamic context in which events are as likely to be caused by individual behaviour as to cause it. When primacy is given to a cognition or behavioural act, the role of

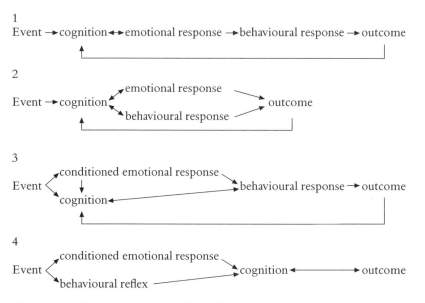

Figure 7.1 Some possible models of response to events

emotional state in the causal chain is excluded or marginalized. Below is such an example:

Cognition → intentional act → event → outcome → emotion

This model is commonly assumed in the field of health promotion, in which it is expected that people are able to make conscious changes to their lifestyle. Feedback loops are not included within this model, and mood or emotional state are rarely taken account of or measured in such situations. Were this to be done, it might emerge that the emotional impact of change could provide a useful indicator of those likely to make or maintain a required change.

A model in which conscious activity appears to play little part in determining outcomes is illustrated below:

Affect ↔ habitual ways of responding and thinking → outcomes

This model may be useful in the field of mental health, particularly in explaining obsessive-compulsive disorders. Here, affect is seen as having a causal impact on ways of automatically responding and hence gaining (or not gaining) control over events. Equally, habitual ways of responding and thinking impact on both emotional state and control over events.

A systems approach

Hyland (1987) presented a systems control interpretation of depression, which he entitled 'motivational control theory'. This model appears to resolve many of the anomalies identified above. According to Hyland, depression is caused by prolonged discrepancy between the system reference criterion (goal or purpose) and perceptual input. He termed this 'prolonged control mismatch'. Transient mismatch, or mismatch in terms of a single goal, is unlikely to result in depression. Depression results from a mismatch between goals and perceived reality involving many different goals.

According to Hyland (1988), motivational control theory is an integrative framework in which different theories are seen to reflect different aspects of a single underlying process. In these two papers, Hyland did not attempt to explain anxiety, although systems theory is well able to do this. Any system that receives inadequate or conflicting information, or is unable to process information to meet the reference criterion, is unable to function properly. Anxiety may represent this chaotic or uncontrolled state. These issues are considered further in Chapter 8.

Concluding comments

It is clear that although most theories of emotion were not based on the concept of control, each appears to reflect some aspects of loss or lack of control. It is a matter of debate whether emotions should be considered as a cause (affect) or consequence (effect). A systems approach appears to render this argument irrelevant by proposing that emotions represent the state of the system at any particular point in time. The emotions most neglected are positive emotions that reflect control, rather than lack or loss of control. In the next chapter, I present an analysis that addresses many of the issues raised here by integrating all the concepts reviewed in this book.

Further reading

Blaney, P. H. (1977) Contemporary theories of depression: critique and comparison. *Journal of Abnormal Psychology*, 86: 203–23.

Gilbert, P. (1992) *Depression: The Evolution of Powerlessness*. Hove: Lawrence Erlbaum Associates.

Graham, S. and Weiner, B. (1986) From an attributional theory of emotion to development psychology: a round-trip ticket? *Social Cognition*, 4(2): 152–79.

Gray, J. A. (1987) *The Psychology of Fear and Stress*, 2nd edn. Cambridge: Cambridge University Press.

Mirowsky, J. and Ross, C. E. (1989) *Social Causes of Psychological Distress*. New York: Aldine de Gruyter.

A unifying theory of control

Introduction: perceived control revisited

The previous chapters have set out a range of concepts that relate to the control or lack of control that people have, or believe that they have, over their lives. These have been developed by different theorists and researchers over the past 40 years, yet little attempt has been made to integrate these concepts into a single unifying theory of control. The result is that researchers in the fields of health and illness use measures of self-efficacy, locus of control, social support and emotional response with little clear understanding of the nature of the relationship between these variables. This chapter presents my own analysis of control, which seeks to integrate the concepts previously reviewed and explain many of the anomalies identified.

This chapter focuses on a theoretical analysis that formed the basis for a series of studies into the impact of chronic pain (Walker 1989; Walker *et al.* 1990, 1999; Walker and Sofaer 1998). I started out with a particular need to make sense of the relationship between pain and distress, but soon found that confusions in terminology and theoretical assumptions were abundant within the literature. Researchers frequently omitted definitions of their use of terms such as coping and control, while basic theoretical assumptions were often neither explicit nor entirely logical. I decided to approach my analysis not from previous theories and assumptions, but from first principles, using the simple example of a headache.

Perceived control over headache

When I have a headache, my immediate concern is to get rid of it by any means possible. Gaining control over the headache implies gaining relief from pain. But relief may come from alternative sources. Normally, I expect to relieve it myself using simple remedies. However, should these fail, I expect to gain medical help to relieve it. I have mapped these two options on to the axes of a contingency space given in Figure 8.1.

A contingency space in this context is based on axes that represent the perceived probability of achieving a successful outcome, given two different behavioural options. In the case of headache, the axes represent beliefs about personal and external sources of control over outcomes. This implies two orthogonal dimensions of locus of control: internal and external (powerful other).

An alternative language may be used to represent the phenomenon described above. Faced with a simple acute condition, such as a headache, people commonly engage in self-care or seek medical help. Essentially the two axes of the contingency space illustrated in Figure 8.1 represent the perceived probability of gaining a satisfactory outcome through 'personal control' and/or 'social support'. Social support in this context is in the form of informational and instrumental support provided by the doctor.

To the extent that perceived personal control is outcome oriented, it is analogous to internal locus of control. Equally, to the extent that social support promotes relief of the headache, social support in this context is analogous to external (powerful other) locus of control. I deal with other levels of complexity below.

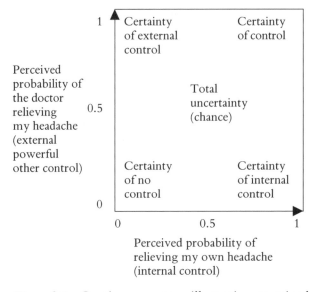

Figure 8.1 Contingency space illustrating perceived control over a headache

Figure 8.1 identifies areas of certainty and uncertainty associated with perceived control over outcomes.

Control, anxiety, fear and depression

Having established that a two-dimensional contingency space represents the perceived available control options in a relatively simple situation, the next step was to map on to it the emotions likely to be experienced at any particular point. For this purpose, it is assumed that the onset of a headache represents a potential threat that evokes stress and coping responses. Figure 8.2 illustrates the likely occurrence of the stress-related emotional responses of anxiety, fear and depression, together with emotions associated with positive outcomes. Faced with a headache, a high perceived probability of pain relief from any source is likely to be associated with feelings of optimism and confidence, whether self-confidence or confidence in the doctor. Uncertainty in either own ability or that of the doctor to relieve the headache is likely to be associated with feelings of anxiety. Lack of any prospect of getting rid of the headache is likely to be associated with mounting fear, sense of hopelessness and eventual depression.

Time is an important factor in the development of stress-related emotions. Initial confidence gives way to anxiety at the point when it becomes apparent that the headache is not responding to treatment. Over time, anxiety and

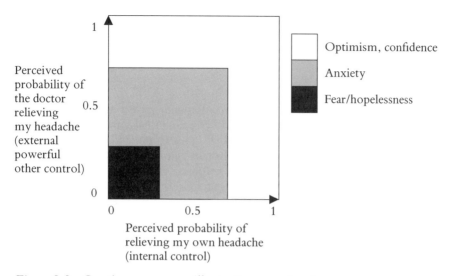

Figure 8.2 Contingency space illustrating emotional responses to perceived control

mounting fear about the possible reason for the headache may give way to hopelessness when no relief is to be found or a sinister diagnosis is suspected. The extent and duration of depression are likely to depend on previous history of dealing with stress, other current demands, extent and duration of mismatch between control demands and reality, and the coping strategies employed to deal with these and with the persistent pain and its underlying cause. Locus of causality is important insofar as it is a good predictor of the likely outcome and of ways of dealing with it. In most Western cultures, lack of knowledge about the cause of an illness generates uncertainty and anxiety. Another important factor is the globality and stability of positive or negative beliefs about outcomes. While it is possible that optimism and pessimism may be heritable personality traits, there is plenty of evidence to indicate that childhood experiences influence future expectations of both probability and source of control. Therefore, someone with a life history of uncertainty and lack of control, combined with poor life skills and lack of social support, is likely to be at high risk of anxiety disorders and/or depressive illness.

The analysis presented in Figure 8.2 distinguishes between anxiety and fear. Anxiety is associated with uncertainty about the likely outcome. Fear is associated with the prediction of a negative outcome. Faced with a situation where the outcome is unknown, it is likely that people faced with a threat may oscillate between optimism and anxiety, anxiety and fear. The area of the contingency space that represents a low probability of a positive outcome from any source represents both fear and hopelessness. One difference is that fear is usually regarded as a specific and relatively unstable emotion, whereas hopelessness attributions are likely to be global and more stable.

Defining control

I have indicated that a theory of control demands a clear and unambiguous definition of what is meant by 'control'. Here, control is defined in terms of the attainment of desired outcomes, analogous to Hyland's system goal or 'reference criterion' (Hyland 1987). Human beings live in a social world in which they depend on both their own resources and those of others for personal survival. If I do nothing for myself and others do nothing to help me meet my basic needs (food, water, warmth etc.), I will certainly die. Some needs arise from basic instincts directed at ecological rather than personal survival. For example, sexual instincts serve to promote the survival of the species. There are also higher order needs, some of which are culturally determined or learned and subject to individual or group differences. I have included the meeting of all of these needs under the general heading of 'desired outcomes'. I have also defined control in terms of both process and outcome:

Control (verb) refers to actions taken by self and/or others to attain a desired outcome.

Control (noun) refers to the attainment of a desired outcome through actions taken by self and/or others.

It is important to note that these definitions make no distinction between control achieved by self and control achieved by others. The human baby is entirely reliant on others to meet all needs. Thus our first life experiences are of external control. At an early stage, however, babies learn that their actions have certain effects on their own bodies, on their environment and on those caring for them. They quickly learn to use their own actions to master tasks and manipulate others to achieve desired outcomes. At this point, the distinction between personal and external control inevitably becomes somewhat blurred.

During the process of development, individuals learn how to look after themselves (take personal control or engage in self-care) and when and how to obtain help from others (seek social support or achieve 'other' control). During this process, control includes the attainment of outcomes that are socially desirable as well as those that are necessary for personal survival. Predictions or expectations of how to gain and maintain control are built up through life experiences during childhood, and at a general level become relatively stable, as reflected in the concept of locus of control. None the less, new experiences and additions to the repertoire of skills have the potential to change control expectancies, particularly in specific domains. In adult life, expectations of personal or external control over outcomes (locus of control) determine both emotional and motivational states. If individuals believe, in certain situations, that a desired outcome depends on their own actions, they are motivated to take personal action. A successful outcome reinforces perceptions of personal control and cultivates a sense of self-efficacy or personal mastery. This promotes self-confidence in future situations and motivates future independent action.

If, on the other hand, individuals believe that an outcome is dependent on the actions of someone else, whether in the form of advice or deed, they are likely to seek help (social support). A successful outcome may reinforce beliefs in external (other) control and may reduce sense of self-efficacy and lead to dependence. Uncertainty about the outcome, whether from own actions or those of others, will be associated with feelings of anxiety, which increase as the certainty of success decreases. In terms of systems theory, this reflects a system that is unable to function properly in the face of inadequate, discrepant or conflicting perceptual inputs. When the expected outcome is negative, regardless of own actions or those of others, loss of control is certain and may, if total or persistent, lead to hopelessness and depression.

The relationship of uncertainty and unpredictability with control

In earlier chapters, it was evident that some researchers had attempted, somewhat unsuccessfully, to distinguish between unpredictability and uncontrollability. The analysis presented in this chapter has also introduced the issue of uncertainty. In line with the proposition of Miller (1979), it is proposed that uncertainty and unpredictability are both sufficient, though not necessary, causes of uncontrollability. I have defined these concepts in terms of personal experience:

◆ Uncertainty: I don't know what is going on.
◆ Unpredictability: I don't know what is going to happen.
◆ Uncontrollability: There is nothing I/they can do about it.

In conditions of uncertainty and unpredictability, it is not possible to know how to respond in a way that will guarantee a successful outcome. Therefore the individual lacks control. This, of course, highlights the importance of informational support and information-giving in health care. Even so, a successful outcome can be expected to occur some of the time by chance. This may offer another explanation for the illusion of control. Furthermore, most people have developed generalized strategies for dealing with situations and are likely to be reasonably assured of gaining a successful outcome most of the time despite uncertainty.

The fact that I know what is happening or what is going to happen in a given situation is no guarantee that I can achieve a desired outcome. For example, knowing what is wrong with me and what my prognosis is does not mean that I will be able to identify the resources for dealing with a condition, either by myself or with the help of others. This is why in health care, teaching appropriate coping strategies and making available suitable supportive resources are as important as providing information. Teaching self-care skills not only provides a sense of self-efficacy but also assures a successful outcome.

The definitions given above refer to actual uncertainty, unpredictability and control. However, in line with systems theory (Hyland 1987), the main focus of the analysis presented in this chapter is on perceived control.

The relationship between perceived personal control and perceived support

The perceived probabilities of gaining control through own actions or those of others, together with the emotional and motivational consequences, are illustrated in Figure 8.3. The contingency analysis in Figure 8.3 indicates that high levels of perceived personal control and perceived social support are independently associated with feelings of confidence and psychological well-being. Feelings of psychological distress are predicted to increase as perceived control and support both decrease, with maximum distress occurring at the point of minimal perceived control and support.

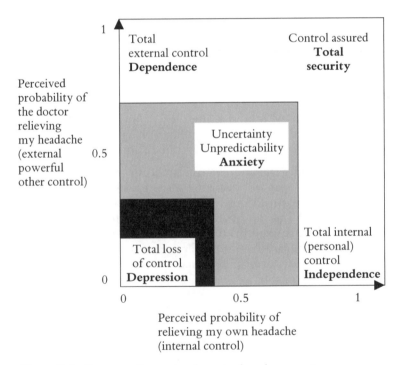

Figure 8.3 Impact of perceived control and support

Figure 8.3 fits exactly with data from the 1985 Illinois Survey of Well-Being (Ross and Mirowsky 1989: 214). This was a large-scale telephone survey in which residents were asked about levels of control and support in their lives and completed the CES-D Scale as a measure of psychological distress. From this, Ross and Mirowsky concluded that control and support substitute for each other as a means of decreasing psychological distress: a low level of one is remedied by a high level of the other. The CES-D Scale was designed as a measure of depression for use with general populations but includes items that reflect general distress as well as positive items (evidence from the previous chapter indicates a high level of common variance between anxiety and depression). The findings would appear, therefore, to lend substantial support to the analysis proposed here.

Figure 8.3 supports the view that depression and anxiety are not independent states, but depend on the extent of perceived control afforded by self and others in a particular context at a particular time. Uncertainty about the level of control likely or possible is associated with anxiety, while perceived loss of control is associated with depression. This analysis supports the observation that individuals frequently oscillate between anxiety and depression.

The advantages of personal control and independence

In Figure 8.3, high expectations of social support accompanied by low expectations of personal control are associated with dependence, while independence is associated with high expectations of personal control. This, together with the findings of Ross and Mirowsky, suggests no advantage of relying on personal control, rather than social support. Yet the literature indicates substantial findings in favour of personal control, self-efficacy, personal mastery, self-care and independence. For example, in the field of chronic pain, active coping strategies have been found to be associated with reports of less pain, less depression, less functional impairment and higher general self-efficacy, compared to the use of passive coping strategies (Brown and Nicassio 1987; Affleck et al. 1992). Why the apparent contradiction?

One answer lies in the inherent lack of reliability of support. In terms of Hyland's motivational control theory (Hyland 1988), there may be a discrepancy between the system reference criterion (goal) and the extent to which this is actually met by others. Reliance on others for instrumental support depends largely on either payment for services rendered or a relationship of trust. Paid carers can rarely be relied upon to provide the level of care that, given the opportunity, individuals would wish for themselves. Paid carers do not work seven days a week; they take annual leave and change their job periodically. Care is likely to be shared among several carers who have different ways of doing things. They may not be committed to the best interests of their patients or clients. Thus dependence on a paid carer is very likely to be associated with a relatively high degree of uncertainty, unpredictability and lack of control. Even when the carer is a committed spouse or trusted friend, illness or death can intervene to remove this main source of social support. In fact, sickness among lay carers is a well recognized phenomenon. In any of these situations, it makes sense to have back-up means of support rather than to be dependent on one individual. Other possibilities relate to the type of support provided, the extent to which it supports the self-efficacy and personal control of the recipient, and the extent to which support may be reciprocated in other ways or at a later date (see Chapter 6, on social support).

Empowerment: the right balance of personal control *and* social support

The proposed model (see Figure 8.3) would appear to indicate that the most adaptive position is one in which individuals maximize personal control and social support. This requires that they do as much for themselves as they can while they can and take action to ensure that they have a supportive network to assist in the event of an inability to achieve a desired outcome. This provides maximum insurance against sudden loss of personal control or social support and is in accordance with Hobfoll's notion of social support as both resource and investment (Hobfoll 1988).

Empowerment, according to this analysis, should involve achieving the right balance of control and support to meet the needs of the individual in the longer term. Where there is a discrepancy between perceived needs of the patient/client and those believed to be needed by professionals or carers, this requires careful negotiation. Where there is a mismatch between the desired or perceived needs of the patient/client and the resources available to meet these (including the health of a carer), this also requires careful negotiation. Empowerment should enable the patient/client to maximize personal control and provide sufficient social support to meet residual needs. If the balance is right, the patient/client will feel confident and satisfied and the carer able to maintain the care required.

Clearly, this is not the first time that control and support have been linked (for example, see Miller 1980). Furthermore, the resulting approaches to intervention are well documented in the health and social care literature. In particular, Orem's self-care model of nursing (Orem 1995) proposed that patients' needs can be met through a combination of self-care and dependent care, the balance influenced by developmental stage. Self-care deficits, using Orem's terminology, are influenced by factors that include lack of education, problems of social adaptation, loss of relative support or occupational security, poor health or disability. Orem's model, like the one proposed in this chapter, illustrates that focusing on only one aspect of control or

Example

Bereavement is an important and common reason for sudden loss of emotional support. The model in Figure 8.3 indicates that it is important in such circumstances to maintain or increase personal control and find alternative sources of social support. The need to replace lost support may help to explain why so many people rush precipitously into a replacement relationship soon after losing a loved one. On the other hand, some people cope by throwing themselves into activities that enhance their sense of control. Bereavement counselling should aim to provide a balance between these two alternatives. It provides an interim source of emotional support, while aiming in the longer term to encourage individuals to regain personal control over their lives and engage in activities that will bring them into contact with alternative sources of support.

support is likely to result in recurrence of the problems and lack or loss of control. The approach required is perhaps well summed up by Ray (1982: 343–4) in relation to patients with chronic pain:

> it is important to adopt a balanced approach in the care and management of the person in pain, helping him to help himself while at the same time providing the sympathy and reassurance to reduce anxiety and prevent despair.

Distinguishing between personal control and social support

In the social world, the distinction between personal control and social support is not clear-cut. People often have to work hard to recruit and retain social support. Indeed, Hobfoll (1988) identified friendship as an insurance against future need. Those who are unable to engage with others to make or sustain social relationships may eventually find themselves socially isolated. This may help to explain why extraverts are less prone to depression and why social skills are so important in preventing depression.

Some individuals are very good at manipulating others to gain desired outcomes. As Langer (1983) observed, control is dependent on the frame of reference. An actor may perceive himself as having a high level of personal control, while observers regard him as engaging in illness behaviour, over-dependent on others. Some years ago, while interviewing someone who had cancer, I listened while she berated the home care organizer for failure to provide continuity of care, then ticked off a young neighbour, who had offered to shop for her, for failing to buy the right brand of coffee. This woman scored high on psychological well-being, reflecting her perception of a high level of personal control and social support, but from the perspectives of others, she exhibited a high level of dependence and deviant ungrateful behaviour. Her level of social support was unlikely to be sustained if she outlived the sympathy of her supporters.

Smith *et al.* (1991) hypothesized that perceived support should bolster perceived competence, thus explaining the influence of social support on adjustment in chronic pain. In testing this hypothesis in a longitudinal study of people with rheumatoid arthritis, they used the CES-D as an outcome measure of psychosocial adjustment. They found that perceived competence exerted a strong effect on adjustment, regardless of pain and functional impairment. Perceived availability of instrumental support was related to future depression. It is unfortunate that perceived emotional support was not measured, since this is the aspect predicted to enhance personal control.

Some people may, wittingly or unwittingly, enhance their own perceptions of personal control by exerting power over another person and forcing on them a state of dependence. This type of 'social support' is probably most damaging, but is likely to be familiar to marriage guidance counsellors and to those caring for vulnerable groups, such as those with chronic illness and mental health problems. It is not unusual for the victim of such circumstances to improve psychologically once the relationship has ended.

Some people with mental health problems engage in socially deviant behaviour that makes it difficult to maintain the social relationships that would provide them with social support. It has been argued that good social skills are an important way of gaining and ensuring good social support. Disordered beliefs and behaviour are capable of depriving people of both personal control and social support, exposing them to increased likelihood of anxiety and depression on top of their other mental health problems. People with mental health problems are among those with the greatest need for social support, yet are likely to be among those least likely to obtain it. It is little wonder that many people with major psychiatric disorders such as schizophrenia, lacking both personal control and social support, also suffer from depression.

Perceived control versus actual control

The reality of the world in which we live is one where miracles rarely occur, where we are expected to take responsibility for taking care of ourselves and others, and where personal and ecological survival depends on personal and collective action. In situations of high certainty and predictability, perceived input will normally reflect reality. However, we live in an uncertain world in which much 'reality' is culturally determined and interpreted. In such a world, we cannot always know the 'truth', if, indeed, there is one. North *et al.* (1996) found that there was poor agreement between self-reported and externally assessed control in the workplace, and their work serves to emphasize that perceived control is not the same as 'objective' control. Measurement of one does not imply measurement of the other.

Assuming that there is an objective reality, some people may be better able than others to draw accurate inferences about it and make accurate predictions about likely outcomes. Some people may have inherited or acquired belief systems that are in some way distorted, making it difficult for them to make accurate predictions about the appropriateness of personal control or social support. Some of these people are likely to be categorized as suffering from major mental illness or personality disorders. Others may be regarded as eccentric. Some people are more likely to see situations in terms of black or white certainty. Some are better able to tolerate uncertainty than others. Some are more accurate in judging the probability of occurrences than others. Some people may have inherited biases towards optimism, pessimism or a tendency to swing between one extreme and the other. Some people have natural skills that enable them to achieve more successful outcomes than others, or recruit more social support. These abilities may all be important in shaping our perceptions of the world and our responses to it.

According to the analysis presented above, what matters in determining our emotional and behavioural responses is our perceptions of the world, rather than the actual nature of the world. Thus if researchers wish to study emotional responses, it is necessary to understand perceptions, rather than actual circumstances. This may help to explain why laboratory experiments can tend to produce conflicting results. While researchers control the actual conditions of the experiment, they cannot control what goes on in people's heads. Similarly, the issue of social response bias makes it difficult to know precisely what people are thinking about at any given time.

Control, support and other emotional states

The axes of a contingency space can be used to examine the relationship of other emotions to control and support. Figure 8.4 maps likely emotional responses under conditions of low personal control and low social support in terms of the match or mismatch between expectations and reality. The greater the mismatch, the more intense the emotional response. These emotions highlight the need to distinguish between perceived and actual control and support. The range of probability within which these emotions occur is, of course, only indicative.

Clearly, the intensity and persistence of the emotions identified in Figure 8.4 depends on the intensity and duration of the discrepancy. These contingency spaces are presented to illustrate their potential for understanding

(a) Emotional response to social support, given low perceived personal control

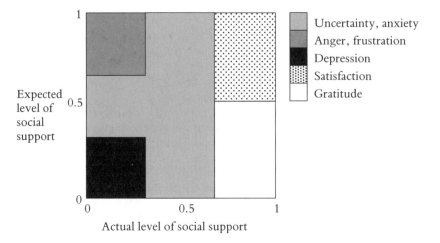

(b) Emotional response to personal control, given low perceived social support

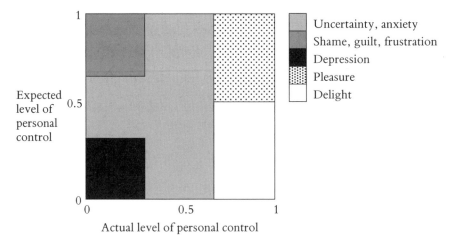

Figure 8.4 Emotional responses under different conditions of control and support

different emotions and the circumstances likely to give rise to them. There are clearly far more permutations than presented here. For example, emotions such as anger are not restricted to the circumstances illustrated in Figure 8.4a, and the reader is encouraged to apply this type of analysis to aid understanding of emotional responses in different types of situation.

Chance locus of control and the third dimension of control

Locus of control is usually described in terms of three dimensions: internal, external (powerful others) and chance. The contingency space used in Figure 8.3 is two-dimensional and does not contain an axis that represents external (chance) locus of control. Chance attributions are associated with beliefs in luck, fate or chance, which appear to divide logically into two quite discrete components. Beliefs in chance or luck reflect uncertainty about the outcome and are therefore represented by the central area of the contingency space where the perceived probability of control from both internal and external sources is in the region of 0.5. In contrast, attributions of fate may represent a belief in some external or higher force, such as a guardian angel or God. In such cases they form a third orthogonal dimension. This analysis receives support from studies that indicate a high level of independence between internal and external (powerful other) locus of control, though much shared variance between these and chance locus of control.

Beliefs in an external force, such as God, in situations that are uncertain or difficult to control provide spiritual support and are likely to be beneficial in protecting emotional integrity. Figure 8.5 indicates that depression

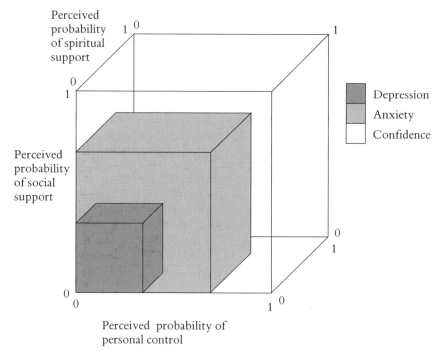

Figure 8.5 Three-dimensional contingency space including spiritual dimension

is less likely to occur among those who are able to maintain a belief in a super-human external source of support (spiritual belief), regardless of its nature. This may in part explain why religious or spiritual beliefs are a source of comfort to those in distress. However, when confronted by the reality of negative events, such beliefs may be associated with higher levels of uncertainty and anxiety when personal control and social support are sacrificed to the power of prayer. Wishing, hoping and praying in the absence of other coping strategies are likely to achieve a desired outcome only by chance. Based on the analyses presented above, and recognizing the reciprocal nature of social support, the saying 'God helps those who help themselves' should perhaps be rephrased 'God help those who help themselves and others'. In reality, faith that occurs within the context of organized religion is usually accompanied by a high level of instrumental and emotional social support, thus adding to the protective nature of religious experience (Walker 1989).

Sudden loss of control

It is generally recognized that post-traumatic stress is associated with anxiety and depression. A single incident of loss of control (or isolated control mismatch) is unlikely to lead to depression in someone who is otherwise in control of his or her life and has good social support. Nevertheless, it is theoretically possible that one incident of complete and sudden loss of control, if viewed as catastrophic, is sufficient to precipitate the cognitive, behavioural and motivational deficits typical of helplessness depression. Those involved in accidents, assaults and natural disasters have their most basic assumptions of safety and routine shattered in one swift blow. In such instances, it may be very difficult to re-establish confidence in one's environment or certain aspects of it. This clearly links with a lack of what Antonovsky termed 'sense of coherence'. If post-traumatic stress is redefined in these terms, it is possible to include a much wider range of events into this category. For example, someone once described experiencing a very sudden and extremely violent bout of diarrhoea and vomiting from which she could easily have died had someone not promptly found her. The losses she experienced included complete loss of bodily control, loss of consciousness, loss of familiar surroundings and time (waking up in hospital a day later) and loss of dignity, which health care staff did little to redeem. This total loss of 'system control' in someone who had previously had complete control over her life had a dramatic effect. She experienced a severe bout of depression accompanied by loss of self-confidence and fear of being left alone that lasted for many months.

Post-traumatic stress presents an interesting distinction between helplessness depression and hopelessness depression. Sudden loss of control leads to strong feelings of helplessness, but may or may not include hopelessness.

Helplessness is likely to occur when all basic routine assumptions about the world are suddenly violated, leading to total loss of control. This is typical of the helplessness anxiety identified by Mandler (1972), and contrasts with hopelessness depression, which is associated with prolonged inability to attain desired outcomes through either personal control or social support. Overall, analyses of depression that distinguish between sudden loss of control and chronic lack of personal control or support may be helpful in developing our understanding of different types of anxiety and depression.

When considering the distinctions between helplessness and hopelessness, it is helpful to revisit Seligman's model of learned helplessness and explain how and why it might have failed to fulfil its early promise.

Critique of learned helplessness

The model of control proposed in this chapter appears to bear considerable resemblance to the original and the reformulated theories of learned helplessness, but it contains some important differences. First compare the proposed model of control with the original model of learned helplessness proposed by Seligman (1975).

Seligman based his model on observations in the animal laboratory. The outcome used was the termination of an aversive stimulus (similar to the example of headache used earlier in this chapter). Seligman's axes represented 'outcome given a response' or 'outcome given no response'. This does not reflect what happens in the real world where all positive and negative outcomes, other than those under the control of an external force, are dependent on making a response. Seligman's original formulation of learned helplessness/uncontrollability fails to take account of the actual external force responsible for starting and ending the shock. The shock administered to the yoked dog in Seligman and Maier's experiment was programmed by the experimenter to be turned off by the response of the other dog. We cannot possibly know what the beliefs of the yoked dogs were. However, given that they were harnessed in an unnatural situation by human experimenters, it is extremely unlikely that they would have attributed (if dogs do make attributions) the commencement or the termination of uncontrollable shock to their own action and certainly not to their inaction. It is much more likely that their 'beliefs' would have reflected the probability that responsibility lay with the humans who had placed them in that situation. Certainly any attempt to translate this experimental situation into a human context would have to take account of such attributions.

If the second dimension of Seligman's contingency space is relabelled to reflect the role of an external 'powerful other', it starts to look very different and much more like the reformulated version of learned helplessness (Abramson *et al.* 1980: 10). Figure 8.6 compares the model of control proposed in this chapter (8.6a) with three versions of Seligman's learned

(a) Proposed model of control

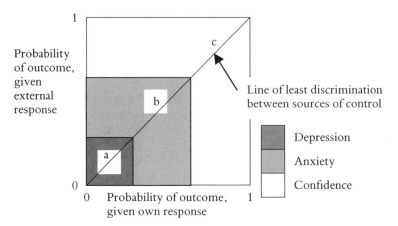

(b) Seligman's original model of learned helplessness

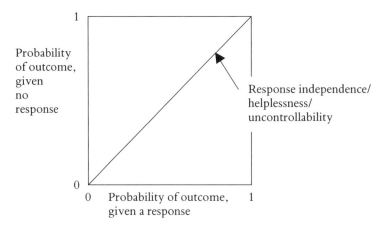

Figure 8.6 Comparison of different models of control and learned helplessness

helplessness: Seligman's original formulation, 8.6b (Seligman 1975), the reformulated model of learned helplessness, 8.6c (Abramson *et al.* 1978) and the analysis presented by Garber *et al.* (1980: 148), 8.6d.

In Seligman's original formulation, helplessness or uncontrollability occurs along the diagonal line that represents the same probability of outcome whether or not the animal makes a response. In the proposed new model, the diagonal line represents the equal probability of obtaining the same outcome whether the dog or the experimenter (or the other dog as proxy)

Figure 8.6 cont'd

(c) Personal and universal helplessness (Abramson *et al*. 1978)

Person expects	Outcome contingent on own response	Outcome contingent **not** contingent on own response
Outcome contingent on response of other	Not relevant	Personal helplessness (internal attribution)
Outcome not contingent on response of other	Not relevant (internal attribution)	Universal helplessness (external attribution)

(d) Beliefs about control (Garber *et al*. 1980: 148)

1	Controllable Certain	Controllable Uncertain	Uncontrollable Certain Hopeless
Probability of *bad* outcome given no response	Controllable Uncertain	Uncontrollable Uncertain Helpless	Controllable Uncertain
0	Uncontrollable Certain Helpless	Controllable Uncertain	Controllable Certain
	0 Probability of *bad* outcome given a response 1		

terminates the shock. Along this line, blocking or overshadowing (Mackintosh 1971) may occur, but it does not represent helplessness or uncontrollability along its entire length. Nevertheless, there are some interesting phenomena associated with the diagonal line.

At point 'a' in Figure 8.6a, the organism is likely to experience the emotional, cognitive and motivational deficits, described by Seligman, typical of depression. It will feel hopeless or helpless, believe it has no control and is unable to gain control by any means. At point 'b', the organism is likely to experience an emotional deficit, anxiety, caused by uncertainty, and cognitive deficit associated with confusion or inability to make a decision or choice. At this point, the organism is likely to search for all possible means of dealing with the situation and is likely to experience heightened motivation, rather than motivational deficit, at least in the short term. In the longer term, some kind of neurosis or chronic anxiety disorder would be expected. At point 'c', there is no emotional deficit, but there may be cognitive and motivational deficits if beliefs in personal control are blocked or overshadowed by beliefs in external control. This could result in the longer term in reduced sense of self-efficacy and unnecessary dependence, but does not reflect uncontrollability, since the outcome is assured.

The attribution reformulation, Figure 8.6c (Abramson *et al.* 1978), distinguished between the actions of self and others, and between personal and universal helpless. But it failed to identify that the person who is able to rely on someone else to achieve a desired outcome is not in any true sense of the word 'helpless'. It is hardly surprising, therefore, that this model failed to gain experimental support. The analysis offered by Garber *et al.* (1980), Figure 8.6d, relied on the axes derived from the original formulation, resulting in the same or worse confusions. In their model, a low probability of achieving a bad outcome from either action or inaction is associated with uncontrollability and hence helplessness. This makes little sense, particularly if it is assumed that lack of a bad outcome implies a satisfactory outcome.

The analysis offered in this chapter offers new opportunities for research in the field of learned helplessness. It retains the intuitive appeal of the original concept of learned helplessness, while resolving many of the outstanding anomalies of the original and reformulated versions. It integrates the concepts reviewed in this book, each of which has made an important contribution to our understanding of control with particular reference to health care. This has been achieved by a relatively small shift in perspective that need not detract from the importance of Seligman's theory.

Control and mood: affect or effect?

The assumption throughout this chapter has been that attributions of control cause mood states, rather than the other way round. This is in contrast to the theoretical stance adopted by some other researchers that mood has an effect on attributions (e.g. Forgas *et al.* 1990). There are a number of good reasons why it may be difficult to distinguish between mood state as an independent and dependent variable in relation to perceived control including:

◆ Changes in mood and cognitive states occur (to all intents and purposes) concurrently.
◆ It is difficult to manipulate mood in isolation from cognitive state. Even if beliefs relative to the task in question are not targeted, feedback from a happy or sad physiological state is likely to influence cognitive set because of the covariation normally experienced between mood and cognition.
◆ Some measures of emotional state include aspects of cognitive set that are identical to, or covary directly with, control beliefs. Measures of mood state such as the POMS (see Table 7.1) avoid this.

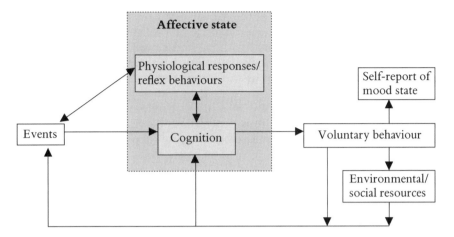

Figure 8.7   Hypothetical relationship between cognition, affect, mood and behaviour

Although mood manipulation may influence control beliefs in the short term, feedback from the external and internal environment is necessary to sustain these beliefs in the longer term. In terms of systems theory, emotions reflect the state of the system at any particular point in time. Thus it covaries with physiological, cognitive and activation state at any particular point in time. Figure 8.7 distinguishes between the affective state of the system and self-report of mood state, which is conceptualized as a voluntary act that follows a process of cognitive reflection.

A unifying theory of control

The unifying theory presented in this chapter contains a number of theoretical propositions that are detailed below.

◆ Control reflects the attainment of desired outcomes (the systems reference criteria) in a given situation.
◆ Control may be achieved through the actions of self or others.
◆ Perceived control normally reflects actual control, though illusions of control may occur under normal conditions by chance. It is also influenced by past history of control and lack of control.
◆ External (other) control relates directly to the achievement of desired outcomes through the actions of others and is equivalent to instrumental social support.
◆ Chance locus of control may reflect uncertainty about the availability of internal or external (other) control, or may reflect a third orthogonal (spiritual) dimension.

♦ Perceived uncertainty and perceived unpredictability are sufficient but not necessary conditions for perceived uncontrollability.
♦ Perceived control is associated with confidence and optimism.
♦ Perceived uncertainty and unpredictability are associated with anxiety.
♦ Perceived uncontrollability is associated with fear, anxiety and/or depression.
♦ Sudden total loss of control may result in helplessness anxiety and depression, which is distinct from hopelessness depression.
♦ Perceived personal control and perceived social support should be viewed as complementary variables in relation to control.
♦ Personal control is preferable to social support, since it is more reliable and sustainable.
♦ Emotional and informational support should be interpreted as the types of support that enhance sense of personal control.
♦ Instrumental support is adaptive if it fulfils needs that cannot be met through self-care. It is maladaptive if it usurps personal control and leads to a relationship of dependence.
♦ Sense of control may be bolstered by spiritual beliefs (represented by belief in an external source of support). Whether this is real or illusory is a matter of personal belief.
♦ Perceived control and support are dependent on frame of reference. What observers view as dependence may be perceived by the actor as control.
♦ It is important to ensure that back-up control and support strategies are in place to protect vulnerable individuals against sudden loss of one or the other in the longer term.
♦ Positive and negative emotions associated with confidence, optimism, fear, anxiety and depression reflect the degree of perceived control available from any source (self, others or spiritual) at a particular point in time.

The relationship between concepts associated with control and support reviewed in this book is illustrated in Figure 8.8. Figure 8.8 represents a new unifying theory of control.

Research design issues

Research designs need to be tailored to meet the demands of the situation. Figure 8.9 presents a list of variables likely to be associated with psychological adjustment to situations of threat. Perceptions of control and support are predicted to have a direct effect on mood state, though these are closely related to beliefs and predictions based on past experiences.

Primary prevention may need to be treated quite differently because there is often no perception of immediate threat. In the field of preventive health, perceived behavioural control has been identified as an important variable (Ajzen 1988, 1991). Control measures necessary to reflect perceived control

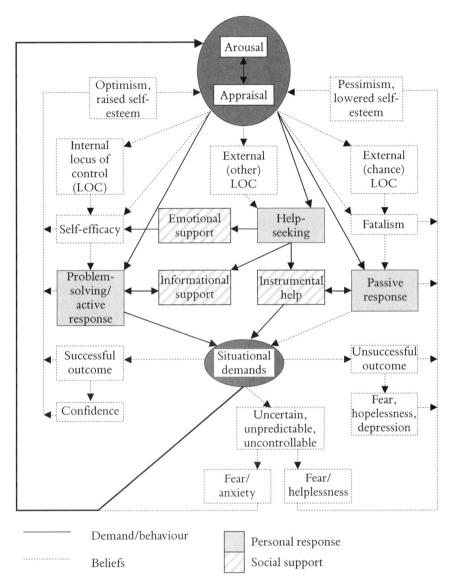

Figure 8.8 Links between control, support, situational demands and outcomes

should include self-efficacy (agency control), locus of control (outcome control), health value (outcome strength), desire for control and perceived support from others for behaviour change. Even so, it has been identified that many health-related behaviours are habits and not normally under

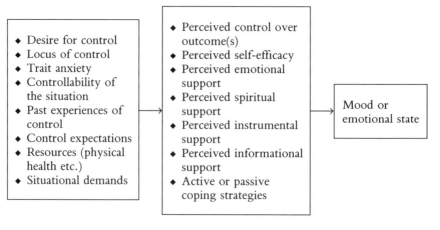

Figure 8.9 Variables associated with psychological adjustments to situations of threat

voluntary control. Models are unlikely to predict behaviour change in the absence of some event or occurrence that brings these behaviours under mindful control (see Hunt and Martin 1988).

Research applications of the unifying control theory

An earlier and less well developed version of the theoretical framework presented above has been used to identify important sources of control and support (or lack of them) in relation to patients with chronic pain (Walker 1989; Walker *et al.* 1990; Walker and Sofaer 1998). A bipolar measure of psychological well-being/distress was developed for use in accordance with the theoretical model (see Walker and Sofaer 1998). In the first study (Walker 1989; Walker *et al.* 1990), 58 per cent of the variance associated with psychological distress, for those in later life with persistent pain, was predicted by a combination of self-reports of:

- Perceived lack of control over pain.
- Feeling inadequately informed about the painful condition.
- Feeling unoccupied (associated with active involvement).
- Personal problems (associated with perceived situational demands).
- Regrets about the past. This variable was identified as important during early interviews and accounted for the largest proportion of the variance.

Each of these variables was measured using a single-item question with a five-point scale of intensity. Perceived control over pain and personal problems represented two of the most important goal deficits in patients' lives.

Lack of adequate information represented an important source of uncertainty and unpredictability. Feeling occupied was shown to reflect active involvement (e.g. cooking, cleaning, hobbies) but not passive pastimes such as watching television. Regrets appeared to focus on salient events associated with loss of control or support in the past (retrospective control: Thompson 1981). This is particularly important in the elderly who, according to Schultz *et al.* (1991), tend increasingly to reflect on past competencies. Clinical practice has confirmed that one or a combination of these variables is usually capable of identifying important causes of psychological distress in older people with pain and is extremely useful in terms of planning therapeutic interventions.

In a second study, which used the same theoretical framework and similar methodology (Walker and Sofaer 1998) but was based on chronic pain patients of all ages, 60 per cent of the variance associated with psychological distress was predicted by a combination of self-reports of:

- Fears about the future. This explained the largest proportion of the variance. Correlations indicated that this variable was associated with financial/health problems and pain intensity (situational demands), perceived control over pain, information about the pain.
- Regrets about the past.
- Age. Older people with chronic pain tended to have better psychological adjustment.
- Feeling unoccupied.
- Practical help (negative relationship). This question related directly to the extent of instrumental help required in everyday life, even when controlling for pain intensity and perceived control over pain.
- Personal relationship problems. This was associated with lack of emotional support and financial problems. Women reported lower levels of emotional support than men.

Clinical applications

The emergent variables from these studies have been incorporated into a questionnaire for my own use in clinical practice to assess patients with chronic pain attending pain clinics. It is used to help to identify key issues that need to be addressed, and inform and prioritize appropriate therapeutic interventions. People who are anxious or depressed normally have good reasons to feel anxious or depressed. These include:

- Their situation is currently beyond their control.
- They lack information that would enable them to gain control.
- They carry negative predictions about present and future control based on early, sustained or catastrophic life experiences.
- They have not learned to cope effectively with the problems they face.

- They have lost the person on whom they previously relied for emotional support.
- Others, either intentionally or unintentionally, have deprived them of their role or sense of purpose.
- They have no spiritual belief to support them in times of difficulty and hardship.
- Their resources are insufficient to meet potentially controllable demands due to physical illness or social exclusion.

Each of these factors can reduce sense of control and needs to be addressed in order to help people to regain control over current and future situations. But in order to address these issues satisfactorily, it is necessary to see them from the patient's point of view and not impose our own frame of reference. The process of negotiation with patients in a clinical situation should therefore include the following:

- What are they able to do for themselves and what more could they do for themselves (promote personal control)? Ideally, carers need to be involved in this discussion to promote independence and avoid unnecessary dependence.
- What do they need to know in order to help themselves (informational support)?
- What skills do they need to acquire or develop in order to help themselves (promote self-efficacy)?
- What type and level of support is available to them as part of their social network (establish available emotional support)?
- What can the health professional do to help them cope in their present situation and with situations likely to occur in the future (provide instrumental, emotional, informational support)?

Concluding comments

This chapter presents a theoretical analysis that is capable of integrating the concepts reviewed in this book. Control is conceptualized as a balance of perceived personal control, perceived social support and perceived spiritual support. Different aspects of control and support interact with each other to promote well-being or cause distress. The emotions of confidence, anxiety and depression are predicted to result from the extent of perceived control (from internal or external sources) at any particular moment in time. Other emotions, including anger, guilt and shame, may also result from an interaction between control and support expected, perceived and received. It is hoped that this theoretical approach will assist researchers in identifying variables likely to predict psychological adjustment, given different types of situational demand.

References

Abbott, M. W. (1984) Locus of control and treatment outcome in alcoholics. *Journal of Studies on Alcohol*, 45(1): 46–52.

Abrahamson, D., Schulderman, S. and Schulderman, E. (1973) Replication of dimensions of locus of control. *Journal of Consulting and Clinical Psychology*, 41: 320.

Abramson, L. Y. and Martin, D. J. (1981) Depression and the causal inference process, in J. H. Harvey, W. J. Ickes and R. F. Kidd (eds) *New Directions in Attribution Research, Volume 3*. Hillsdale, NJ: Lawrence Erlbaum Associates, pp. 117–70.

Abramson, L. Y., Garber, J. and Seligman, M. E. P. (1980) Learned helplessness in humans: an attributional analysis, in J. Garber and M. E. P. Seligman (eds) *Human Helplessness: Theory, and Applications*. London: Harcourt Brace Jovanovich.

Abramson, L. Y., Metalsky, G. I. and Alloy, L. B. (1989) Hopelessness depression: a theory-based subtype of depression. *Psychological Review*, 96(2): 358–72.

Abramson, L. Y., Seligman, M. E. P. and Teasdale, J. D. (1978) Learned helplessness in humans: critique and reformulation. *Journal of Abnormal Psychology*, 87(1): 49–74.

Affleck, G., Tennen, H., Pfeiffer, C. and Fifield, J. (1987) Appraisals of control and predictability in adapting to a chronic disease. *Journal of Personality and Social Psychology*, 53(2): 273–9.

Affleck, G., Urrows, S., Tennen, H. and Higgins, P. (1992) Daily coping with pain from rheumatoid arthritis: patterns and correlates. *Pain*, 51: 221–9.

Ajzen, I. (1988) *Attitudes, Personality and Behaviour*. Milton Keynes: Open University Press.

Ajzen, I. (1991) The theory of planned behaviour. *Organizational Behaviour and Human Decision Processes*, 50: 179–211.

Alden, L. (1987) Attributional responses of anxious individuals to different patterns of social feedback: nothing succeeds like improvement. *Journal of Personality and Social Psychology*, 52(1): 100–6.

Alloy, L. B. and Abramson, L. Y. (1982) Learned helplessness, depression and the illusion of control. *Journal of Personality and Social Psychology*, 42: 1114–26.

Alloy, L. B., Abramson, L. Y., Metalsky, G. I. and Hartlage, S. (1988) The hopelessness theory of depression: attributional aspects. *British Journal of Clinical Psychology*, 27: 5–21.

Alloy, L. B., Abramson, L. Y. and Viscusi, D. (1981) Induced mood and the illusion of control. *Journal of Personality and Social Psychology*, 41(6): 1129–40.

Anderson, C. A., Horowitz, L. M. and French, R. (1983) Attributional style of lonely and depressed people. *Journal of Personality and Social Psychology*, 45: 127–36.

Anderson, C. A. and Jennings, D. L. (1980) When experiences of failure promote expectations of success: the impact of attributing failure to ineffective strategies. *Journal of Personality*, 48(3): 393–407.

Anderson, C. R. (1977) Locus of control, coping behaviours and performance in a stress setting: a longitudinal study. *Journal of Applied Psychology*, 62(4): 446–51.

Anisman, H. and Zacharko, R. M. (1982) Depression: the predisposing influence of stress. *Behavioural and Brain Sciences*, 5: 89–137.

Antonovsky, A. (1979) *Health, Stress, and Coping*. San Francisco: Jossey-Bass.

Antonovsky, A. (1985) *Health, Stress, and Coping*, 2nd edn. San Francisco: Jossey-Bass.

Antonovsky, A. (1993) The structure and properties of the sense of coherence scale. *Social Science and Medicine*, 36: 725–33.

Antonucci, T. C. and Jackson, J. S. (1990) The role of reciprocity in social support, in B. R. Sarason, I. G. Sarason and G. R. Pierce (eds) *Social Support: An Interactional View*. New York: John Wiley, pp. 173–96.

Apter, M. J. (1991) Reversal theory and the structure of emotional experience, in C. D. Spielberger, I. G. Sarason, Z. Kulcsar and G. L. van Heck (eds) *Stress and Emotion, Volume 14*. New York: Hemisphere, pp. 17–30.

Argyle, M. (1992) Benefits produced by supportive social relationships, in H. O. F. Veiel and U. Baumann (eds) *The Meaning and Measurement of Social Support*. New York, Hemisphere, pp. 13–32.

Arnkoff, D. B. and Mahoney, M. J. (1979) The role of perceived control in psychopathology, in L. C. Perlmuter and R. A. Monty (eds) *Choice and Perceived Control*. Hillsdale, NJ: John Wiley, pp. 155–74.

Arntz, A. and Schmidt, A. J. M. (1989) Perceived control and the experience of pain, in A. Steptoe and A. Appels (eds) *Stress, Personal Control and Health*. Chichester: John Wiley, pp. 131–62.

Arsenow, J. R. and Carlson, G. A. (1985) Depression self-rating scale: utility with child psychiatric inpatients. *Journal of Consulting and Clinical Psychology*, 53(3): 491–9.

Averill, J. R. (1973) Personal control over aversive stimuli and its relationship to stress. *Psychological Bulletin*, 80(4): 286–303.

Bachiocco, V., Morselli, A. M., Mastrorilli, M. and Carli, G. (1993) Self-control expectancy and post surgical pain: relationships to previous pain, behaviour in past pain, familial pain tolerance models and personality. *Journal of Pain and Symptom Management*, 8: 205–14.

Baer, J. S., Holt, C. S. and Lichtenstein, E. (1986) Self-efficacy and smoking reexamined: construct validity and clinical utility. *Journal of Consulting and Clinical Psychology*, 34(6): 846–52.

Balcazar, F. E., Seekins, T., Fawcett, S. B. and Hopkins, B. L. (1990) Empowering people with physical disabilities through advocacy skills training. *American Journal of Community Psychology*, 18(2): 281–98.

Balch, P. and Ross, A. W. (1975) Predicting success in weight reduction as a function of locus of control: a unidimensional and multidimensional approach. *Journal of Consulting and Clinical Psychology*, 43: 119.

Baltes, M. M. and Baltes, P. B. (eds) (1986) *The Psychology of Control and Aging*. Hillsdale, NJ: Erlbaum.

Baltes, M. M. and Skinner, E. A. (1983) Cognitive performance deficits and hospitalization: learned helplessness, instrumental passivity or what? *Journal of Personality and Social Psychology*, 45: 1013–16.

Baltes, P. B. (1987) Theoretical propositions of life-span developmental psychology: on the dynamics between growth and decline. *Developmental Psychology*, 23(5): 611–26.

Bandura, A. (1977a) *Social Learning Theory*. Englewood Cliffs, NJ: Prentice Hall.

Bandura, A. (1977b) Self-efficacy: towards a unifying theory of behavioural change. *Psychological Review*, 84(2): 191–215.

Bandura, A. (1978) Reflections on self-efficacy. *Advances in Behaviour Research and Therapy*, 1: 237–69.

Bandura, A. (1982) Self-efficacy mechanism in human agency. *American Psychologist*, 37(2): 122–47.

Bandura, A. (1984) Recycling misconceptions of perceived self-efficacy. *Cognitive Therapy and Research*, 8: 231–55.

Bandura, A. (1988) Organisational applications of social cognitive theory. *Australian Journal of Management*, 13: 275–302.

Bandura, A. (1997a) *Self-efficacy: The Exercise of Control*. New York: W. H. Freeman.

Bandura, A. (1997b) Self-efficacy and health behaviour, in A. Baum, S. Newman, J. Weinman, R. West and C. McManus (eds) *Cambridge Handbook of Psychology, Health and Medicine*. Cambridge: Cambridge University Press, pp. 160–2.

Bandura, A., Adams, N. E. and Beyer, J. (1977) Cognitive processes mediating behavioural change. *Journal of Personality and Social Psychology*, 35: 125–39.

Bandura, A., Adams, N. E., Hardy, A. B. and Howells, G. N. (1980) Tests of the generality of self-efficacy theory. *Cognitive Therapy and Research*, 4: 39–66.

Bandura, A. and Cervone, D. (1983) Self-evaluative and self-efficacy mechanisms governing the motivational effects of goal systems. *Journal of Personality and Social Psychology*, 45: 1017–28.

Bandura, A., O'Leary, A., Taylor, C. B., Gauthier, J. and Gossard, D. (1987) Self-efficacy and pain control: opioid and nonopioid mechanisms. *Journal of Personality and Social Psychology*, 53: 563–71.

Barden, C. J. (1990) A test of the self-help model: learned response to chronic illness experience. *Nursing Research*, 39(1): 42–7.

Bardy, J. V., Porter, R. W., Conrad, D. G. and Mason, J. W. (1958) Avoidance behaviour and the development of gastroduodenal ulcers. *Journal of Experimental Analysis of Behaviour*, 1(1): 69–72.

Barrera, M. (1986) Distinctions between social support concepts, measures, and models. *American Journal of Community Psychology*, 14(4): 413–45.

Barrera, M. and Ainlay, S. L. (1983) The structure of social support: a conceptual and empirical analysis. *Journal of Community Psychology*, 11: 133–43.

Bartholomew, K., Cobb, R. J. and Poole, J. A. (1997) Adult attachment patterns and social support processes, in G. R. Pierce, B. Lakey, I. G. Sarason and B. R. Sarason (eds) *Sourcebook of Social Support and Personality*. New York: Plenum, pp. 359–78.

Batson, C. D. (1975) Attribution as a mediator of bias in helping. *Journal of Personality and Social Psychology*, 32: 455–66.

Batson, C. D. and Marz, B. (1979) Dispositional bias in trained therapists' diagnoses: does it exist? *Journal of Applied Social Psychology*, 9: 479–86.

Battle, E. and Rotter, J. B. (1963) Children's feelings of personal control as related to social class and ethnic groups. *Journal of Personality*, 31: 482–90.

Baum, A., Aiello, J. R. and Calesnick, L. E. (1978) Crowding and personal control: social density and the development of learned helplessness. *Journal of Personality and Social Psychology*, 36(9): 1000–11.

Baum, A. and Gatchel, R. J. (1981) Cognitive determinants of reaction to uncontrollable events: development of reactance and learned helplessness. *Journal of Personality and Social Psychology*, 40(6): 1078–89.

Baum, A., Newman, S., Weinman, J., West, R. and McManus, C. (eds) (1997) *Cambridge Handbook of Psychology, Health and Medicine*. Cambridge: Cambridge University Press.

Bazerman, H. M. (1982) Impact of personal control on performance: is added control always beneficial? *Journal of Applied Psychology*, 67(4): 472–9.

Beck, A. T. (1974) The development of depression: a cognitive model, in R. J. Friedman and M. M. Katz (eds) *The Psychology of Depression: Contemporary Theory and Research*. Washington, DC: V. H. Winston, pp. 3–28.

Beck, A. T. (1976) *Cognitive Therapy and the Emotional Disorders*. London: Penguin.

Beck, A. T., Steer, R. A. and Brown, G. K. (1997) *Beck Depression Inventory – II*. London: Psychological Corporation.

Beck, A. T., Ward, C. H., Mendelson, M., Mock, J. and Erbaugh, J. (1961) An inventory for measuring depression. *Archives of General Psychiatry*, 4: 561–71.

Beck, A. T., Weissman, A., Lester, D. and Trexler, L. (1974) The measurement of pessimism: the hopelessness scale. *Journal of Consulting and Clinical Psychology*, 42: 861–5.

Beck, K. H. (1980) Development and validation of a dental health locus of control scale. *Journal of Preventive Dentistry*, 6: 327–32.

Beresford, P. and Croft, S. (1989) Empowerment: an idea whose time has come? *Social Work Today*, 30(20): 17.

Berkowitz, L. (ed.) (1975) *Advances in Experimental Social Psychology, Volume 21: Social Psychological Studies of the Self*. San Diego: Academic Press.

Berman, R. L. H. and Iris, M. A. (1998) Approaches to self-care in late life. *Qualitative Health Research*, 8(2): 224–36.

Bernstein, J. and Carmel, S. (1987) Trait anxiety and the sense of coherence. *Psychological Reports*, 60: 1000.

Berry, J. M. and West, R. L. (1993) Cognitive self-efficacy in relation to personal mastery and goal setting across the life span. *International Journal of Behavioural Development*, 16(2): 351–79.

Berzins, J. I. and Ross, W. F. (1973) Locus of control among opiate addicts. *Journal of Consulting and Clinical Psychology*, 40: 84–91.

Bialer, I. (1961) The locus of control scale for children. *Journal of Personality*, 29: 303–20.

Bishop, R. and Solomon, E. (1989) Sex differences in career development: locus of control and career commitment effects. *Psychological Reports*, 65: 107–14.

Blackman, S. (1962) Some factors affecting the perception of events as chance determined. *Journal of Psychology*, 54: 197–202.

Blaney, P. H. (1977) Contemporary theories of depression: critique and comparison. *Journal of Abnormal Psychology*, 86: 203–23.

Blaney, P. H. and Ganellen, R. J. (1990) Hardiness and social support, in B. R. Sarason, I. G. Sarason and G. R. Pierce (eds) *Social Support: An Interactional View*. New York: John Wiley, pp. 297–313.

Blankenstein, K. R. (1984) Psychophysiology and perceived locus of control: critical review, theoretical speculation and research directions, in H. M. Lefcourt (ed.) *Research with the Locus of Control Construct, Volume 3: Extensions and Limitations*. New York: Academic Press, pp. 73–208.

Boland, E. A. and Grey, M. (1996) Coping strategies of school-age children with diabetes mellitus. *The Diabetic Educator*, 22(6): 592–7.

Borkovec, T. D. (1978) Self-efficacy: cause of reflection of behavioural change. *Advances in Behaviour Research and Therapy*, 1: 163–70.

Bosma, H., Marmot, M. G., Hemingway, H. *et al.* (1997) Low job control and risk of coronary heart disease in Whitehall II (prospective cohort) study. *British Medical Journal*, 314: 558–65.

Bowers, K. S. (1968) Pain anxiety and perceived control. *Journal of Consulting and Clinical Psychology*, 32(5): 596–602.

Bowling, A. (1991) *Measuring Health: A Review of Quality of Life Measurement*. Buckingham: Open University Press.

Bowling, A. (1995) *Measuring Disease*. Buckingham: Open University Press.

Bradburn, N. M. (1969) *The Structure of Psychological Well-Being*. Chicago: Aldine.

Braden, C. J. (1990) A test of the self-help model: learned response to chronic illness experience. *Nursing Research*, 39(1): 42–7.

Bradley, C., Brewin, C. R., Gamusa, D. X. and Moses, J. L. (1984) Development of scales to measure perceived control of diabetes mellitis and diabetes-related health beliefs. *Diabetic Medicine*, 1: 213–18.

Bradley, C., Lewis, K. S., Jenings, A. M. and Ward, J. D. (1990) Scales to measure perceived control developed specifically for people with tablet-treated diabetes. *Diabetic Medicine*, 7: 685–94.

Brady, J. V., Porter, R. W., Conrad, D. G. and Mason, J. W. (1958) Avoidance behaviour and the development of gastroduodenal ulcers. *Journal of the Experimental Analysis of Behaviour*, 1(1): 69–72.

Brafford, L. J. and Beck, K. H. (1991) Development and validation of a condom self-efficacy scale for college students. *Journal of American College Health*, 39: 219–25.

Brandt, P. A. and Weinert, C. (1981) The PRQ: a social support measure. *Nursing Research*, 30(5): 277–80.

Brecher, M. and Denmark, F. L. (1972) Locus of control: effects of a serendipitous manipulation. *Psychological Reports*, 30: 461–2.

Brewin, C. R. (1985) Depression and causal attributions: what is their relation? *Psychological Bulletin*, 98(2): 297–309.

Brewin, C. R. and Shapiro, D. A. (1984) Beyond locus of control: attribution of responsibility for positive and negative outcomes. *British Journal of Psychology*, 75: 43–9.

Brickman, P. (1978) Is it real? in J. H. Harvey, W. J. Ickes and R. F. Kidd (eds) *New Directions in Attribution Research, Volume 2*. Hillsdale, NJ: Lawrence Erlbaum Associates, pp. 6–35.

Brickman, P., Rabinowitz, V., Karuza, J. *et al.* (1982) Models of helping and coping. *American Psychologist*, 37: 368–84.

Broadhead, W. E., Gehlbach, S. H., de Gruy, F. V. and Kaplan, B. H. (1988) The Duke-UNC Functional Social Support Questionnaire: measurement of social support in family medicine patients. *Medical Care*, 26(7): 709–21.

Brown, G. K. and Nicassio, P. M. (1987) Development of a questionnaire for the assessment of active and passive coping strategies in chronic pain patients. *Pain*, 31: 53–64.

Brown, G. K., Nicassio, P. M. and Wallston, K. A. (1989a) Pain coping strategies and depression in rheumatoid arthritis. *Journal of Consulting and Clinical Psychology*, 57(5): 652–7.

Brown, G. K., Wallston, K. A. and Nicassio, P. M. (1989b) Social support and depression in rheumatoid arthritis: a one year prospective study. *Journal of Applied Social Psychology*, 19: 1164–81.

Brown, G. W. and Harris, T. (1978) *Social Origins of Depression: A Study of Psychiatric Disorder in Women*. New York: Tavistock.

Brown, I. (1979) Learned helplessness through modeling: self-efficacy and social comparison processes, in L. C. Perlmuter and R. A. Monty (eds) *Choice and Perceived Control*. Hillsdale, NJ: John Wiley, pp. 107–20.

Brown, I. and Inouye, D. K. (1978) Learned helplessness through modeling: the role of perceived similarity in competence. *Journal of Personality and Social Psychology*, 36(8): 900–8.

Brown, J. D. and Siegel, J. M. (1988) Attributions for negative life events and depression: the role of perceived control. *Journal of Personality and Social Psychology*, 54(2): 316–22.

Buchwald, A. M., Coyne, J. C. and Cole, C. S. (1978) A critical evaluation of the learned helplessness model of depression. *Journal of Abnormal Psychology*, 87(1): 180–93.

Buckelow, S. P., Shutty, M. S., Hewett, J. *et al.* (1995) Health locus of control, gender differences and adjustment to persistent pain. *Pain*, 42: 287–94.

Bullers, S. (1994) Women's roles and health: the mediating effect of perceived control. *Women and Health*, 22(2): 11–30.

Bulman, R. J. and Wortman, C. B. (1977) Attribution of blame and coping in the real world: severe accident victims react to their lot. *Journal of Personality and Social Psychology*, 35: 351–63.

Bumberry, W., Oliver, J. M. and McClure, J. N. (1978) Validation of the Beck Depression Inventory in a university population using psychiatric estimate as the criterion. *Journal of Consulting and Clinical Psychology*, 40: 150–5.

Bunch, J. M. and Schneider, H. G. (1991) Smoking-specific locus of control. *Psychological Reports*, 69: 1075–81.

Burger, J. M. (1989) Negative reactions to increases in perceived personal control. *Journal of Personality and Social Psychology*, 56: 246–56.

Burger, J. M. and Arkin, R. M. (1980) Prediction, control and learned helplessness. *Journal of Personality and Social Psychology*, 38(3): 482–91.

Burger, J. M. and Cooper, H. M. (1979) The desirability of control. *Motivation and Emotion*, 3: 381–93.

Burish, T. G., Carey, M. P., Wallston, K. A. *et al.* (1984) Health locus of control and chronic disease: an external orientation may be advantageous. *Journal of Social and Clinical Psychology*, 2: 326–32.

Buschmann, M. T. and Hollinger, L. M. (1994) Influence of social support and control on depression in the elderly. *Clinical Gerontologist*, 14(4): 13–28.

Calhoun, L. G., Cheney, T. and Dawes, A. S. (1974) Locus of control, self-reported depression and perceived causes of depression. *Journal of Consulting and Clinical Psychology*, 42: 736.

Callahan, L. F., Brooks, R. H. and Pincus, T. (1988) Further analysis of learned helplessness in rheumatoid arthritis using a 'rheumatoid attitudes index'. *Journal of Rheumatology*, 15(3): 418–25.

Calnan, M. (1989) Control over health and patterns of health-related behaviour. *Social Science and Medicine*, 29(2): 131–6.

Campis, L. K., Lyman, R. D. and Prentice-Dunn, S. (1986) The Parental Locus of Control Scale: development and validation. *Journal of Clinical Child Psychology*, 15: 260–7.

Carlson, J. G. (1982) Some concepts of perceived control and their relationship to bodily self-control. *Biofeedback and Self-Regulation*, 7(3): 341–75.

Carlson, R. and Levy, N. (1968) Brief methods for assessing social-personal orientation. *Psychological Reports*, 23: 911–14.

Chambliss, C. A. and Murray, E. J. (1979) Efficacy attribution, locus of control and weight loss. *Cognitive Therapy and Research*, 3: 349–54.

Champion, R. A. (1950) Studies of experimentally induced disturbance. *Australian Journal of Psychology*, 2: 90–9.

Chapman, M., Skinner, E. A. and Baltes, P. B. (1990) Interpreting correlations between children's perceived control and cognitive performance: control, agency, or means–ends beliefs? *Developmental Psychology*, 26(2): 246–53.

Chewning, B. and Sleath, B. (1996) Medication decision-making and management: a client-centred model. *Social Science and Medicine*, 42(3): 389–98.

Clark, J. V. and Arkowitz, H. (1975) Social anxiety and self-evaluation of interpersonal performance. *Psychological Reports*, 36: 211–21.

Clark, N. M., Evans, D., Zimmerman, B. J., Levison, M. J. and Mellins, R. B. (1994) Patient and family management of asthma: theory-based techniques for the clinician. *Journal of Asthma*, 31(6): 427–35.

Coates, V. E. and Boore, J. R. P. (1996) Knowledge and diabetes self-management. *Patient Education and Counselling*, 29: 99–108.

Cobb, S. (1976) Social support as a moderator of life stress. *Psychosomatic Medicine*, 38(5): 300–14.

Cochran, S. D. and Hammen, C. L. (1985) Perceptions of stressful life events and depression: a test of attributional models. *Journal of Personality and Social Psychology*, 48(6): 1562–71.

Cohen, F. and Hoberman, J. (1983) Positive events and social support as buffers of life change stress. *Journal of Applied Social Psychology*, 13: 99–125.

Cohen, L. H., Hettler, T. R. and Park, C. L. (1997) Social support, personality and life stress adjustment, in G. R. Pierce, B. Lakey, I. G. Sarason and B. R. Sarason (eds) *Sourcebook of Social Support and Personality*. New York: Plenum, pp. 215–28.

Cohen, S. and Wills, T. A. (1985) Stress, social support and the buffering hypothesis. *Psychological Bulletin*, 98(2): 310–57.

Coleman, P. G. (1984) Assessing self esteem and its sources in elderly people. *Ageing and Society*, 4(2): 117–35.

Colletti, G. and Supnick, J. A. (1985) The smoking self-efficacy questionnaire SSEQ: preliminary scale development and validation. *Behavioural Assessment*, 7: 249–60.

Collins, B. E. (1974) Four separate components of the Rotter I–E Scale: belief in a difficult, a just world, a predictable world and a politically responsive world. *Journal of Personality and Social Psychology*, 29: 381–91.

Collins, R. L. and di Paula, A. (1997) Personality and the provision of support: emotions felt and signaled, in G. R. Pierce, B. Lakey, I. G. Sarason and B. R. Sarason (eds) *Sourcebook of Social Support and Personality*. New York: Plenum, pp. 429–44.

Condiotte, M. M. and Lichtenstein, E. (1981) Self-efficacy and relapse in smoking cessation programs. *Journal of Consulting and Clinical Psychology*, 49(5): 648–58.

Connelly, C. E. (1987) Self-care and the chronically ill patient. *Nursing Clinics of North America*, 22(3): 621–9.

Conner, M. and Norman, P. (eds) (1995a) *Predicting Health Behaviour*. Buckingham: Open University Press.

Conner, M. and Norman, P. (1995b) The role of social cognition in health behaviours, in M. Conner and P. Norman (eds) *Predicting Health Behaviour*. Buckingham: Open University Press, pp. 1–22.

Conner, M. and Sparks, P. (1995) The theory of planned behaviour and health behaviours, in M. Conner and P. Norman (eds) *Predicting Health Behaviour*. Buckingham: Open University Press, pp. 121–62.

Conner-Warren, R. L. (1996) Pain intensity and home pain management of children with sickle cell disease. *Issues in Comprehensive Pediatric Nursing*, 19: 183–95.

Connolly, D. S. G. (1980) Changing expectancies – a counselling model based on locus of control. *Personnel and Guidance Journal*, 59: 176–80.

Conrad, K. M., Flay, B. R. and Hill, D. (1992) Why children start smoking cigarettes: predictors of onset. *British Journal of Addiction*, 87: 1711–24.

Coombs, D. W., Roberts, R. W. and Crist, D. A. (1989) Effects of social support on depression following coronary artery bypass graft surgery. *Psychology and Health*, 3: 29–35.

Cooper, C. L. and Payne, R. (eds) (1991) *Personality and Stress: Individual Differences in the Stress Process*. Chichester: John Wiley.

Coopersmith, S. (1967) *The Antecedents of Self-Esteem*. San Francisco: W. H. Freeman.

Corah, N. L. and Boffa, J. (1970) Perceived control, self-observation and response to aversive stimulation. *Journal of Personality and Social Psychology*, 16(1): 1–4.

Cormier-Daigle, M. and Stewart, M. (1997) Support and coping of male hemodialysis-dependent patients. *International Journal of Nursing Studies*, 34(6): 420–30.

Costello, C. G. (1976) *Anxiety and Depression: The Adaptive Emotions*. Montreal: McGill-Queen's University Press.

Costello, C. G. (1978) A critical review of Seligman's laboratory experiments on learned helplessness and depression in humans. *Journal of Abnormal Psychology*, 87(1): 21–31.

Costello, C. G. and Comrey, A. L. (1967) Scales for measuring depression and anxiety. *Journal of Psychology*, 66: 303–13.

Costello, R. M. and Manders, K. R. (1974) Locus of control and alcoholism. *British Journal of Addiction*, 69: 11–17.

Covington, M. V. and Omelich, C. L. (1979) Are causal attributions causal? A path analysis of the cognitive model of achievement motivation. *Journal of Personality and Social Psychology*, 37(9): 1487–504.

Cowen, E. L. (1982) Help is where you find it: four informal helping groups. *American Psychologist*, 37(4): 385–95.

Cowen, E. L., Work, W. C., Hightower, A. D. *et al.* (1991) Toward the development of a measure of perceived self-efficacy in children. *Journal of Clinical Child Psychology*, 20: 169–78.

Cox, J. L., Chapman, G., Murray, D. and Jones, P. (1996) Validation of the Edinburgh Postnatal Depression Scale (EPDS) in non-postnatal women. *Journal of Affective Disorders*, 39(3): 185–9.

Coyne, J. C., Ellard, J. H. and Smith, D. A. (1990) Social support, interdependence and the dilemmas of helping, in B. R. Sarason, I. G. Sarason and G. R. Pierce (eds) *Social Support: An Interactional View*. New York: John Wiley, pp. 129–49.

Coyne, J. C. and Gotlib, I. H. (1983) The role of cognition in depression: a critical appraisal. *Psychological Bulletin*, 94(3): 472–505.

Creer, T. L. (1987) Self-management in the treatment of childhood asthma. *Journal of Allergy and Clinical Immunology*, 80(3): 500–4.

Creer, T. L., Stein, R. E. K., Rappaport, L. and Lewis, C. (1992) Behavioural consequences of illness: childhood asthma as a model. *Pediatrics*, 90(5): 808–15.

Crisson, J. E. and Keefe, F. J. (1988) The relationship of locus of control to pain coping strategies and psychological distress in chronic pain patients. *Pain*, 35: 147–54.

Culbertson, F. M. and Spielberger, C. D. (1996) Relations of anger expression and depression to blood pressure in high school students, in C. D. Spielberger, I. G. Sarason, J. M. T. Brebner *et al.* (eds) *Stress and Emotion: Anxiety, Anger and Curiosity, Volume 16*. Washington, DC: Taylor and Francis, pp. 193–202.

Cummins, R. C. (1988) Perceptions of social support, receipt of supportive behaviours and locus of control as moderators of the effects of chronic stress. *American Journal of Community Psychology*, 16: 685–700.

D'Amato, M. R. and Gumenik, W. E. (1960) Some effects of immediate versus randomly delayed shock on an instrumental response and cognitive processes. *Journal of Abnormal and Social Psychology*, 60(1): 64–7.

Davis, F. W. and Yates, B. T. (1982) Self-efficacy expectancies versus outcome expectancies as determinants of performance deficits and depressive affect. *Cognitive Therapy and Research*, 6(1): 23–35.

Davis, W. L. and Phares, E. J. (1967) Internal–external control as a determinant of information-seeking in a social influence situation. *Journal of Personality*, 35: 547–61.

Dean, D. G. (1961) Alienation: its meaning and measurement. *American Sociological Review*, 26: 753–8.

DeCharms, R. (1968) *Personal Causation: The Internal Affective Determinants of Behaviour*. New York: Academic Press.

DeCharms, R. (1979) Personal causation and perceived control, in L. C. Perlmuter and R. A. Monty (eds) *Choice and Perceived Control*. Hillsdale, NJ: John Wiley, pp. 29–40.

DeCharms, R. (1981) Personal causation and locus of control: two different traditions and two uncorrelated measures, in H. M. Lefcourt (ed.) *Research with the Locus of Control Construct. Volume 1, Assessment Methods*. New York: Academic Press, pp. 337–58.

DeGood, D. E. and Kiernan, B. (1996) Perception of fault in patients with chronic pain. *Pain*, 64: 153–9.

de Jong-Gierveld, J. (1989) Personal relationship, social support and loneliness. *Journal of Social and Personal Relationships*, 6(2): 197–221.

Dennis, K. E. (1990) Patients' control and the information imperative: clarification and confirmation. *Nursing Research*, 39(3): 162–6.

Depner, C. E., Withington, E. and Ingersoll-Dayton, B. (1984) Social support: methodological issues in design and measurement. *Journal of Social Issues*, 40(4): 37–54.

Depue, R. A. and Monroe, S. M. (1978) Learned helplessness in the perspective of the depressive disorders: conceptual and definitional issues. *Journal of Abnormal Psychology*, 87(1): 3–20.

DeVellis, R. F. and Callahan, L. F. (1993) A brief measure of helplessness in rheumatoid disease: the helplessness subscale of the rheumatology attitudes index. *Journal of Rheumatology*, 20: 866–9.

DeVellis, R. F., DeVellis, B. M., Blanchard, L. W. *et al.* (1993) Development and validation of the Parent Health Locus of Control (PHLOC) Scales. *Health Education Quarterly*, 20: 211–25.

DeVellis, R. F., DeVellis, B. M., Revicki, D. A. *et al.* (1985) Development and validation of the Child Improvement Locus of Control (CILC) scales. *Journal of Social and Clinical Psychology*, 3: 307–24.

DeVellis, R. F., DeVellis, B. M., Wallston, B. S. and Wallston, K. A. (1980) Epilepsy and learned helplessness. *Basic and Applied Social Psychology*, 1: 241–54.

DiClemente, C. C. (1986) Self-efficacy and the addictive behaviours. *Journal of Social and Clinical Psychology*, 4: 302–15.

DiClemente, C. C., Prochaska, J. O. and Gilbertine, M. (1985) Self-efficacy and the stages of self-change of smoking. *Cognitive Therapy and Research*, 9: 181–200.

Dielman, T. E., Campanelli, P. C., Shope, J. T. and Butchart, A. T. (1987) Susceptibility to peer pressure, self-esteem and health locus of control as correlates of adolescent substance abuse. *Health Education Quarterly*, 14: 207–21.

Diener, C. I. and Dweck, C. S. (1978) An analysis of learned helplessness: continuous changes in performance, strategy and achievement cognitions following failure. *Journal of Personality and Social Psychology*, 36: 451–62.

Diener, E. (1984) Subjective well-being. *Psychological Bulletin*, 95(3): 542–75.

Diener, E. (1994) Subjective well-being. *Psychological Bulletin*, 95: 542–75.

DiLorio, L., Maibach, E., O'Leary, A., Sanderson, C. A. and Celentano, D. (1997) Measurement of condom use self-efficacy and outcome expectancies in a geographically diverse group of STD patients. *AIDS Education and Prevention*, 9(1): 1–13.

Dixon, D. N., McKee, C. S. and McRae, B. C. (1976) Dimensionality of three adult, objective locus of control scales. *Journal of Personality Assessment*, 40: 310–19.

Dobbins, C. and Eaddy, J. (1986) Mood, health behaviours, perceived life control: excellent predictors of metabolic control. *Diabetes* (Supplement 1), 35(21A): 81.

Dohrenwend, B. S., Dohrenwend, B. P., Dodson, M. and Shrout, P. E. (1984) Symptoms, hassles, social supports and life events: problem of confounded measures. *Journal of Abnormal Psychology*, 93(2): 222–30.

Dohrenwend, B. S. and Martin, J. L. (1979) Personal versus situational determination of anticipation and control of the occurrence of stressful life events. *American Journal of Community Psychology*, 7: 453–68.

Dolce, J. J., Doleys, D. M., Raczynski, J. M. *et al.* (1986) The role of self-efficacy expectancies in the prediction of pain tolerance. *Pain*, 27: 261–72.

Donovan, D. M. and O'Leary, M. R. (1978) The drinking-related locus of control scale. *Journal of Studies on Alcohol*, 39: 759–84.

Donovan, D., O'Leary, M. and Walker, B. (1979) Validation of a subjective helplessness measure. *Journal of Personality Assessment*, 43: 461–7.

DSM-IV (1994) *Diagnostic and Statistical Manual of Mental Disorders*, 4th edn. Washington, DC: American Psychological Association.

DuCette, J. and Wolk, S. (1972) Locus of control and extreme behaviour. *Journal of Consulting and Clinical Psychology*, 39: 253–8.

Dunkel-Schetter, C. (1984) Social support and cancer. Findings based on patient interviews and their implications. *Journal of Social Issues*, 40: 77–98.

Dunkel-Schetter, C. and Bennett, T. L. (1990) Differentiating the cognitive and behavioural aspects of social support, in B. R. Sarason, I. G. Sarason and G. R. Pierce (eds) *Social Support: An Interactional View*. New York: John Wiley, pp. 267–96.

Dunkel-Schetter, C., Folkman, S. and Lazarus, R. S. (1987) Correlates of social support receipt. *Journal of Personality and Social Psychology*, 53: 71–80.

Dweck, C. S. (1975) The role of expectations and attributions in the alleviation of learned helplessness. *Journal of Personality and Social Psychology*, 31: 674–85.

Dweck, C. S., Davidson, W., Nelson, S. and Enna, B. (1978) Sex differences in learned helplessness. II, The contingencies of evaluative feedback in the classroom. III, An experimental analysis. *Developmental Psychology*, 14(3): 268–76.

Dweck, C. S. and Goetz, T. E. (1978) Attributions and learned helplessness, in J. H. Harvey, W. J. Ickes and R. F. Kidd (eds) *New Directions in Attribution Research, Volume 2*. Hillsdale, NJ: Lawrence Erlbaum Associates, pp. 158–81.

Dweck, C. S. and Wortman, C. B. (1982) Learned helplessness, anxiety, and achievement motivation: neglected parallels in cognitive, affective and coping responses, in H. W. Krohne and L. Laux (eds) *Achievement, Stress, and Anxiety*. Washington, DC: Hemisphere, pp. 95–125.

Dyal, J. A. (1984) Cross-cultural research with the locus of control construct, in H. M. Lefcourt (ed.) *Research with the Locus of Control Construct. Volume 3, Extensions and Limitations*. New York: Academic Press, pp. 209–306.

Edelstein, J. and Linn, M. W. (1987) Locus of control and the control of diabetes. *Diabetes Educator*, 13: 51–4.

Egan, K. J. and Ready, L. B. (1994) Patient satisfaction with intravenous PCA or epidural morphine. *Canadian Journal of Anaesthetics*, 41(1): 6–11.

Elderen, T. van, Maes, S. and Komproe, I. (1997) The development of an anger expression and control scale. *British Journal of Health Psychology*, 2: 269–81.

Epstein, R. and Komita, S. S. (1971) Self-esteem, success–failure and locus of control in Negro children. *Development Psychology*, 4(1): 2–8.

Evans, R. G. (1981) The relationship of two measures of perceived control to depression. *Journal of Personality Assessment*, 45(1): 66–70.

Eysenck, M. (1991) Trait anxiety and cognition, in C. D., Spielberger, I. G. Sarason, Z. Kulcsar and G. L. van Heck (eds) *Stress and Emotion, Volume 14*. New York: Hemisphere, pp. 77–84.

Fallowfield, L. (1990) *The Quality of Life: The Missing Measurement in Health Care*. London: Souvenir.

Feather, N. T. (1967) Some personality correlates of external control. *Australian Journal of Psychology*, 19(3): 253–60.

Feldman, H. R. (1986) Self-esteem, types of attributional style and sensation and distress pain ratings in males. *Journal of Advanced Nursing*, 11: 75–86.

Felton, B. J. and Revenson, T. A. (1984) Coping with chronic illness: a study of illness controllability and the influence of coping strategies on psychological adjustment. *Journal of Consulting and Clinical Psychology*, 52: 343–53.

Felton, B. J. and Shinn, M. (1992) Social integration and social support: moving 'social support' beyond the individual level. *Journal of Community Psychology*, 20: 103–15.

Feltz, D. L. (1982) Path analysis of the causal elements in Bandura's theory of self-efficacy and an anxiety-based model of avoidance behaviour. *Journal of Personality and Social Psychology*, 42(4): 764–81.

Fernandez, E. and Turk, D. C. (1995) The scope and significance of anger in the experience of chronic pain. *Pain*, 61: 165–75.

Ferraro, L. A., Price, J. H., Desmond, S. M. and Roberts, S. M. (1987) Development of a diabetes locus of control scale. *Psychological Reports*, 61: 763–70.

Ferster, C. B. (1973) A functional analysis of depression. *American Psychologist*, 28(10): 857–70.

Fiedler, K. (1982) Causal schemata: review and criticism of research on a popular construct. *Journal of Personality and Social Psychology*, 42: 1001–13.

Findley, M. J. and Cooper, H. M. (1983) Locus of control and academic achievement: a literature review. *Journal of Personality and Social Psychology*, 44: 419–27.

Fiore, M., Becker, J. and Coppel, D. B. (1983) Social network interactions: a buffer or a stress. *American Journal of Community Psychology*, 11: 423–39.

Fisher, K. and Johnston, M. (1998) Emotional distress and control cognitions as mediators of the impact of chronic pain on disability. *British Journal of Health Psychology*, 3: 225–36.

Fitch, G. (1970) Effects of self-esteem, perceived performance and choice on causal attributions. *Journal of Personality and Social Psychology*, 16: 311–15.

Flor, H., Kerns, R. D. and Turk, D. C. (1987) The role of spouse reinforcement, perceived pain and activity levels of chronic pain patients. *Journal of Psychosomatic Research*, 31: 251–9.

Folkman, S. (1984) Personal control and stress and coping processes: a theoretical analysis. *Journal of Personality and Social Psychology*, 46(4): 839–52.

Folkman, S. and Lazarus, R. S. (1980) An analysis of coping in a middle-age community sample. *Journal of Health and Social Behaviour*, 21: 219–39.

Folkman, S. and Lazarus, R. S. (1988) The relationship between coping and emotion: implications for theory and research. *Social Science and Medicine*, 26(3): 309–17.

Folkman, S. and Lazarus, R. S. (1991) The concept of coping, in A. Monat and R. S. Lazarus (eds) *Stress and Coping: An Anthology*, 3rd edn. New York: Columbia University Press, pp. 207–27.

Follette, V. and Jacobson, N. (1987) Importance of attributions as a predictor of how people cope with failure. *Journal of Personality and Social Psychology*, 52: 1205–11.

Fonagy, P. and Higgitt, A. (1984) *Personality Theory and Clinical Practice*. London: Methuen.

Fordyce, W. E. (ed.) (1996) *Back Pain in the Workplace*. Seattle: IASP Press.

Forgas, J. P., Bower, G. H. and Moylan, S. J. (1990) Praise or blame? Affective influences on attributions for achievement. *Journal of Personality and Social Psychology*, 39(4): 809–19.

Forgays, D. G., Sosnowski, T. and Wrzesniewski, K. (eds) (1992) *Anxiety: Recent Developments in Cognitive, Psychophysiological and Health Research*. Washington, DC: Hemisphere.

Fowles, D. C. (1992) Motivational approach to anxiety disorders, in D. G. Forgays, T. Sosnowski and K. Wrzesniewski (eds) *Anxiety: Recent Developments in Cognitive, Psychophysiological and Health Research*. Washington, DC: Hemisphere, pp. 181–92.

Freud, S. (1936) *The Problem of Anxiety, 1926*. New York: Norton.

Friedman, R. J. and Katz, M. M. (eds) (1974) *The Psychology of Depression: Contemporary Theory and Research*. Washington, DC: V. H. Winston.

Froman, R. D. (1997) Response to 'Bandura's theory of self-efficacy: applications to oncology'. *Scholarly Inquiry for Nursing Practice*, 11(1): 39–43.

Frost, T. F. and Clayson, D. E. (1991) The measurement of self-esteem, stress-related events and locus of control among unemployed and employed blue-collar workers. *Journal of Applied Social Psychology*, 21(17): 1402–17.

Fry, P. S. (ed.) (1989) *Psychological Perspectives of Helplessness and Control in the Elderly*. Amsterdam: North-Holland.

Ganster, D. C. and Victor, B. (1988) The impact of social support on mental and physical health. *Journal of Medical Psychology*, 61: 17–36.

Garber, J. and Hollon, S. D. (1980) Universal versus personal helplessness in depression: belief in uncontrollability or incompetence? *Journal of Abnormal Psychology*, 89(1): 56–66.

Garber, J., Miller, S. M. and Abramson, L. Y. (1980) On the distinction between anxiety and depression: perceived control, certainty and probability of goal attainment, in J. Garber and M. E. P. Seligman (eds) *Human Helplessness: Theory and Applications*. Orlando, FL: Academic Press, pp. 131–69.

Garber, J. and Seligman, M. E. P. (eds) (1980) *Human Helplessness: Theory and Applications*. Orlando, FL: Academic Press.

Gatchel, R. J. and Proctor, J. D. (1976) Physiological correlates of learned helplessness in man. *Journal of Abnormal Psychology*, 85(1): 27–34.

Gecas, V. (1989) The social psychology of self-efficacy. *Annual Review of Sociology*, 15: 291–316.

Geer, J., Davison, G. C. and Gatchel, R. J. (1970) Reduction of stress in humans through nonveridical perceived control of aversive stimulation. *Journal of Personality and Social Psychology*, 16: 731–8.

Geer, J. H. and Maisl, E. (1972) Evaluating the effects of the prediction control confound. *Journal of Personality and Social Psychology*, 23: 314–19.

Geisser, M. E., Robinson, M. E., Keefe, F. J. and Weiner, M. L. (1994) Catastrophizing, depression and the sensory, affective and evaluative aspects of chronic pain. *Pain*, 59: 79–83.

Georgiou, A. and Bradley, C. (1992) The development of a smoking-specific locus of control scale. *Psychology and Health*, 6: 227–46.

Gerin, W., Litt, M. D., Deigh, J. and Pickering, T. G. (1995) Self-efficacy as a moderator of perceived control effects on cardiovascular reactivity: is enhanced control always beneficial? *Psychosomatic Medicine*, 57: 390–7.

Gilbert, P. (1992) *Depression: The Evolution of Powerlessness*. Hove: Lawrence Erlbaum Associates.

Gilmor, T. M. and Minton, L. H. (1974) Internal versus external attribution of task performance as a function of locus of control, initial confidence and success–failure outcome. *Journal of Personality*, 42: 159–74.

Girodo, M. and Wood, D. (1979) Talking yourself out of pain: the importance of believing that you can. *Cognitive Therapy and Research*, 3: 23–33.

Glass, D. C., McKnight, J. D. and Valdimarsdottir, H. (1993) Depression, burnout and perceptions of control in hospital nurses. *Journal of Consulting and Clinical Psychology*, 61(1): 147–55.

Glass, D. C., Reim, B. and Singer, J. E. (1971) Behavioural consequences of adaptation to controllable and uncontrollable noise. *Journal of Experimental Social Psychology*, 7: 244–57.

Glass, D. C., Singer, J. E. and Freidman, L. N. (1969) Psychic cost of adaptation to an environmental stressor. *Journal of Personality and Social Psychology*, 12(3): 200–10.

Glynn, L. M., Christenfeld, N. and Gerin, W. (1999) Gender, social support and cardiovascular responses to stress. *Psychosomatic Medicine*, 61: 234–42.

Goffman, E. (1961) *Asylums: Essays on the Social Situation of Mental Patients and Other Inmates*. London: Penguin.

Goldberg, D. P. and Hillier, V. F. (1979) A scaled version of the General Health Questionnaire. *Psychological Medicine*, 9: 139–45.

Gonzalez, V. M., Geoppinger, J. and Lorig, K. (1990) Four psychosocial theories and their application to patient education and clinical practice. *Arthritis Care and Research*, 3(3): 132–43.

Goodstadt, B. E. and Hjelle, L. A. (1973) Power to the powerless: locus of control and the use of power. *Journal of Personality and Social Psychology*, 27: 190–6.

Gorin, A., Weisberg, J. N., Drozd, M. A. and Gallagher, R. M. (1996) The relationship between pain severity and locus of control in chronic pain patients, the mediating effect of depression. Paper presented at 8th World Congress on Pain, Vancouver, August.

Gorman, P., Jones, L. and Holman, I. (1980) Generalizing American locus of control norms to Australian populations: a warning. *Australian Psychologist*, 15: 125–7.

Gottesfield, J. and Dozier, G. (1966) Changes in feelings of powerlessness in a community action program. *Psychological Reports*, 19: 978.

Gottlieb, B. H. (1978) The development and application of a classification scheme of informal helping behaviours. *Canadian Journal of Behavioural Science*, 10: 105–15.

Gottlieb, B. H. (1983) Social support as a focus for integrative research in psychology. *American Psychologist*, 38: 278–87.

Gottlieb, B. H. (1985) Social support and the study of personal relationships. *Journal of Social and Personal Relationships*, 2: 351–75.

Gozali, J. and Bialer, I. (1968) Children's locus of control scale: independence from response set bias among retardates. *American Journal of Mental Deficiency*, 72: 622–5.

Graham, S. and Weiner, B. (1986) From an attributional theory of emotion to development psychology: a round-trip ticket? *Social Cognition*, 4(2): 152–79.

Gray, J. A. (1987) *The Psychology of Fear and Stress*, 2nd edn. Cambridge: Cambridge University Press.

Gray, R. E., Doan, B. D. and Church, K. (1990) Empowerment and persons with cancer: politics in cancer medicine. *Journal of Palliative Care*, 6(2): 33–45.

Greenglass, E. R. (1996) Anger suppression, cynical distrust and hostility: implications for coronary heart disease, in C. D. Spielberger, I. G. Sarason, J. M. T.

Brebner, *et al.* (eds) *Stress and Emotion: Anxiety, Anger and Curiosity, Volume 16.* Washington, DC: Taylor & Francis, pp. 205–26.

Gregory, W. L. (1978) Locus of control for positive and negative outcomes. *Journal of Personality and Social Psychology*, 36: 840–9.

Gregory, W. L. (1981) Expectancies for controllability, performance attributions and behavior, in H. M. Lefcourt (ed.) *Research with the Locus of Control Construct. Volume 1, Assessment Methods.* New York: Academic Press, pp. 67–124.

Grob, A., Little, T. D., Wanner, B. and Wearing, A. J. (1996) Adolescents' well-being and perceived control across 14 sociocultural contexts. *Journal of Personality and Social Psychology*, 71(4): 785–95.

Gunnar-Vongnechten, M. R. (1978) Changing a frightening toy into a pleasant toy by allowing the infant to control its actions. *Development Psychology*, 14(2): 157–62.

Gurin, P., Gurin, G., Lao, R. and Beattie, M. (1969) Internal–external control in the motivational dynamics of Negro youth. *Journal of Social Issues*, 25: 29–53.

Hage, J. N., Halfern, P. L. and Moore, B. S. (1977) Effects of personal causation and perceived control on response to an aversive environment: the more control, the better. *Journal of Experimental Social Psychology*, 13: 14–27.

Haggard, E. A. (1943) Experimental studies in affective processes: 1. Some effects of cognitive structure and active participation on certain autonomic reactions during and following experimentally induced stress. *Journal of Experimental Psychology*, 33(4): 257–84.

Hammer, M. (1981) Social supports, social networks and schizophrenia. *Schizophrenia Bulletin*, 7(1): 45–56.

Hanusa, B. A. and Schultz, R. (1977) Attributional mediation of learned helplessness. *Journal of Personality and Social Psychology*, 35: 602–11.

Härkäpää, K., Järvikoski, A., Mellin, G., Hurri, H. and Luoma, J. (1991) Health locus of control beliefs and psychological distress as predictors for treatment outcomes in low-back pain patients: results of a 3-month follow-up of a controlled intervention study. *Pain*, 46: 35–41.

Härkäpää, K., Järvikoski, A. and Estlander, A.-M. (1996) Health optimism and control beliefs as predictors for treatment outcome of a multimodal back treatment program. *Psychology and Health*, 12: 123–34.

Harvey, D. M. (1981) Depression and attributional style: interpretations of important personal events. *Journal of Abnormal Psychology*, 90(2): 134–42.

Harvey, J. H. and Harris, B. (1975) Determinants of perceived choice and the relationship between perceived choice and expectancy about feelings of internal control. *Journal of Personality and Social Psychology*, 31: 101–6.

Harvey, J. H., Ickes, W. J. and Kidd, R. F. (eds) (1976) *New Directions in Attribution Research, Volume 1.* Hillsdale, NJ: Lawrence Erlbaum Associates.

Harvey, J. H., Ickes, W. J. and Kidd, R. F. (eds) (1978) *New Directions in Attribution Research, Volume 2.* Hillsdale, NJ: Lawrence Erlbaum Associates.

Harvey, J. H., Ickes, W. J. and Kidd, R. F. (eds) (1981) *New Directions in Attribution Research, Volume 3.* Hillsdale, NJ: Lawrence Erlbaum Associates.

Harvey, J. H. and Weary, G. (1984) Current issues in attribution theory and research. *Annual Review of Psychology*, 35: 427–59.

Haseth, K. J. (1996) The Norwegian adaptation of the State-trait Anger Expression Inventory, in C. D. Spielberger, I. G. Sarason, J. M. T. Brebner *et al.* (eds) *Stress and Emotion: Anxiety, Anger and Curiosity, Volume 16.* Washington, DC: Taylor and Francis, pp. 83–106.

Hawley, D. J., Wolfe, F. and Cathey, M. A. (1992) The sense of coherence question-naire in patients with rheumatic disorders. *Journal of Rheumatology*, 19: 1912–18.

Heckhausen, H. and Weiner, B. (1974) The emergence of a cognitive psychology of motivation, in B. Weiner (ed.) *Achievement Motivation and Attribution Theory*. Morriston, NJ: General Learning Press, pp. 49–67.

Heider, F. (1944) Social perception and phenomenal causality. *Psychological Review*, 51: 358–74.

Heider, F. (1958) *The Psychology of Interpersonal Relations*. New York: John Wiley.

Hemingway, H., Shipley, M. J., Stansfield, S. and Marmot, M. (1997) Sickness absence from back pain, psychosocial work characteristics and employment grade among office workers. *Scandinavian Journal of Work Environment and Health*, 23: 121–9.

Hewstone, M. (1989) *Causal Attribution: From Cognitive Processes to Collective Beliefs*. Oxford: Blackwell.

Hickey, T. (1988) Self-care behaviour of older adults. *Family and Community Health*, 11(3): 23–32.

Hill, D. J. and Bale, R. M. (1981) Measuring beliefs about where psychological pain originates and who is responsible for its alleviation: two new scales for clinical researchers, in H. M. Lefcourt (ed.) *Research with the Locus of Control Construct. Volume 1, Assessment Methods*. New York: Academic Press, pp. 281–320.

Hirano, P. C., Laurent, D. D. and Lorig, K. (1994) Arthritis patient education studies 1987–1991: a review of the literature. *Patient Education and Counselling*, 24: 9–54.

Hiroto, D. S. (1974) Locus of control and learned helplessness. *Journal of Experimental Psychology*, 102(2): 187–93.

Hiroto, D. S. and Seligman, M. E. P. (1975) Generality of learned helplessness in man. *Journal of Personality and Social Psychology*, 31: 311–27.

Hirsch, B. J. (1979) Psychological dimensions of social networks: a multimethod analysis. *American Journal of Community Psychology*, 7(3): 263–77.

Hjelle, L. A. (1971) Social desirability as a variable in the locus of control scale. *Psychological Reports*, 28: 807–16.

Hjelle, L. A. and Clouser, R. (1970) Susceptibility to attitude change as a function of internal–external control. *Psychological Record*, 20: 305–10.

Hobfoll, S. (1988) *The Ecology of Stress*. New York: Hemisphere.

Hoff, E.-H. and Hohner, H.-U. (1986) Occupational careers, work and control, in M. M. Baltes and P. B. Baltes (eds) *The Psychology of Control and Aging*. Hillsdale, NJ: Erlbaum, pp. 345–71.

Hofstetter, C. R., Sallis, J. F. and Hovell, M. F. (1990) Some health dimensions of self-efficacy: analysis of theoretical specificity. *Social Science and Medicine*, 31(9): 1051–6.

Holahan, C. K. and Holahan, C. J. (1987) Self-efficacy, social support and depression in aging: a longitudinal analysis. *Journal of Gerontology*, 42: 65–8.

Holden, F., Mocher, M. S., Schinke, S. P. and Barker, K. M. (1990) Self-efficacy of children and adolescents: a meta-analysis. *Psychological Reports*, 66: 1044–6.

Holman, J. and Lorig, K. (1992) Perceived self-efficacy in self-management of chronic disease, in R. Schwarzer (ed.) *Self-Efficacy Through Control of Activity*. Washington, DC: Hemisphere, pp. 305–23.

House, J. S. (1981) *Work Stress and Social Support*. Reading, MA: Addison-Wesley.

Houston, B. K. (1972) Control over stress, locus of control and response to stress. *Journal of Personality and Social Psychology*, 21: 249–55.

Houston, B. K. and Holmes, D. S. (1974) Effect of avoidant thinking and reappraisal for coping with threat involving temporal uncertainty. *Journal of Personality and Social Psychology*, 30(3): 382–8.

Houts, P. S., Quann, P. and Scott, R. A. (1979) Staff perception of client initiative and control, in L. C. Perlmuter and R. A. Monty (eds) *Choice and Perceived Control*. Hillsdale, NJ: John Wiley, pp. 143–53.

Huckstadt, A. (1987) Locus of control among alcoholics, recovering alcoholics, and non-alcoholics. *Research in Nursing and Health*, 10: 23–8.

Huesman, L. R. (1978) Cognitive processes and models of depression. *Journal of Abnormal Psychology*, 87(1): 194–8.

Hunt, S. M. and Martin, C. J. (1988) Health-related behavioural change: a test of a new model. *Psychology and Health*, 2(3): 209–30.

Hupcey, J. E. (1998) Social support: assessing conceptual coherence. *Qualitative Health Research*, 8(3): 304–18.

Hutner, N. L. and Locke, S. E. (1984) Health locus of control: a potential moderator variable for the relationship between life stress and psychopathology. *Psychotherapy and Psychosomatics*, 41: 186–94.

Hyland, M. E. (1987) Control theory interpretation of psychological mechanisms of depression: comparison and integration of several theories. *Psychological Bulletin*, 102(1): 109–21.

Hyland, M. E. (1988) Motivational control theory: an integrative framework. *Journal of Personality and Social Psychology*, 55(4): 642–51.

Ickes, W. J. and Kidd, R. F. (1976) An attributional analysis of helping behaviour, in J. H. Harvey, W. J. Ickes and R. F. Kidd (eds) *New Directions in Attribution Research, Volume 1*. Hillsdale, NJ: Lawrence Erlbaum Associates, pp. 311–33.

Janis, I. L. (1983) Foreword, in E. J. Langer, *The Psychology of Control*. Beverly Hills, CA: Sage, pp. 9–11.

Jenkins, H. M. and Ward, W. C. (1965) Judgment of contingency between responses and outcomes. *Psychological Monographs*, 79 (1, whole no. 594).

Jennings, B. M. and Staggers, N. (1994) A critical analysis of hardiness. *Nursing Research*, 43(5): 274–81.

Jensen, M. P. and Karoly, P. (1991) Control beliefs, coping efforts and adjustment to chronic pain. *Journal of Consulting and Clinical Psychology*, 59(3): 431–8.

Jensen, M. P., Turner, J. A. and Romano, J. M. (1991) Self-efficacy and outcome expectancies: relationship to chronic pain coping strategies and adjustment. *Pain*, 44: 263–9.

Joe, V. C. (1971) Review of the internal–external control construct as a personality variable. *Psychological Reports*, 28: 619–40.

Joe, V. C. (1972) Social desirability and the I–E scale. *Psychological Reports*, 30: 44–6.

Johnson, J. H. and Sarason, I. G. (1978) Life stress, depression and anxiety: internal–external control as a moderator variable. *Journal of Psychosomatic Research*, 22: 205–8.

Johnson, L. R., Magnani, B., Chan, V. and Ferrante, F. M. (1989) Modifiers of patient-controlled analgesia efficacy. I, Locus of control. *Pain*, 39: 17–22.

Julian, J. W., Lichtman, C. M. and Ruckman, R. J. (1968) Internal–external control and need to control. *Journal of Social Psychology*, 76: 43–8.

Julkunen, J. (1996) Suppressing your anger: good manners, bad health?, in C. D. Spielberger, I. G. Sarason, J. M. T. Brebner *et al.* (eds) *Stress and Emotion*,

Volume 16: Anxiety, Anger and Curiosity. Washington, DC: Taylor and Francis, pp. 227–40.

Kanfer, F. H. and Goldfoot, D. A. (1966) Self-control and tolerance of noxious stimulation. *Psychological Reports*, 18: 79–85.

Kanfer, F. H. and Karoly, P. (1972) Self-control: a behavioristic excursion into the lion's den. *Behavior Therapy*, 3: 398–416.

Kanfer, R. and Zeiss, A. M. (1984) Depression, interpersonal standard-setting, and judgments of self-efficacy. *Journal of Abnormal Psychology*, 92: 319–29.

Kaplan, B. H., Cassel, J. C. and Gore, S. (1977) Social support and health. *Medical Care*, 15(5), supplement.

Kaplan, G. D. and Cowles, A. (1978) Health locus of control and health value in the prediction of smoking reduction. *Health Education Monographs*, 6: 129–37.

Kaplan, R. M., Atkins, C. J. and Reinsch, S. (1984) Specific efficacy expectations mediate exercise compliance in patients with COPD. *Health Psychology*, 3(3): 223–42.

Kaplan, R. M., Ries, A. L., Prewitt, I. M. and Eakin, E. (1994) Self-efficacy expectations predict survival for patients with chronic obstructive pulmonary disease. *Health Psychology*, 13(4): 366–8.

Karniol, R. and Ross, M. (1976) The development of causal attributions in social perception. *Journal of Personality and Social Psychology*, 34(3): 455–64.

Karpinski, C. K. (1992) The development of a cancer locus of control scale and its utility in predicting attendance at smoking cessation programs. *Dissertation Abstracts International*, 52(7): 2419.

Kasl, S. V. and Cooper, C. L. (eds) (1987) *Research Methods in Stress and Health Psychology*. Chichester: John Wiley.

Kavanagh, D. J., Pierce, M., Lo, S. K. and Shelley, J. (1993) Self-efficacy and social support as predictors of smoking after a quit attempt. *Psychology and Health*, 8: 231–42.

Kazdin, A. E. and Petti, T. A. (1982) Self-report and interview measures of childhood and adolescent depression. *Journal of Child Psychology and Psychiatry*, 23: 437–57.

Kelley, H. H. (1973) The processes of causal attribution. *American Psychologist*, 28: 107–28.

Kelley, H. H. and Michela, J. L. (1980) Attribution theory and research. *Annual Review of Psychology*, 31: 457–501.

Kellogg, R. and Baron, R. S. (1975) Attribution theory, insomnia and the reverse placebo effect: a reversal of Storm and Nisbett's findings. *Journal of Personality and Social Psychology*, 32: 231–6.

Kelly, G. A. (1955) *A Theory of Personality: The Psychology of Personal Constructs.* New York: W. W. Norton.

Kelner, M. J. and Bourgeault, I. L. (1993) Patient control over dying: responses of health care professionals. *Social Science and Medicine*, 36(6): 757–65.

Kickbusch, I. (1989) Self-care in health promotion. *Social Science and Medicine*, 29(2): 125–30.

Kincey, J. (1981) Internal–external control and weight loss in the obese: predictive and discriminant validity and some possible clinical implications. *Journal of Clinical Psychology*, 37: 100–3.

Kjervik, D. K. (1990) Empowerment and the elderly. *Journal of Professional Nursing*, 6(2): 74.

Klein, D. C., Fencil-Morse, E. and Seligman, M. E. P. (1976) Learned helplessness, depression and the attribution of failure. *Journal of Personality and Social Psychology*, 33: 508–16.

Klein, D. C. and Seligman, M. E. P. (1976) Reversal of performance deficits and perceptual deficits in learned helplessness and depression. *Journal of Abnormal Psychology*, 85(1): 11–26.

Klosterhalfen, W. and Klosterhalfen, S. (1983) A critical analysis of the animal experiments cited in support of learned helplessness. *Psycholgische Beitrage*, 25(3/4): 436–85.

Kobasa, S. C. (1979) Stressful life events, personality and health: an inquiry into hardiness. *Journal of Personality and Social Psychology*, 37: 1–11.

Kobasa, S. C., Maddi, S. R. and Courington, S. (1981) Personality and constitution as mediators in the stress–illness relationship. *Journal of Health and Social Behaviour*, 22: 368–78.

Kobasa, S. C., Maddi, S. R. and Kahn, S. (1982) Hardiness and health: a prospective study. *Journal of Personality and Social Psychology*, 42(1): 168–77.

Kobasa, S. C., Maddi, S. R., Puccetti, M. C. and Zola, M. A. (1985) Effectiveness of hardiness, exercise and social support as resources against illness. *Journal of Psychosomatic Research*, 29(5): 525–33.

Kobasa, S. C. and Puccetti, M. C. (1983) Personality and social resources in stress-resistance. *Journal of Personality and Social Psychology*, 45: 839–50.

Koeske, G. F. and Koeske, R. D. (1992) Parenting locus of control: measurement, construct validation, and a proposed conceptual model. *Social Work Research and Abstracts*, 28(3): 37–46.

Kores, R. C., Murphy, W. D., Rosenthal, T. L., Elias, D. B. and North, W. C. (1990) Predicting outcome of chronic pain treatment via a modified self-efficacy scale. *Behaviour Research and Therapy*, 28(2): 165–9.

Krantz, D. S., Baum, A. and Wideman, M. V. (1980) Assessment of preferences for self-treatment and information in health care. *Journal of Personality and Social Psychology*, 39(5): 977–90.

Krause, N. (1987a) Chronic strain, locus of control and distress in older adults. *Psychology and Aging*, 2: 375–82.

Krause, N. (1987b) Understanding the stress process: linking social support with locus of control beliefs. *Journal of Gerontology*, 42(6): 589–93.

Krause, N. (1993) Early parental loss and personal control in later life. *Journal of Gerontology: Psychological Sciences*, 48(3): 117–26.

Krause, N. (1997) Social support and feelings of personal control in later life, in G. R. Pierce, B. Lakey, I. G. Sarason and B. R. Sarason (eds) *Sourcebook of Social Support and Personality*. New York: Plenum, pp. 335–58.

Krohne, H. W. and Laux, L. (eds) (1982) *Achievement, Stress, and Anxiety*. Washington, DC: Hemisphere.

Krovetz, M. L. (1974) Explaining success or failure as a function of one's locus of control. *Journal of Personality*, 42: 175–89.

Kuhl, J. (1986) Aging and models of control: the hidden costs of wisdom, in M. M. Baltes and P. B. Baltes (eds) *The Psychology of Control and Aging*. Hillsdale, NJ: Erlbaum, pp. 1–33.

Kuiper, N. A. (1978) Depression and causal attributions for success and failure. *Journal of Personality and Social Psychology*, 36: 236–46.

Kun, A. and Weiner, B. (1973) Necessary versus sufficient causal schemata for success and failure. *Journal of Research in Personality*, 7: 197–207.

Labs, S. M. and Wurtele, S. K. (1986) Fetal health locus of control scale: development and validation. *Journal of Consulting and Clinical Psychology*, 54(6): 814–19.

Lacey, H. M. (1979) Control, perceived control, and the methodological role of cognitive constructs, in L. C. Perlmuter and R. A. Monty (eds) *Choice and Perceived Control*. Hillsdale, NJ: John Wiley, pp. 7–16.

Lachman, M. E. (1986a) Personal control in later life: stability, change and cognitive correlates, in M. M. Baltes and P. B. Baltes (eds) *The Psychology of Control and Aging*. Hillsdale, NJ: Erlbaum, pp. 207–36.

Lachman, M. E. (1986b) Locus of control in aging research: a case for multi-dimensional and domain-specific assessment. *Journal of Psychology and Aging*, 1: 34–40.

Lachman, M. E. (1991) Perceived control over memory aging: developmental and intervention perspectives. *Journal of Social Issues*, 47(4): 159–75.

Laffrey, S. C. and Isenberg, M. (1983) The relationship of internal locus of control, value placed on health, perceived importance of exercise, and participation in physical activity during leisure. *International Journal of Nursing Studies*, 20(3): 187–96.

Lakey, B. and Drew, J. B. (1997) A social-cognitive perspective on social support, in G. R. Pierce, B. Lakey, I. G. Sarason and B. R. Sarason (eds) *Sourcebook of Social Support and Personality*. New York: Plenum, pp. 107–40.

LaMontagne, L. L. and Hepworth, J. T. (1991) Issues in the measurement of children's locus of control. *Western Journal of Nursing Research*, 31(1): 67–83.

Lange, R. V. and Tiggemann, M. (1978) Dimensionality and reliability of the Rotter internal–external locus of control scale. *Journal of Personality Assessment*, 45: 398–406.

Langer, E. J. (1975) The illusion of control. *Journal of Personality and Social Psychology*, 32(2): 311–28.

Langer, E. J. (1979) The illusion of incompetence, in L. C. Perlmuter and R. A. Monty (eds) *Choice and Perceived Control*. Hillsdale, NJ: John Wiley, pp. 301–13.

Langer, E. J. (ed.) (1983) *The Psychology of Control*. Beverly Hills, CA: Sage.

Langer, E. J. and Abelson, R. P. (1974) A patient by any other name. *Journal of Consulting and Clinical Psychology*, 42(1): 4–9.

Langer, E. J., Janis, I. L. and Wolfer, J. A. (1975) Reduction of psychological stress in surgical patients. *Journal of Experimental Social Psychology*, 11: 155–65.

Langer, E. J., Johnson, T. and Botwinick, H. (1983) Nothing succeeds like success, except . . . in E. J. Langer (ed.) *The Psychology of Control*. Beverly Hills, CA: Sage, pp. 241–50.

Langer, E. J. and Rodin, J. (1976) The effects of choice and enhanced personal responsibility for the aged: a field experiment in an institutional setting. *Journal of Personality and Social Psychology*, 34(2): 191–8.

Langer, E. J. and Saegert, S. (1977) Crowding and cognitive control. *Journal of Personality and Social Psychology*, 35(3): 175–82.

Langford, C. P. H., Bowsher, J., Maloney, J. P. and Lillis, P. P. (1997) Social support: a conceptual analysis. *Journal of Advanced Nursing*, 25: 95–100.

Larde, J. and Clopton, J. R. (1983) Generalized locus of control and health locus of control of surgical patients. *Psychological Reports*, 52: 599–602.

Laschinger, H. K. S. and Shamian, J. (1994) Staff nurses' and nurse managers' perceptions of job-related empowerment and managerial self-efficacy. *Journal of Nurse Administration*, 24(10): 38–47.

Lau, R. R. and Ware, J. F. (1981) Refinements in the measurement of health-specific locus-of-control beliefs. *Medical Care*, 19(11): 1147–57.

Lau, R. S. (1982) Origins of health locus of control beliefs. *Journal of Personality and Social Psychology*, 42(2): 322–34.

Lazarus, A. A. (1968) Learning theory and the treatment of depression. *Behavior Research and Therapy*, 6: 83–9.

Lazarus, R. S. (1966) *Psychological Stress and the Coping Process*. New York: McGraw-Hill.

Lazarus, R. S. and Averill, J. R. (1972) Emotion and cognition: with special reference to anxiety, in C. D. Spielberger (ed.) *Anxiety: Current Trends in Therapy and Research, Volume II*. New York: Academic Press, pp. 241–60.

Lazarus, R. S. and Folkman, S. (1984) Coping and adaptation, in W. D. Gentry (ed.) *Handbook of Behavioural Medicine*. New York: Guilford Press, pp. 282–319.

Lazarus, S. R., DeLongis, A., Folkman, S. and Gruen, R. (1985) Stress and adaptational outcomes. *American Psychologist*, 40(7): 770–9.

Lee, C. and Bobko, P. (1994) Self-efficacy beliefs: comparison of five measures. *Journal of Applied Psychology*, 79: 364–9.

Lefcourt, H. M. (1966a) Belief in personal control: research and implications. *Journal of Individual Psychology*, 22: 185–95.

Lefcourt, H. M. (1966b) Internal versus external control of reinforcement: a review. *Psychological Bulletin*, 65(4): 206–20.

Lefcourt, H. M. (1973) The function of the illusions of control and freedom. *American Psychologist*, 28: 418–25.

Lefcourt, H. M. (1979) Locus of control for specific goals, in L. C. Perlmuter and R. A. Monty (eds) *Choice and Perceived Control*. Hillsdale, NJ: John Wiley, pp. 209–20.

Lefcourt, H. M. (ed.) (1981a) *Research with the Locus of Control Construct. Volume 1, Assessment Methods*. New York: Academic Press.

Lefcourt, H. M. (1981b) The construction and development of the multidimensional-multiattributional causality scales, in H. M. Lefcourt (ed.) *Research with the Locus of Control Construct. Volume 1, Assessment Methods*. New York: Academic Press, pp. 245–77.

Lefcourt, H. M. (ed.) (1982) *Locus of Control: Current Trends in Theory and Research*, 2nd edn. Hillsdale, NJ: Lawrence Erlbaum Associates.

Lefcourt, H. M. (ed.) (1984) *Research with the Locus of Control Construct. Volume 3, Extensions and Limitations*. Orlando, FL: Academic Press.

Lefcourt, H. M., Martin, R. A. and Saleh, W. E. (1984) Locus of control and social support: interactive moderators of stress. *Journal of Personality and Social Psychology*, 47: 378–89.

Lev, E. L. (1997) Bandura's theory of self-efficacy: applications to oncology. *Scholarly Inquiry for Nursing Practice*, 11(1): 21–37.

Levenson, H. (1973a) Multidimensional locus of control in psychiatric patients. *Journal of Consulting and Clinical Psychology*, 41(3): 397–404.

Levenson, H. (1973b) Perceived parental antecedents of internal, powerful others, and chance locus of control orientations. *Developmental Psychology*, 9(2): 268–74.

Levenson, H. (1974) Activism and powerful others: distinctions within the concept of internal–external control. *Journal of Personality Assessment*, 38: 377–83.

Levenson, H. (1981) Differentiating among internality, powerful others, and chance, in H. M. Lefcourt (ed.) *Research with the Locus of Control Construct. Volume 1, Assessment Methods*. New York: Academic Press, pp. 377–83.

Levin, L. S. and Idler, E. L. (1983) Self care in health. *Annual Review of Public Health*, 4: 181–210.

Levinson, R. A. (1986) Contraceptive self-efficacy: a perspective on teenage girls' contraceptive behaviour. *Journal of Sex Research*, 22: 347–69.

Levinson, R. A. (1995) Reproductive and contraceptive knowledge, contraceptive self-efficacy and contraceptive behaviour among teenage women. *Adolescence*, 30(117): 65–85.

Lewinsohn, P. M. (1974) A behavioural approach to depression, in R. J. Friedman and M. M. Katz (eds) (1974) *The Psychology of Depression: Contemporary Theory and Research*. Washington, DC: V. H. Winston, pp. 157–86.

Lewinsohn, P. M., Mischel, W., Chaplin, W. and Barton, R. (1980) Social competence and depression: the role of illusory self-perceptions. *Journal of Abnormal Psychology*, 89: 203–12.

Lewis, F. M., Morisky, D. E. and Flynn, B. S. (1978) A test of construct validity of health locus of control: effects of self-reported compliance for hypertensive patients. *Health Education Monographs*, 6: 138–48.

Lin, N., Dean, A. and Ensel, W. (1981) Social support scales: a methodological note. *Schizophrenia Bulletin*, 7(1): 73–89.

Lin, N., Ensel, W. M., Semeone, R. S. and Kuo, W. (1979) Social support, stressful life events and illness: a model and empirical test. *Journal of Health and Social Behaviour*, 20: 108–19.

Linn, J. G., Lewis, F. M., Cain, V. A. and Kimbrough, G. A. (1993) HIV-illness, social support, sense of coherence, and psychosocial well-being in a sample of help-seeking adults. *AIDS Education and Prevention*, 5(3): 254–62.

Lipchik, G. L., Milles, K. and Covington, E. C. (1993) The effects of multidisciplinary pain management treatment on locus of control and pain beliefs in chronic non-terminal pain. *Clinical Journal of Pain*, 9: 49–57.

Litt, M. D. (1988) Self-efficacy and perceived control: cognitive mediators of pain tolerance. *Journal of Personality and Social Psychology*, 54: 149–60.

Lord, R. G. and Levy, P. E. (1994) Moving from cognition to action: a control theory perspective. *Applied Psychology: An International Review*, 43: 335–98.

Lorig, K., Chastain, R., Ung, E., Shoor, S. and Holman, H. (1989) Development and evaluation of a scale to measure the perceived self-efficacy of people with arthritis. *Arthritis and Rheumatism*, 32(1): 37–44.

Lorig, K. and Holman, H. R. (1989) Long-term outcomes of an arthritis self-management study: effects of reinforcement efforts. *Social Science and Medicine*, 29(2): 221–4.

Lorig, K., Lubeck, D., Kraines, R. G., Seleznick, M. and Holman, H. R. (1985) Outcomes of self-help education for patients with arthritis. *Arthritis and Rheumatism*, 28: 680–5.

Lorig, K. R., Mazonson, P. D. and Holman, H. R. (1993) Evidence suggesting that health education for self-management in patients with chronic arthritis has sustained health benefits while reducing health care costs. *Arthritis and Rheumatism*, 36(4): 439–46.

Lorr, M. and McNair, D. M. (1984) *Manual for Profile of Mood States, BiPolar Form (POMS-BI)*. San Diego: Educational and Industrial Testing Service.

Lowery, B. J. and Ducette, J. P. (1976) Disease-related learning and disease-related control as a function of locus of control. *Nursing Research*, 25: 358–62.

Lubin, B. (1965) Adjective checklist for measurement of depression. *Archives of General Psychiatry*, 12: 57–62.

Ludtke, H. A. and Schneider, H. G. (1996) Habit-specific locus of control scales for drinking, smoking and eating. *Psychological Reports*, 78: 363–9.

Lumpkin, J. R. (1986) The relationship between locus of control and age: new evidence. *Journal of Social Behaviour and Personality*, 1: 245–52.

Lust, J. A., Celuch, K. G. and Showers, L. S. (1993) A note on issues concerning the measurement of self-efficacy. *Journal of Applied Social Psychology*, 23(17): 1426–34.

MacDonald, A. P. Jr (1971) Internal external locus of control: parental antecedents. *Journal of Consulting and Clinical Psychology*, 37: 141–7.

McDowell, I. and Newell, C. (1987) *Measuring Health: A Guide to Rating Scales and Questionnaires*. Oxford: Oxford University Press.

McFarlane, A. H., Neale, K. A., Norman, G. R., Roy, R. G. and Streiner, D. L. (1981) Methodological issues in developing scale to measure social support. *Schizophrenia Bulletin*, 7: 90–100.

McGhee, P. E. and Crandall, V. C. (1968) Beliefs in internal–external control of reinforcement and academic performance. *Child Development*, 39: 91–102.

McGinnies, E. and Ward, C. D. (1974) Persuadability as a function of source credibility and locus of control: five cross cultural experiments. *Journal of Personality*, 42: 360–71.

McGuiness, S. (1996) Learned helplessness in the multiple sclerosis population. *Journal of Neuroscience Nursing*, 28(3): 163–70.

McKinney, J. P. (1981) The construct of engagement style: theory and research, in H. M. Lefcourt (ed.) *Research with the Locus of Control Construct. Volume 1, Assessment Methods*. New York: Academic Press, pp. 359–80.

Mackintosh, N. J. (1971) An analysis of overshadowing and blocking. *Quarterly Journal of Experimental Psychology*, 23(1): 118–25.

MacLachlan, M., Ager, A. and Brown, J. (1996) Health locus of control in Malawi: a failure to support the cross-cultural validity of the HLOCQ. *Psychology and Health*, 12: 33–8.

McLean, J. and Pietroni, P. (1990) Self-care – who does best? *Social Science and Medicine*, 5: 591–6.

McLelland, D. C. (1965) Toward a theory of motive acquisition. *American Psychologist*, 20: 321–33.

McLelland, D. C. (1966) Longitudinal trends in the relation of thought to action. *Journal of Consulting Psychology*, 30(6): 479–83.

McMahan, I. D. (1973) Relationships between causal attributions and expectancy of success. *Journal of Personality and Social Psychology*, 28: 108–14.

McMahan, I. D. (1974) Relationships between causal attributions and expectancy of success, in B. Weiner (ed.) *Achievement Motivation and Attribution Theory*. Morriston, NJ: General Learning Press, pp. 114–24.

Maddux, J. E. and Stanley, M. A. (1986) Self-efficacy theory in contemporary psychology: an overview. *Journal of Social and Clinical Psychology*, 4: 249–55.

Mahor, B., Cozzarelli, C., Sciacchitano, A. M. *et al.* (1990) Perceived social support, self-efficacy and adjustment to abortion. *Journal of Personality and Social Psychology*, 593: 452–63.

Maibach, E. and Murphy, D. A. (1995) Self-efficacy in health promotion research and practice: conceptualization and measurement. *Health Education Research*, 10(1): 37–50.

Maier, S. F. and Seligman, M. E. P. (1976) Learned helplessness: theory and evidence. *Journal of Experimental Psychology: General*, 105(1): 3–46.

Major, B., Cozzarelli, C., Sciacchitano, A. M. *et al.* (1990) Perceived social support, self-efficacy and adjustment to abortion. *Journal of Personality and Social Psychology*, 59(3): 452–63.

Malin, N. and Teasdale, K. (1991) Caring versus empowerment: considerations for nursing practice. *Journal of Advanced Nursing*, 16: 657–62.

Mancini, J. A. and Blieszner, R. (1992) Social provisions in adulthood: concepts and measurement in close relationships. *Journal of Gerontology and Psychological Sciences*, 44(1): 14–28.

Mandler, G. (1972) Helplessness: theory and research in anxiety, in C. D. Spielberger (ed.) *Anxiety: Current Trends in Therapy and Research, Volume II*. New York: Academic Press, pp. 359–78.

Mandler, G. (1982) Stress and thought processes, in L. Goldberger and S. Bresnitz (eds) *Handbook of Stress: Theoretical and Clinical Aspects*. New York, Free Press.

Mankowski, E. S. and Wyer, R. S. (1997) Cognitive causes and consequences of perceived social support, in G. R. Pierce, B. Lakey, I. G. Sarason and B. R. Sarason (eds) *Sourcebook of Social Support and Personality*. New York: Plenum, pp. 141–68.

Manning, M. and Wright, T. L. (1983) Self-efficacy expectancies, outcome expectancies and the persistence of pain control in childbirth. *Journal of Personality and Social Psychology*, 45: 421–31.

Manuck, S. B., Hinrichson, J. J. and Ross, E. O. (1975a) Life-stress, locus of control and state and trait anxiety. *Psychological Reports*, 36: 413–14.

Manuck, S. B., Hinrichson, J. J. and Ross, E. O. (1975b) Life-stress, locus of control and treatment-seeking. *Psychological Reports*, 37: 589–90.

Marks, G., Richardson, J. L., Graham, J. W. and Levine, A. (1986) Role of locus of control beliefs and expectations of treatment efficacy in adjustment to cancer. *Journal of Personality and Social Psychology*, 51: 443–50.

Marks, M. (1993) *The Quit for Life Programme: An Easier Way to Stop Smoking and Not Start Again*. Leicester: The British Psychological Society.

Marmot, M. (1999) Introduction, in M. Marmot and R. G. Wilkinson (eds) *Social Determinants of Health*. Oxford: Oxford University Press, pp. 1–16.

Marmot, M. and Wilkinson, R. G. (eds) (1999) *Social Determinants of Health*. Oxford, Oxford University Press.

Marshall, G. N. (1991) A multidimensional analysis of internal health locus of control beliefs: separating the wheat from the chaff. *Journal of Personality and Social Psychology*, 61(3): 483–91.

Marshall, G. N., Burnam, M. A., Koegel, P., Sullivan, G. and Benjamin, B. (1996) Objective life circumstances and life satisfaction: results from the course of homelessness study. *Journal of Health and Social Behaviour*, 37 (March): 44–58.

Marteau, T. and Bekker, H. (1992) The development of a six-item short-form of the state scale of the Spielberger State–Trait Anxiety Inventory (STAI). *British Journal of Clinical Psychology*, 31(3): 301–6.

Martin, N. J., Holroyd, K. A. and Penzien, D. B. (1990) The headache-specific locus of control scale: adaptation to recurrent headaches. *Headache*, 30: 729–34.

Maslow, A. (1970) *Motivation and Personality*, 2nd edn. New York: Van Nostrand-Reinhold.

Mercer, S. and Kane, R. A. (1979) Helplessness and hopelessness among the institutionalized aged: an experiment. *Health and Social Work*, 4: 91–116.

Metalsky, G. I., Halberstadt, L. J. and Abramson, L. Y. (1987) Vulnerability to depressive mood reactions: toward a more powerful test of the diathesis–stress and causal mediation components of the reformulated theory of depression. *Journal of Personality and Social Psychology*, 52: 386–93.

Metalsky, G. I. and Joiner, T. E. Jr (1992) Vulnerability to depressive symptomatology: a prospective test, the diathesis-stress and causal mediation components of the hopelessness theory of depression. *Journal of Personality and Social Psychology*, 63: 667–75.

Michotte, A. (1963) *The Perception of Causality*. London, Methuen.

Mikulincer, M. (1986) Attributional processes in the learned helplessness paradigm: behavioral effects of global attributions. *Journal of Personality and Social Psychology*, 51(6): 1248–56.

Miller, D. T. and Ross, M. (1975) Self-serving biases in the attribution of causality: fact or fiction? *Psychological Bulletin*, 82(2): 213–25.

Miller, I. W. III and Norman, W. H. (1979) Learned helplessness in humans: a review and attribution-theory model. *Psychological Bulletin*, 86(1): 93–118.

Miller, J. F. (1992a) *Coping with Chronic Illness: Overcoming Powerlessness*, 2nd edn. Philadelphia: F. A. Davis.

Miller, J. F. (1992b) Analysis of coping with illness, in J. F. Miller, *Coping with Chronic Illness: Overcoming Powerlessness*, 2nd edn. Philadelphia: F. A. Davis, pp. 19–49.

Miller, J. F. (1992c) Concept development of powerlessness: a nursing diagnosis, in J. F. Miller, *Coping with Chronic Illness: Overcoming Powerlessness*, 2nd edn. Philadelphia: F. A. Davis, pp. 50–81.

Miller, P. C., Lefcourt, H. M. and Ware, E. E. (1983) The construction and development of the Miller Locus of Control Scale. *Canadian Journal of Behavioural Science*, 15: 266–79.

Miller, S. M. (1979) Controllability and human stress: method, evidence and theory. *Behaviour Research and Therapy*, 17(4): 287–304.

Miller, S. M. (1980) Why having control reduces stress: if I can stop the roller coaster, I don't want to get off, in J. Garber and M. E. P. Seligman (eds) *Human Helplessness: Theory and Applications*. Orlando, FL: Academic Press, pp. 71–95.

Miller, S. M. (1987) Monitoring and blunting: validation of questionnaire to assess styles of information seeking under threat. *Journal of Personality and Social Psychology*, 52: 345–53.

Miller, S. M., Brody, D. and Summerton, J. (1988) Styles of coping with threat: implications for health. *Journal of Personality and Social Psychology*, 54: 142–8.

Miller, S. M., Lack, E. R. and Asroff, S. (1985) Preference for control and the coronary-prone behaviour pattern: 'I'd rather do it myself'. *Journal of Personality and Social Psychology*, 49: 492–9.

Miller, W. R. and Seligman, M. E. P. (1973) Depression and the perception of reinforcement. *Journal of Abnormal Psychology*, 82(1): 62–73.

Miller, W. R. and Seligman, M. E. P. (1975) Depression and learned helplessness in man. *Journal of Abnormal Psychology*, 84(3): 228–38.

Miller, W. R., Seligman, M. E. P. and Kurlander, H. M. (1975) Learned helplessness, depression and anxiety. *Journal of Nervous and Mental Disease*, 161: 347–57.

Mills, T. and Krantz, D. S. (1979) Information, choice and reactions to stress: a field experiment in a blood bank with laboratory analogue. *Journal of Personality and Social Psychology*, 37: 608–20.

Mineka, S. and Hendersen, R. W. (1985) Controllability and predictability in acquired motivation. *Annual Review of Psychology*, 36: 495–529.

Mirels, H. L. (1970) Dimensions of internal versus external control. *Journal of Consulting and Clinical Psychology*, 34: 226–8.

Mirowsky, J. and Ross, C. E. (1989) *Social Causes of Psychological Distress*. New York: Aldine de Gruyter.

Mirowsky, J. and Ross, C. E. (1990) Control or defense: depression and the sense of control over good and bad outcomes. *Journal of Health and Social Behavior*, 31(1): 71–86.

Mirowsky, J. and Ross, C. E. (1996) Fundamental analysis in research on well-being: distress and the sense of control. *The Gerontologist*, 36(5): 584–94.

Mischel, W., Zeiss, R. and Zeiss, A. (1974) Internal–external control and persistence: validation and implications of the Stanford Preschool Internal–External Scale. *Journal of Personality and Social Psychology*, 29: 265–78.

Mishel, M. H. (1981) The measurement of uncertainty in illness. *Nursing Research*, 30(5): 258–63.

Moch, S. D. (1988) Toward a personal control/uncontrol balance. *Journal of Advanced Nursing*, 13: 119–23.

Monat, A., Averill, J. R. and Lazarus, R. S. (1972) Anticipatory stress and coping reactions under various conditions of uncertainty. *Journal of Personality and Social Psychology*, 24(2): 237–53.

Monat, A. and Lazarus, R. S. (eds) (1991) *Stress and Coping: An Anthology*, 3rd edn. New York: Columbia University Press.

Mook, J., Ploeg, H. M. van der and Kleijn, W. C. (1990) Anxiety, anger and depression: relationships at the trait level. *Anxiety Research*, 3(1): 1–72.

Mowrer, O. H. and Viek, P. (1948) An experimental analogue of fear from a sense of helplessness. *Journal of Abnormal and Social Psychology*, 43: 193–200.

Murphy, S. A. (1987) Self-efficacy and social support mediators of stress on mental health following a natural disaster. *Western Journal of Nursing Research*, 9: 58–86.

Nadler, A. (1997) Personality and help seeking: autonomous versus dependent seeking of help, in G. R. Pierce, B. Lakey, I. G. Sarason and B. R. Sarason (eds) *Sourcebook of Social Support and Personality*. New York: Plenum, pp. 379–408.

Nagy, V. T. and Wolfe, G. R. (1983) Chronic illness and health locus of control beliefs. *Journal of Social and Clinical Psychology*, 1: 58–65.

Nelson, D. W. and Cohen, J. H. (1983) Locus of control and control perceptions and the relationship between life stress and psychological disorder. *American Journal of Community Psychology*, 11: 705–22.

Newcomb, M. and Harlow, L. (1986) Life events and substance use among adolescents: mediating effects of perceived loss of control and meaninglessness in life. *Journal of Personality and Social Psychology*, 51(3): 564–77.

Nicassio, P. M., Wallston, K. A., Callahan, L. F., Herbert, M. and Pincus, T. (1985) The measurement of helplessness in rheumatoid arthritis: the development of the Arthritis Helplessness Index. *Journal of Rheumatology*, 12: 462–7.

Nolen-Hoeksema, S., Girgus, J. S. and Seligman, M. E. P. (1986) Learned helplessness in children: a longitudinal study of depression, achievement and explanatory style. *Journal of Personality and Social Psychology*, 51: 28–33.

Norbeck, J. (1981) Social support: a model for clinical research and application. *Advances in Nursing Science*, 3(4): 43–59.

Norbeck, J., Lindsey, A. and Carrierie, V. (1981) The development of an instrument to measure social support. *Nursing Research*, 30: 264–9.

Norbeck, J., Lindsey, A. and Carrierie, V. (1983) Further development of the Norbeck Social Support Questionnaire: normative data and validity testing. *Nursing Research*, 32: 4–9.

Norman, P. (1991) Social learning theory and the prediction of attendance at screening. *Psychology and Health*, 5: 231–9.

Norman, P. and Bennett, P. (1995) Health locus of control, in M. Conner and P. Norman (eds) *Predicting Health Behaviour*. Buckingham: Open University Press, pp. 62–94.

Norman, P., Bennett, P., Smith, C. and Murphy, S. (1998) Health locus of control and health behaviour. *Journal of Health Psychology*, 3(2): 171–80.

North, F. M., Syme, S. L., Feeney, A., Shipley, M. and Marmot, M. (1996) Psychosocial work environment and sickness absence among British civil servants: the Whitehall II Study. *American Journal of Public Health*, 86(3): 332–40.

Nowicki, S. Jr and Hopper, A. E. (1974) Locus of control correlates in an alcoholic population. *Journal of Consulting and Clinical Psychology*, 42: 735.

Nowicki, S. and Strickland, B. R. (1973) A locus of control scale for children. *Journal of Consulting and Clinical Psychology*, 40(1): 148–54.

Oakley, A. (1992) *Social Support and Motherhood*. Oxford: Blackwell.

Oberle, K. (1991) A decade of research in locus of control: what have we learned? *Journal of Advanced Nursing*, 16: 800–6.

Obitz, F. W. and Oziel, L. J. (1978) Change in general and specific perceived locus of control in alcoholics as a function of treatment exposure. *International Journal of the Addictions*, 13: 995–1001.

O'Brien, G. E. (1981) Locus of control, previous occupation and satisfaction with retirement. *Australian Journal of Psychology*, 33(3): 305–18.

O'Brien, G. E. (1984) Locus of control, work and retirement, in H. Lefcourt (ed.) *Research with the Locus of Control Construct. Volume 3, Extensions and Limitations*. New York: Academic Press, pp. 53–72.

O'Brien, G. E. and Kabanoff, B. (1981) Australian norms and factor analyses of Rotter's Internal–External Control Scale. *Australian Psychologist*, 16: 184–202.

O'Connell, J. K. and Price, J. H. (1985) Development of a heart disease locus of control scale. *Psychological Reports*, 56: 159–64.

O'Leary, A. (1985) Self-efficacy and health. *Behaviour Research and Therapy*, 23: 537–51.

O'Leary, A., Shoor, S., Lorig, K. and Holman, H. R. (1988) A cognitive-behavioural treatment for rheumatoid arthritis. *Health Psychology*, 7(6): 527–44.

O'Leary, M., Donovan, D., Cysewski, B. and Chaney, E. (1977) Perceived locus of control, experienced control and depression: a trait description of the learned helplessness model of depression. *Journal of Clinical Psychology*, 33: 164–8.

O'Leary, M. R., Donovan, D. M., Hague, W. H. and Shea, R. A. (1975) Shifts in component factors of locus of control as a function of treatment in male alcoholics. *Journal of Clinical Psychology*, 31: 359–61.

O'Leary, M. R., Donovan, D. M. and O'Leary, D. E. (1976) Changes in perceived and experienced control among inpatient alcoholics. *Journal of Clinical Psychology*, 32: 500–4.

Oleson, O., Iverson, L. and Sabroe, S. (1991) Age and the operationalization of social support. *Social Support and Medicine*, 32(7): 767–71.

Opie, A. (1998) 'Nobody's asked me for my view': users' empowerment by multidisciplinary health teams. *Qualitative Health Research*, 8(2): 188–206.

Orem, D. E. (1995) *Nursing: Concepts of Practice*, 5th edn. St Louis: Mosby.

Oswald, L. M., Walker, G. C., Reilly, E., Krajewski, K. J. and Parker, C. A. (1992) Measurement of locus of control in cocaine abusers. *Issues in Mental Health Nursing*, 13: 81–94.

Overmeier, J. B. and Seligman, M. E. P. (1967) Effects of inescapable shock upon subsequent escape and avoidance responding. *Journal of Comparative and Physiological Psychology*, 63(1): 28–33.

Ozer, E. M. and Bandura, A. (1990) Mechanisms governing empowerment effects: a self-efficacy analysis. *Journal of Personality and Social Psychology*, 58: 472–86.

Oziel, L. J., Obitz, F. W. and Keyson, M. (1972) General and specific perceived locus of control in alcoholics. *Psychological Reports*, 30: 957–8.

Palenzuela, D. L. (1984) Critical evaluation of locus of control: towards a reconceptualization of the construct and its measurement. *Psychological Reports*, 54: 683–709.

Parcel, G. S. and Meyer, M. P. (1978) Development of an instrument to measure children's health locus of control. *Health Education Monographs*, 6: 149.

Parish, T. (1982) Locus of control as a function of father loss and the presence of stepfathers. *Journal of Genetic Psychology*, 140: 321–2.

Parker, L. E. (1994) Working together – perceived self-efficacy and collective efficacy at the workplace. *Journal of Applied Social Psychology*, 24(1): 43–59.

Parker, M. (1990) Patients and empowerment (letter). *Australian Family Physician*, 19(9): 1454.

Parkes, K. R. (1984) Locus of control, cognitive appraisal and coping in stressful episodes. *Journal of Personality and Social Psychology*, 46: 655–68.

Parkes, K. R. (1986) Coping in stressful episodes: the role of individual differences, environment factors and situational characteristics. *Journal of Personality and Social Psychology*, 51(6): 1277–92.

Partridge, C. and Johnston, M. (1989) Perceived control of recovery from physical disability: measurement and prediction. *British Journal of Clinical Psychology*, 28: 53–9.

Pasch, L. A., Bradbury, T. N. and Sullivan, K. T. (1997) Social support in marriage: an analysis of intraindividual and interpersonal components, in G. R. Pierce, B. Lakey, I. G. Sarason and B. R. Sarason (eds) *Sourcebook of Social Support and Personality*. New York: Plenum, pp. 229–56.

Pauhus, D. and Christie, R. (1981) Spheres of control: an interactionist approach to assessment of perceived control, in H. M. Lefcourt (ed.) *Research with the Locus of Control Construct. Volume 1, Assessment Methods*. New York: Academic Press, pp. 161–88.

Paykel, E. S., Cooper, Z., Ramana, R. and Hayhurst, H. (1996) Life events, social support and marital relationships in the outcome of severe depression. *Psychological Medicine*, 26: 121–33.

Payne, R. L. and Jones, J. G. (1987) Measurement and methodological issues in social support, in S. V. Kasl and C. L. Cooper (eds) *Research Methods in Stress and Health Psychology*. Chichester: John Wiley, pp. 167–205.

Pearlin, L. and Schooler, C. (1978) The structure of coping. *Journal of Health and Social Behaviour*, 19: 2–21.

Pearlin, L. I. and Turner, J. A. (1987) The family as a context of the stress process, in S. V. Kasl and C. L. Cooper (eds) *Research Methods in Stress and Health Psychology*. Chichester: John Wiley, pp. 143–65.

Pearson, J. E. (1986) The definition and measurement of social support. *Journal of Counselling and Development*, 64(6): 390–5.

Pekrun, R. (1992) Expectancy-value theory of anxiety: overview and implications, in D. C. Forgays, T. Sosnowski and K. Wrzesniewski (eds) *Anxiety: Recent Developments in Cognitive, Psychophysiological and Health Research*. Washington, DC: Hemisphere, pp. 23–41.

Penk, W. E. (1969) Age changes and correlates of internal–external locus of control scale. *Psychological Reports*, 25: 856.

Pennebaker, J. W., Burnam, M. A., Shaeffer, M. A. and Harper, D. C. (1977) Lack of control as a determinant of perceived physical symptoms. *Journal of Personality and Social Psychology*, 24: 237–53.

Perlmuter, L. C. and Monty, R. A. (eds) (1979) *Choice and Perceived Control*. Hillsdale, NJ: John Wiley.

Perlmuter, L. C., Monty, R. A. and Chan, F. (1986) Choice, control and cognitive functioning, in M. M. Baltes and P. B. Baltes (eds) *The Psychology of Control and Aging*. Hillsdale, NJ: Erlbaum, pp. 91–118.

Pervin, L. A. (1963) The need to predict and control under conditions of threat. *Journal of Personality*, 31: 570–87.

Peterson, C. and Raps, C. S. (1984) Helplessness and hospitalization: more remarks. *Journal of Personality and Social Psychology*, 46(1): 82–3.

Peterson, C., Rosenbaum, A. C. and Conn, M. K. (1985) Depressive mood reaction to breaking up: testing the learned helplessness model of depression. *Journal of Social and Clinical Psychology*, 3(2): 161–9.

Peterson, C., Schwartz, S. M. and Seligman, M. E. P. (1981) Self-blame and depressive symptoms. *Journal of Personality and Social Psychology*, 41: 253–9.

Peterson, C. and Seligman, M. E. P. (1984) Causal explanation as a risk factor for depression: theory and evidence. *Psychological Review*, 91(3): 347–74.

Peterson, C. and Seligman, M. E. P. (1987) Explanatory style and illness. *Journal of Personality*, 55(2): 237–65.

Peterson, C., Seligman, M. E. P. and Vaillant, G. E. (1988) Pessimistic explanatory style is a risk factor for physical illness: a thirty-five year longitudinal study. *Journal of Personality and Social Psychology*, 55: 23–7.

Peterson, C., Semmel, A., von Baeyer, C., Abramson, L., Metalsky, G. and Seligman, M. E. P. (1982) The attributional style questionnaire. *Cognitive Therapy and Research*, 6: 297–300.

Peterson, C. and Stunkard, A. J. (1989) Personal control and health promotion. *Social Science and Medicine*, 28(8): 819–28.

Petrie, K. and Chamberlain, K. (1983) Hopelessness and social desirability as moderator variables in predicting suicidal behaviour. *Journal of Consulting and Clinical Psychology*, 51: 485–7.

Petterson, N. (1987) A conceptual difference between internal–external locus of control and causal attributions. *Psychological Reports*, 60: 203–9.

Phares, E. J. (1957) Expectancy changes in skill and chance situations. *Journal of Abnormal and Social Psychology*, 54: 339–42.

Phares, E. J. (1976) *Locus of Control in Personality*. Morristown, NJ: General Learning Press.

Phares, E. J. (1979) Defensiveness and perceived control, in L. C. Perlmuter and R. A. Monty (eds) *Choice and Perceived Control*. Hillsdale, NJ: John Wiley, pp. 195–208.

Phares, E. J. (1990) *Introduction to Personality*, 3rd edn. New York: HarperCollins.

Phares, E. J., Ritchie, D. E. and Davis, W. L. (1968) Internal–external control and reaction to threat. *Journal of Personality and Social Psychology*, 10: 402–5.

Pierce, G. R., Lakey, B., Sarason, I. G. and Sarason, B. R. (eds) (1997) *Sourcebook of Social Support and Personality*. New York: Plenum.

Pilisuk, M. and Froland, C. (1978) Kinship, social networks, social support and health. *Social Science and Medicine*, 12: 273–80.

Pill, R. and Stott, N. C. H. (1985) Choice or chance: further evidence on ideas of illness and responsibility for health. *Social Science and Medicine*, 20: 981–91.

Pines, H. A. (1973) An attributional analysis of locus of control orientation and source of informational dependence. *Journal of Personality and Social Psychology*, 26: 262–72.

Piper, A. I. and Langer, E. J. (1986) Aging and mindful control, in M. M. Baltes and P. B. Baltes (eds) *The Psychology of Control and Aging*. Hillsdale, NJ: Erlbaum, pp. 71–89.

Plous, S. and Zimbardo, P. G. (1986) Attributional biases among clinicians: a comparison of psychoanalysts and behaviour therapists. *Journal of Consulting and Clinical Psychology*, 54: 568–70.

Pollack, L. and Harris, R. (1983) Measurement of social support. *Psychological Reports*, 53: 466.

Pollock, S. E. (1987) Adaptation to chronic illness: analysis of nursing research. *Nursing Clinics of North America*, 22(3): 631–44.

Powell, A. and Vega, M. (1972) Correlates of adult locus of control. *Psychological Reports*, 30: 455–60.

Procidano, M. E. and Heller, K. (1983) Measures of perceived social support from friend and from family: three validation studies. *American Journal of Community Psychology*, 11(1): 1–24.

Prohaska, T. R., Keller, M. L., Lenenthal, E. A. and Leventhal, H. (1987) Impact of symptoms and aging on attribution on emotions and coping. *Health Psychology*, 6(6): 495–514.

Pruyn, J. and van den Heuvel, W. (1991) Anxiety, control and information-seeking behavior in screening for cancer, in D. C. Forgays, T. Sosnowski and K. Wrzesniewski (eds) *Anxiety: Recent Developments in Cognitive, Psychophysiological and Health Research*. Washington, DC: Hemisphere, pp. 183–95.

Punamaki, R.-L. and Aschan, H. (1994) Self-care and mastery among primary health care patients. *Social Science and Medicine*, 39(5): 733–41.

Quinless, F. W. and Nelson, M. A. M. (1988) Development of a measure of learned helplessness. *Nursing Research*, 37(1): 11–15.

Radloff, L. S. (1977) The CES-D scale: a self-report depression scale for research in the general population. *Applied Psychological Measurement*, 1: 385–401.

Rael, E. G. S., Stansfield, S. A., Shipley, M. *et al.* (1995) Sickness absence in the Whitehall II study, London: the role of social support and material problems. *Journal of Epidemiological and Community Health*, 49: 474–81.

Rappaport, J. (1987) Terms of empowerment/exemplars of prevention: toward a theory for community psychology. *American Journal of Community Psychology*, 15(2): 121–45.

Raps, C. S., Peterson, C., Jonas, M. and Seligman, M. E. P. (1982) Patient behaviour in hospitals: helplessness, reactance or both? *Journal of Personality and Social Psychology*, 42(6): 1036–41.

Raps, C. S., Peterson, C., Reinhard, K. E., Abramson, L. Y. and Seligman, M. E. P. (1982) Attributional style among depressed patients. *Journal of Abnormal Psychology*, 91(2): 102–8.

Ray, P. (1982) Pain, in J. Hall (ed.) *Psychology for Nurses and Health Visitors*. London: British Psychological Society and Macmillan Press.

Ray, W. J. and Katahn, M. (1968) Relation of anxiety to locus of control. *Psychological Reports*, 23: 1196.

Rehm, L. P. (1977) A self-control model of depression. *Behaviour Therapy*, 8: 787–804.

Reich, J. W. and Zautra, A. J. (1990) Dispositional control beliefs and the consequences of a control-enhancing intervention. *Journal of Gerontology: Psychological Sciences*, 45: 46–51.

Reich, J. W. and Zautra, A. J. (1991) Experimental and measurement approaches to internal control in at-risk older adults. *Journal of Social Issues*, 47(4): 143–58.

Reich, J. W. and Zautra, A. J. (1995) Spouse encouragement of self-reliance and other-reliance in rheumatoid arthritis couples. *Journal of Behavioural Medicine*, 18(3): 249–60.

Reid, D. W. (1984) Participatory control and the chronic-illness adjustment process, in H. M. Lefcourt (ed.) *Research with the Locus of Control Construct. Volume 3, Extensions and Limitations*. New York: Academic Press, pp. 361–89.

Reid, D. W., Haas, G. and Hawkings, D. (1977) Locus of desired control and positive self-concept of the elderly. *Journal of Gerontology*, 22: 441–50.

Reid, D. W. and Stirling, G. (1989) Cognitive social learning theory of control and gaining, participatory control and the well-being of elderly persons, in P. S. Fry (ed.) *Psychological Perspectives of Helplessness and Control in the Elderly*. Amsterdam: North-Holland, pp. 217–58.

Reid, D. W. and Ware, E. E. (1973) Multidimensionality of internal–external control: implications for past and future research. *Canadian Journal of Behavioural Science*, 5(3): 264–71.

Reid, D. W. and Ware, E. E. (1974) Multidimensionality of internal–external control: addition a third dimension and non-distinction of self versus others. *Canadian Journal of Behavioural Science*, 6: 131–42.

Reid, D. W. and Ziegler, M. (1980) Validity and stability of a new Desired Control measure pertaining to psychological adjustment of the elderly. *Journal of Gerontology*, 35: 395–402.

Reid, D. W. and Ziegler, M. (1981) The desired control measure and adjustment among the elderly, in H. M. Lefcourt (ed.) *Research with the Locus of Control Construct. Volume 1, Assessment Methods*. New York: Academic Press, pp. 127–60.

Reisenzein, R. (1983) The Schachter theory of emotion: two decades later. *Psychological Bulletin*, 2: 239–64.

Rhodewalt, F. and Davison, J. J. R. (1983) Reactance and the coronary-prone behaviour pattern: the role of self-attribution in responses to reduced behavioural freedom. *Journal of Personality and Psychology*, 44: 220–8.

Ritchie, E. and Phares, E. J. (1969) Attitude change as a function of internal–external control and communicator status. *Journal of Personality*, 37: 429–43.

Roberts, R., Brunner, E. and Marmot, M. (1995) Psychological factors in the relationship between alcohol and cardiovascular morbidity. *Social Science and Medicine*, 41(11): 1513–16.

Rock, D., Green, K., Wise, B. and Rock, R. (1984) Social support social network scales: a psychometric review. *Research in Nursing and Health*, 7: 325–32.

Rock, D. L., Meyerowitz, B. E., Maisto, S. A. and Wallston, K. A. (1987) The derivation and validation of six multidimensional health locus of control scale clusters. *Research in Nursing and Health*, 10: 185–95.

Rodin, J. (1976) Density, perceived choice and response to controllable and uncontrollable outcomes. *Journal of Experimental Social Psychology*, 12: 564–78.

Rodin, J. (1986) Aging and health: effects of the sense of control. *Science*, 233: 1271–6.

Rodin, J. and Langer, E. J. (1977) Long-term effects of a control-relevant intervention with the institutionalized aged. *Journal of Personality and Social Psychology*, 35(12): 897–902.

Rodin, J., Solomon, S. K. and Metcalf, J. (1978) Role of control in mediating perceptions of density. *Journal of Personality and Social Psychology*, 36(9): 988–99.

Rohsenow, D. J. and O'Leary, M. R. (1978) Locus of control research on alcoholic populations: a review. 1. Development, scales and treatment. *International Journal of the Addictions*, 13(1): 55–78.

Rosenbaum, M. (1980) A schedule for assessing self-control behavior: preliminary findings. *Behavior Therapy*, 11: 109–21.

Ross, C. E. (1991) Marriage and the sense of control. *Journal of Marriage and the Family*, 53: 831–8.

Ross, C. E. and Mirowsky, J. (1984) Components of depressed mood in married men and women. *American Journal of Epidemiology*, 119(6): 997–1004.

Ross, C. E. and Mirowsky, J. (1989) Explaining the social patterns of depression: control and problem solving – or support and talking? *Journal of Health and Social Behaviour*, 30: 206–19.

Ross, M. (1989) Relation of implicit theories to the construction of personal histories. *Psychological Review*, 89: 341–7.

Rothbaum, R., Weisz, J. R. and Snyder, S. S. (1982) Changing the world and changing the self. A two-process model of perceived control. *Journal of Personality and Social Psychology*, 42: 5–37.

Rotter, J. B. (1954) *Social Learning and Clinical Psychology*. New York: Prentice Hall.

Rotter, J. B. (1966) Generalized expectancies for internal versus external control of reinforcement. *Psychological Monographs: General and Applied*, 80(1): 1–28.

Rotter, J. B. (1971a) External control and internal control. *Psychology Today*, 5: 37–42, 58–9.

Rotter, J. B. (1971b) Generalized expectancies for interpersonal trust. *American Psychologist*, 26: 443–52.

Rotter, J. B. (1975) Some problems and misconceptions related to the construct of internal versus external control of reinforcement. *Journal of Consulting and Clinical Psychology*, 43(1): 56–67.

Rotter, J. B. (1979) Comments on Section IV: individual differences and perceived control, in L. C. Perlmuter and R. A. Monty (eds) *Choice and Perceived Control*. Hills, NJ: John Wiley, pp. 263–9.

Rotter, J. B., Liverant, S. and Crowne, D. P. (1961) The growth and extinction of expectancies in chance controlled and skilled tasks. *Journal of Psychology*, 52: 161–77.

Rowan, K. (1994) Global questions and scores, in C. Jenkinson (ed.) *Measuring Health and Medical Outcomes*. London: UCL Press, pp. 54–76.

Rubin, Z. (1974) *Doing unto Others*. Englewood Cliffs, NJ: Prentice Hall.

Russell, D. (1982) The causal dimension scale: a measure of how individuals perceive causes. *Journal of Personality and Social Psychology*, 42: 1137–45.

Ryckman, R. M. and Malikiosi, M. X. (1975) Relationship between locus of control and chronological age. *Psychological Reports*, 36: 655–8.

Salovey, P. and Birmbaum, D. (1989) Influence of mood on health-relevant cognitions. *Journal of Personality and Social Psychology*, 57: 539–51.

Saltzer, E. B. (1982) The weight locus of control (WLOC) scale: a specific measure for obesity research. *Journal of Personality Assessment*, 46: 620–8.

Sanders, G. S. and Suls, J. (eds) (1982) *Social Psychology of Health and Illness*. Hillsdale, NJ: Lawrence Erlbaum Associates.

Sandler, I. N. and Lakey, B. (1982) Locus of control as a stress moderator: the role of control perceptions and social support. *American Journal of Community Psychology*, 10(1): 65–80.

Sarason, B. R., Sarason, I. G. and Pierce, G. R. (eds) (1990) *Social Support: An Interactional View*. New York: John Wiley.

Sarason, B. R., Shearin, E. N., Pierce, G. R. and Sarason, I. G. (1987) Interrelations of social support measures: theoretical and practical implications. *Journal of Personality and Social Psychology*, 52(4): 813–32.

Sarason, I. G., Levine, H. M., Basham, R. B. and Sarason, B. R. (1983) Assessing social support: the social support questionnaire. *Journal of Personality and Social Psychology*, 44(1): 127–39.

Sarason, I. G., Sarason, B. R., Brock, D. M. and Pierce, G. R. (1996) Social support: current status, current issues, in C. D. Spielberger, I. G. Sarason, J. M. T. Brebner, *et al.* (eds) *Stress and Emotion: Anxiety, Anger and Curiosity, Volume 16*. Washington, DC: Taylor & Francis, pp. 3–27.

Schachter, S. and Singer, J. E. (1962) Cognitive, social and physiological determinants of emotional state. *Psychological Review*, 69(5): 379–97.

Schlenk, E. A. and Hart, L. K. (1984) Relationship between health locus of control, health value and social support and compliance of personal with diabetes mellitus. *Diabetes Care*, 7: 566–74.

Schulman, P., Keith, D. and Seligman, M. E. P. (1993) Is optimism heritable? A study of twins. *Behaviour Research and Therapy*, 31(6): 569–74.

Schulman, P., Seligman, M. E. P. and Amsterdam, D. (1987) The attributional style questionnaire is not transparent. *Behaviour Research and Therapy*, 25: 391–5.

Schulz, R. (1976) Effects of control and predictability on the physical and psychological well-being of the institutionalized aged. *Journal of Personality and Social Psychology*, 33(5): 563–73.

Schultz, R. and Dwecker, S. (1985) Long-term adjustment to physical disability. The role of social support, perceived control and self-blame. *Journal of Personality and Social Psychology*, 48: 1162–72.

Schultz, R. and Hanusa, B. H. (1978) Long-term effects of control and predictability-enhancing interventions: findings and ethical issues. *Journal of Personality and Social Psychology*, 36(11): 1194–201.

Schultz, R. and Schonpflug, W. (1988) Anxiety as a motivating factor and stressing agent, in C. D. Spielberger, I. G. Sarason and P. B. Defares (eds) *Stress and Anxiety: Vol 11*. Cambridge: Hemisphere.

Schultz, R., Heckhausen, J. and Locher, J. L. (1991) Adult development, control and adaptive functioning. *Journal of Social Issues*, 47(4): 177–96.

Schwarzer, R. and Fuchs, R. (1995) Self-efficacy and health behaviours, in M. Conner and P. Norman (eds) *Predicting Health Behaviour*. Buckingham: Open University Press, pp. 163–96.

Schwarzer, R. and Leppin, A. (1988) Social support: the many faces of help social interactions. *International Journal of Educational Research*, 2: 333–45.

Schwarzer, R. and Leppin, A. (1989) Social support and health: a meta-analysis. *Psychology and Health*, 3: 1–15.

Seale, C. and Addington-Hall, J. (1995) Euthanasia: the role of good care. *Social Science and Medicine*, 40(5): 581–7.

Seeman, M. (1959) On the meaning of alienation. *American Sociological Review*, 24: 783–91.

Seeman, M. and Evans, J. W. (1962) Alienation and learning in a hospital setting. *American Sociological Review*, 27: 772–82.

Seeman, M. and Seeman, T. E. (1983) Health behaviour and personal autonomy: longitudinal study of the sense of control in illness. *Journal of Health and Social Behaviour*, 24: 144–60.

Seligman, M. E. (1974) Depression and learned helplessness, in R. J. Friedman and M. M. Katz (eds) (1974) *The Psychology of Depression: Contemporary Theory and Research*. Washington, DC: V. H. Winston, pp. 83–126.

Seligman, M. E. P. (1975) *Helplessness: on Depression, Development and Death*. New York: W. H. Freeman.

Seligman, M. E. P., Abramson, L. Y., Semmel, A. and von Baeyer, C. (1979) Depressive attributional style. *Journal of Abnormal Psychology*, 88(3): 242–7.

Seligman, M. E. P., Maier, S. F. and Geer, J. H. (1968) Alleviation of learned helplessness in the dog. *Journal of Abnormal Psychology*, 73(3): 256–62.

Seligman, M. E. P. and Maier, S. F. (1967) Failure to escape traumatic shock. *Journal of Experimental Psychology*, 74: 1–9.

Seligman, M. E. P. and Miller, S. M. (1979) The psychology of power: concluding comments, in L. C. Perlmuter and R. A. Monty (eds) *Choice and Perceived Control*. Hillsdale, NJ: John Wiley, pp. 347–70.

Seligman, M. E. P., Peterson, C., Kaslow, N. J. *et al.* (1984) Attributional style and depressive symptoms among children. *Journal of Abnormal Psychology*, 93(2): 235–8.

Seligman, M. E. P., Weiss, J. M., Weinraub, M. and Schulman, A. (1980) Coping behaviour: learned helplessness, physiological change and learned inactivity. *Behaviour Research and Therapy*, 18: 459–512.

Shadish, W. R., Hickman, D. Jr and Arvick, M. C. (1981) Psychological problems of spinal cord injury patients: emotional distress as a function of time and locus of control. *Journal of Clinical and Consulting Psychology*, 49: 297.

Shaver, K. G. and Drown, D. (1986) On causality, responsibility and self-blame: a theoretical note. *Journal of Personality and Social Psychology*, 50: 697–702.

Sherer, M., Maddux, J. E., Mercandante, B. *et al.* (1982) The self-efficacy scale: construction and validation. *Psychological Reports*, 51: 663–71.

Sherrod, D. R., Hage, J. N., Halpern, P. L. and Moore, B. S. (1977) Effects of personal causation and perceived control on responses to an aversive environment: the more control, the better. *Journal of Experimental Social Psychology*, 13: 14–27.

Shinn, M., Lehmann, S. and Wong, N. W. (1984) Social interaction and social support. *Journal of Social Issues*, 40(4): 55–76.

Shipley, R. H., Butt, J. H. and Horowitz, B. (1979) Preparation to reexperience a stressful medical examination: effect of repetitious videotape exposure and coping style. *Journal of Consulting and Clinical Psychology*, 46: 499–507.

Silver, R. L. and Wortman, C. B. (1980) Coping with undesirable life events, in J. Garber and M. E. P. Seligman (eds) *Human Helplessness: Theory and Applications*. Orlando, FL: Academic Press, pp. 279–340.

Simeons, A. T. W. (1960) *Man's Presumptuous Brain: An Evolutionary Interpretation of Psychosomatic Disease*. London: Longman.

Singer, J. E. (1979) Diverse comments on diverse papers about choice and perceived control, in L. C. Perlmuter and R. A. Monty (eds) *Choice and Perceived Control*. Hillsdale, NJ: John Wiley, pp. 339–44.

Skelton, R. (1994) Nursing and empowerment: concepts and strategies. *Journal of Advanced Nursing*, 19: 415–23.

Skevington, S. M. (1979) Pain and locus of control – a social approach, in D. Oborne, M. M. Gruneberg and J. R. Eiser (eds) *Research in Psychology and Medicine. Volume 1, Physical Aspects: Pain, Stress, Diagnosis and Organic Damage*. London: Academic Press, pp. 61–9.

Skevington, S. M. (1983) Chronic pain and depression: universal or personal helplessness? *Pain*, 15: 309–17.

Skevington, S. M. (1990) A standardised scale to measure beliefs about controlling pain (BPCQ): a preliminary study. *Psychology and Health*, 4: 221–32.

Skinner, B. F. (1953) *Science and Human Behavior*. New York: Free Press.

Skinner, E. A. (1985) Action, control judgments, and the structure of control experience. *Psychological Review*, 92(1): 39–58.

Skinner, E. A. and Chapman, M. (1984) Control beliefs in an action perspective? *Human Development*, 27: 129–33.

Skinner, E. A., Chapman, M. and Baltes, P. B. (1988) Control, means–ends and agency beliefs: a new conceptualization and its measurement during childhood. *Journal of Personality and Social Psychology*, 54: 117–33.

Skinner, E. A. and Connell, J. P. (1986) Control understanding: suggestions for a development framework, in M. M. Baltes and P. B. Baltes (eds) *The Psychology of Control and Aging*. Hillsdale, NJ: Erlbaum, pp. 35–69.

Skowronski, J. J. and Carlston, D. E. (1982) Effects of previously experienced outcomes on the desire for choice. *Journal of Personality and Social Psychology*, 43(4): 689–701.

Smarr, K. L., Parker, J. C., Wright, G. E. *et al.* (1997) The importance of enhancing self-efficacy in rheumatoid arthritis. *Arthritis Care and Research*, 10(1): 18–26.

Smith, C. A., Dobbins, C. J. and Wallston, K. A. (1991) The mediational role of perceived competence in psychological adjustment to rheumatoid arthritis. *Journal of Applied Social Psychology*, 21(15): 1218–47.

Smith, R. A., Wallston, B. S., Wallston, K. A., Forsberg, P. R. and King, J. E. (1984) Measuring desire for control of health care processes. *Journal of Personality and Social Psychology*, 47(2): 415–26.

Smith, R. E. (1970) Changes in locus of control as a function of life crisis resolution. *Journal of Abnormal Psychology*, 75(3): 328–32.

Smith, R. E. (1989) Effects of coping skills training on generalized self-efficacy and locus of control. *Journal of Personality and Social Psychology*, 56: 228–33.

Smith, T. W., Peck, J. R. and Ward, J. R. (1990) Helplessness and depression in rheumatoid arthritis. *Health Psychology*, 9: 377–89.

Snaith, R. P., Mehta, A. S. and Hamilton, M. (1971) Assessment of the severity of primary depressive illness. *Psychological Medicine*, 1: 143–9.

Snyder, C. R. (1977) 'A patient by any other name' revisted: maladjustment or attributional locus of problems? *Journal of Consulting and Clinical Psychology*, 45: 101–3.

Snyder, M. (1976) Attribution and behaviour: social perception and social causation, in J. H. Harvey, W. J. Ickes and R. F. Kidd (eds) *New Directions in Attribution Research, Volume 1*. Hillsdale, NJ: Lawrence Erlbaum Associates, pp. 53–71.

Soderhamn, O., Ek, A. and Pörn, I. (1996) The self-care ability scale for the elderly. *Scandinavian Journal of Occupational Health*, 3(2): 69–78.

Soeken, K. L. and Carson, V. J. (1987) Responding to the spiritual needs of the chronically ill. *Nursing Clinics of North America*, 22(3): 603–11.

Sokolov, E. N. (1992) Detector mechanisms of perceptions and emotions, in D. C. Forgays, T. Sosnowski and K. Wrzesniewski (eds) *Anxiety: Recent Developments in Cognitive, Psychophysiological and Health Research*. Washington, DC: Hemisphere, pp. 153–66.

Solomon, K. (1982) Social antecedents of learned helplessness in the health care setting. *The Gerontologist*, 22(3): 282–7.

Solomon, S., Regier, D. A. and Burke, J. D. (1989) Role of perceived control in coping with disaster. *Journal of Social and Clinical Psychology*, 8(4): 376–92.

Spacapan, S. and Oskamp, S. (eds) (1988) *The Social Psychology of Health*. Newbury Park, CA: Sage.

Spielberger, C. D. (ed.) (1972a) *Anxiety: Current Trends in Therapy and Research, Volume I*. New York: Academic Press.

Spielberger, C. D. (ed.) (1972b) *Anxiety: Current Trends in Therapy and Research, Volume II*. New York: Academic Press.

Spielberger, C. D. (1972c) Anxiety as an emotional state, in C. D. Spielberger (ed.) *Anxiety: Current Trends in Therapy and Research, Volume II*. New York: Academic Press, pp. 23–49.

Spielberger, C. D. (1972d) Conceptual and methodological issues in anxiety research, in C. D. Spielberger (ed.) *Anxiety: Current Trends in Therapy and Research, Volume II*. New York: Academic Press, pp. 481–93.

Spielberger, C. D., Crane, R. S., Kearns, W. D. *et al.* (1991a) Anger and anxiety in essential hypertension, in C. D. Spielberger, I. G. Sarason, Z. Kulcsar and G. L. van Heck (eds) *Stress and Emotion, Volume 14*. New York: Hemisphere, pp. 265–83.

Spielberger, C. D., Sarason, I. G., Brebner, J. M. T. *et al.* (eds) (1996) *Stress and Emotion: Anxiety, Anger and Curiosity, Volume 16*. Washington, DC: Taylor & Francis.

Spielberger, C. D., Sarason, I. G. and Defares, P. B. (eds) (1988) *Stress and Anxiety, Volume 11*. Washington, DC: Hemisphere.

Spielberger, C. D., Sarason, I. G., Kulcsar, Z. and van Heck, G. L. (eds) (1991b) *Stress and Emotion, Volume 14*. New York: Hemisphere.

Stansfield, S. A. (1999) Social support and social cohesion, in M. Marmot and R. G. Wilkinson (eds) *Social Determinants of Health*. Oxford: Oxford University Press, pp. 155–78.

Stansfield, S. A., Rael, E. G. S., Head, J., Shipley, M. and Marmot, M. (1997) Social support and psychiatric sickness absence: a prospective study of British civil servants. *Psychological Medicine*, 27: 35–48.

Staub, E., Tursky, B. and Schwartz, G. E. (1971) Self-control and predictability: their effects on reactions to aversive stimulation. *Journal of Personality and Social Psychology*, 18(2): 157–62.

Stein, M. J., Wallston, K. A. and Nicassio, P. M. (1988) Factor structure of the Arthritis Helplessness Index. *Journal of Rheumatology*, 15: 427–32.

Stein, M. J., Wallston, K. A., Nicassio, P. M. and Castner, N. M. (1988) Correlates of a clinical classification schema for the arthritis helplessness subscale. *Arthritis and Rheumatism*, 31: 876–81.

Steiner, I. D. (1979) Three kinds of reported choice, in L. C. Perlmuter and R. A. Monty (eds) *Choice and Perceived Control*. Hillsdale, NJ: John Wiley, 17–21.

Stenström, U., Wikby, A., Andersson, P.-O. and Rydén, O. (1998) Relationship between locus of control beliefs and metabolic control in insulin-dependent diabetes mellitis. *British Journal of Health Psychology*, 3: 15–25.

Steptoe, A. (1983) Stress, helplessness and control: the implications of laboratory studies. *Journal of Psychosomatic Research*, 27(5): 361–7.

Steptoe, A. and Appels, A. (eds) (1989) *Stress, Personal Control and Health*. Chichester: John Wiley.

Sterling, R. C., Gottheil, E., Weinstein, S. P., Lundy, A. and Serota, R. D. (1996) Learned helplessness and cocaine dependence: an investigation. *Journal of Addictive Diseases*, 15(2): 13–24.

Stewart, M. J. (1989) Social support: diverse theoretical perspectives. *Social Science and Medicine*, 28(12): 1275–82.

Stewart, M. J. (1990) Expanding theoretical conceptualizations of self-help groups. *Social Science and Medicine*, 31(9): 1057–66.

Stewart, M. J. (1993) *Integrating Social Support in Nursing*. Newbury Park, CA: Sage.

Stewart, M. J., Hirth, A. M., Klassen, G., Makridish, L. and Wolf, H. (1997) Stress, coping and social support as psychosocial factors in readmissions for ischaemic heart disease. *International Journal of Nursing Studies*, 34(2): 151–63.

Stotland, S. and Zuroff, D. C. (1990) A new measure of weight locus of control: the Dieting Beliefs Scale. *Journal of Personality Assessment*, 54: 191–203.

Strecher, V. J., DeVellis, B. M., Becker, M. H. and Rosenstock, I. M. (1986) The role of self-efficacy in achieving health behaviour change. *Health Education Quarterly*, 13: 73–91.

Strecher, V. J. and Rosenstock, I. M. (1997) The health belief model, in A. Baum, S. Newman, J. Weinman, R. West and C. McManus (eds) *Cambridge Handbook of Psychology, Health and Medicine*. Cambridge: Cambridge University Press, pp. 113–16.

Strelau, J. (1992) Current studies on anxiety from the perspective of research conducted during the last three decades, in D. C. Forgays, T. Sosnowski and K. Wrzesniewski (eds) *Anxiety: Recent Developments in Cognitive, Psychophysiological and Health Research*. Washington, DC: Hemisphere, pp. 1–22.

Strickland, B. R. (1978) Internal–external expectancies and health related behaviour. *Journal of Consulting and Clinical Psychology*, 46(6): 1192–211.

Strickland, B. R. (1979) Internal–external expectancies and cardiovascular functioning, in L. C. Perlmuter and R. A. Monty (eds) *Choice and Perceived Control*. Hillsdale, NJ: John Wiley, pp. 221–9.

Strube, M. J. (1985) Attributional style and the type A coronary-prone behaviour pattern. *Journal of Personality and Social Psychology*, 49: 500–9.

Stuart, K., Borland, R. and McMurray, N. (1994) Self-efficacy, health locus of control and smoking cessation. *Addictive Behaviours*, 19: 1–12.

Sullivan, G. C. (1993) Towards clarification of convergent concepts: sense of coherence, will to meaning, locus of control, learned helplessness and hardiness. *Journal of Advanced Nursing*, 18: 1772–8.

Sullivan, M. D., LaCroix, A. Z., Russo, J. and Katon, W. J. (1998) Self-efficacy and self-reported functional status in coronary heart disease: a six-month prospective study. *Psychosomatic Medicine*, 60: 473–8.

Suls, J. (1982) Social support, interpersonal relations and health: benefits and liabilities, in G. S. Sanders and J. Suls (eds) *Social Psychology of Health and Illness*. Hillsdale, NJ: Lawrence Erlbaum Associates, pp. 255–77.

Sweeney, P. D., Anderson, K. and Bailey, S. (1986) Attributional style in depression: a meta-analytic review. *Journal of Personality and Social Psychology*, 50: 974–91.

Taal, E., Rasker, J. J., Seydel, E. R. and Wiegman, O. (1993) Health status, adherence with health recommendations, self-efficacy and social support in patients with rheumatoid arthritis. *Patient Education and Counselling*, 20: 63–76.

Tait, R., DeGood, D. and Carron, H. (1982) A comparison of health locus of control beliefs in low-back patients from the US and New Zealand. *Pain*, 14: 53–61.

Tanzer, N. K., Sim, C. Q. E. and Spielberger, C. D. (1996) Experience, expression and control of anger in a Chinese society, in C. D. Spielberger, I. G. Sarason, J. M. T. Brebner, *et al.* (eds) *Stress and Emotion: Anxiety, Anger and Curiosity, Volume 16*. Washington, DC: Taylor & Francis, pp. 51–65.

Tardy, C. (1985) Social support measurement. *American Journal of Community Psychology*, 13: 187–202.

Taylor, S. E. (1979) Hospital patient behaviour: reactance, helplessness or control? *Journal of Social Issues*, 35: 156–84.

Taylor, S. E. (1983) Adjustment to threatening events: a theory of cognitive adaptation. *American Psychologist*, 38(11): 1161–73.

Taylor, S. E. and Brown, J. D. (1988) Illusion and well-being: a social psychological perspective on mental health. *Psychological Bulletin*, 103(2): 193–210.

Taylor, S. E. and Dakof, G. A. (1988) Social support and the cancer patient, in S. Spacapan and S. Oskamp (eds) *The Social Psychology of Health*. Newbury Park, CA: Sage, pp. 95–116.

Taylor, S. E., Lichtman, R. R. and Wood, J. V. (1984) Attributions, beliefs about control and adjustment to breast cancer. *Journal of Personality and Social Psychology*, 46(3): 489–502.

Taylor, S. E., Wood, J. V. and Lichtman, R. (1983) It could be worse: selective evaluation as a response to victimization. *Journal of Social Issues*, 39: 19–40.

Teasdale, K. (1993) Information and anxiety: a critical reappraisal. *Journal of Advanced Nursing*, 18: 1125–32.

Tedesco, L. A., Albino, J. E. and Cunat, J. J. (1985) Reliability and validity of the Orthodontic Locus of Control scale. *American Journal of Orthodontics*, 88: 396–401.

Tennen, V. and Herzberger, S. (1987) Depression, self-esteem and the absence of self-protective attributional biases. *Journal of Personality and Social Psychology*, 52: 72–80.

Thoits, P. A. (1982) Conceptual, methodological and theoretical problems in studying social support as a buffer against life stress. *Journal of Health and Social Behaviour*, 23: 145–59.

Thomason, J. A. (1983) Multidimensional assessment of locus of control and obesity. *Psychological Reports*, 53: 1083–6.

Thompson, R. J., Gil, K. M., Abrams, M. R. and Phillips, G. (1992) Stress, coping and psychological adjustment of adults with sickle cell disease. *Journal of Consulting and Clinical Psychology*, 60(3): 433–40.

Thompson, S. C. (1981) Will it hurt less if I can control it? A complex answer to a simple question. *Psychological Bulletin*, 90(1): 89–101.

Thompson, S. C., Cheek, P. and Graham, M. (1988) The other side of perceived control: disadvantages and negative effects, in S. Spacapan and S. Oskamp (eds) *The Social Psychology of Health*. Newbury Park, CA: Sage, pp. 69–93.

Thompson, S. C. and Collins, M. A. (1995) Applications of perceived control to cancer: an overview of theory and measurement. *Journal of Psychosocial Oncology*, 13(1/2): 11–26.

Thompson, S. C., Sobolew-Shubin, A., Galbraith, M. E., Schwankovsky, L. and Cruzen, D. (1993) Maintaining perceptions of control: finding perceived control in low-control circumstances. *Journal of Personality and Social Psychology*, 64(2): 293–304.

Thompson, S. C. and Spacapan, S. (1991) Perceptions of control in vulnerable populations. *Journal of Social Issues*, 47(4): 1–21.

Thornhill, M. A., Thornhill, G. J. and Youngman, M. B. (1975) A computerized and categorized bibliography on locus of control. *Psychological Reports*, 36: 505–6.

Thornton, J. W. and Jacobs, P. D. (1971) Learned helplessness in human subjects. *Journal of Experimental Psychology*, 87(3): 369–72.

Thornton, J. W. and Powell, G. D. (1974) Immunization and alleviation of learned helplessness in man. *American Journal of Psychology*, 87(3): 351–67.

Throop, W. R. and MacDonald, A. P. (1971) Internal–external locus of control: a bibliography. *Psychological Reports*, 28: 175–90.

Tiffany, D. W. (1967) Mental health: a function of experienced control. *Journal of Clinical Psychology*, 23(3): 311–15.

Tiffany, D. W. and Tiffany, P. G. (1973) Social unrest: powerlessness and/or self-direction? *American Psychologist*, 28: 151–4.

Tilden, V. (1985) Issues of conceptualization and measurement of social support in the construction of nursing theory. *Research in Nursing and in Health*, 8: 199–206.

Tilden, V. P. and Weinert, S. C. (1987) Social support and the chronically ill individual. *Nursing Clinics of North America*, 22(3): 613–20.

Tipton, R. M., Harrison, B. M. and Mahoney, J. (1980) Faith and locus of control. *Psychology Reports*, 46: 1151–4.

Tipton, R. M. and Worthington, E. L. (1984) The measurement of generalised self-efficacy: a study of construct validity. *Journal of Personality Assessment*, 48(5): 545–8.

Tobin, D. L., Winder, J. A., Holroyd, K. A. and Creer, T. L. (1987) The 'Asthma Self-Efficacy Scale'. *Annals of Allergy*, 59: 273–7.

Tolor, A. (1978) Some antecedents and personality correlates of health locus of control. *Psychological Reports*, 43: 1159–65.

Tones, K. (1991) Health promotion, empowerment and the psychology of control. *Journal of the Institute of Health Education*, 29(1): 17–27.

Toomey, T. C., Mann, J. D., Abashian, S. W., Carnrike, C. L. M. and Hernandez, J. T. (1993) Pain locus of control scores in chronic pain patients and medical clinic patients with and without pain. *Clinical Journal of Pain*, 9: 242–7.

Toomey, T. C., Mann, J. D., Abashian, S. and Thompson-Pole, S. (1991) Relationship between perceived self-control of pain, pain description, and functioning. *Pain*, 45: 129–33.

Toomey, T. C., Seville, J. L. and Mann, J. D. (1995) The pain locus of control scale: relationship to pain description, self-control skills and psychological symptoms. *Pain Clinic*, 8: 315–22.

Turk, D. C., Okifuji, A. and Scharff, L. (1995) Chronic pain and depression: role of perceived impact and perceived control in different age cohorts. *Pain*, 61: 93–101.

Valecha, G. K. and Ostrom, T. M. (1974) An abbreviated measure of internal–external locus of control. *Journal of Personality Assessment*, 38: 369–76.

Valine, W. J. and Phillips, C. (1984) An examination of perceived helplessness in psychiatric patients. *American Mental Health Counselors Association Journal*, 6(3): 134–43.

van Oostrom, M. A., Tijhuis, M. A. R., de Haes, J. C. J. M., Tempelaar, R. and Krombout, D. (1995) A measurement of social support in epidemiological research: the social experiences checklist tested in a general population in The Netherlands. *Journal of Epidemiological Community Health*, 49: 518–24.

Vaux, A. (1988) *Social Support: Theory, Research, and Intervention*. New York: Praeger.

Veiel, H. O. F. and Baumann, U. (eds) (1992a) *The Meaning and Measurement of Social Support*. New York: Hemisphere.

Veiel, H. O. F. and Baumann, U. (1992b) The many meanings of social support, in H. O. F. Veiel and U. Baumann (eds) *The Meaning and Measurement of Social Support*. New York: Hemisphere, pp. 1–9.

Walker, J., Holloway, I. and Sofaer, B. (1999) In the system: patients' experiences of chronic back pain. *Pain*, 80: 621–8.

Walker, J. M. (1989) The management of elderly patients with pain. Unpublished PhD thesis, Dorset Institute (Bournemouth University).

Walker, J. M. (1993) A social behavioural approach to understanding and promoting condom use, in J. Wilson-Barnett and J. Macleod Clark (eds) *Research in Health Promotion and Nursing*. Basingstoke: Macmillan, pp. 36–42.

Walker, J. M., Akinsanya, J. A., Davis, B. D. and Marcer, D. (1990) The nursing management of elderly patients with pain in the community: study and recommendations. *Journal of Advanced Nursing*, 15: 1154–61.

Walker, J. M., Hall, S. M. and Thomas, M. (1995) The experience of labour: a perspective from those receiving care in a midwife-led unit. *Midwifery*, 11: 120–9.

Walker, J. and Sofaer, B. (1998) Predictors of psychological distress in chronic pain patients. *Journal of Advanced Nursing*, 27: 320–6.

Walker, R. D., Van Ryn, F., Frederick, B., Reynolds, D. and O'Leary, M. R. (1980) Drinking-related locus of control as a predictor of attrition in an alcoholism treatment program. *Psychological Reports*, 476: 871–7.

Walkey, F. H. (1979) Internal control, powerful others, and chance: a confirmation of Levenson's factor structure. *Journal of Personality Assessment*, 43: 532–5.

Wallerstein, N. (1992) Powerlessness, empowerment and health: implications for health promotion programmes. *American Journal of Health Promotion*, 6(3): 197–205.

Wallston, K. (1989) Role of perceived control in rheumatoid arthritis. *Bulletin of the British Psychological Society*, 40: A25.

Wallston, B. S., Alagna, S. W., DeVillis, B. M. and DeVillis, R. F. (1983a) Social support and physical health. *Health Psychology*, 2: 367–91.

Wallston, B. S., Wallston, K. A., Kaplan, G. D. and Maides, S. A. (1976a) Development and validation of the Health Locus of Control (HLC) scale. *Journal of Consulting and Clinical Psychology*, 44: 480–585.

Wallston, K. A. (1992) Hocus-pocus, the focus isn't strictly on locus: Rotter's social learning theory modified for health. *Cognitive Therapy and Research*, 16(2): 183–99.

Wallston, K. A. (1994) Cautious optimism vs cockeyed optimism. *Psychology and Health*, 9: 201–3.

Wallston, K. A. (1997) Perceived control and health behaviour, in A. Baum, S. Newman, J. Weinman, R. West and C. McManus (eds) *Cambridge Handbook of Psychology, Health and Medicine*. Cambridge: Cambridge University Press, pp. 151–3.

Wallston, K. A., Maides, S. and Wallston, B. S. (1976b) Health-related information seeking as a function of health-related locus of control and health value. *Journal of Research in Personality*, 10: 215–22.

Wallston, K. A., Smith, R. A., Forsberg, P. R., Wallston, B. S. and Nagy, V. T. (1983b) Expectancies about control over health: relationship to desire for control of health care. *Personality and Social Psychology Bulletin*, 9(3): 377–85.

Wallston, K. A., Stein, M. J. and Smith, C. A. (1994) Form C of the MHLC scales. *Journal of Personality Assessment*, 63(3): 534–53.

Wallston, K. A. and Wallston, B. S. (1981) Health locus of control scales, in H. M. Lefcourt (ed.) *Research with the Locus of Control Construct. Volume 1, Assessment Methods*. New York: Academic Press, pp. 189–244.

Wallston, K. A. and Wallston, B. S. (1982) Who is responsible for your health? The construct of health locus of control, in G. S. Sanders and J. Suls (eds) *Social Psychology of Health and Illness*. Hillsdale, NJ: Lawrence Erlbaum Associates, pp. 65–95.

Wallston, K. A., Wallston, B. S. and DeVellis, R. (1978) Development of the multidimensional health locus of control (MHLC) scales. *Health Education Monographs*, 6(2): 160–70.

Wallston, K. A., Wallston, B. S., Smith, S. and Dobbins, C. J. (1987) Perceived control and health. *Current Psychology – Research and Reviews*, 6(1): 5–25.

Watson, D. (1967) Relationship between locus of control and anxiety. *Journal of Personality and Social Psychology*, 6: 91–2.

Watson, D. and Baumal, E. (1967) Effect of locus of control and expectation of future control upon present performance. *Journal of Personality and Social Psychology*, 6: 212–15.

Watson, J. M. (1981) A note on the dimensionality of the Rotter locus of control scale. *Australian Journal of Psychology*, 33(3): 319–30.

Weary, G., Elbin, S. and Hill, M. G. (1987) Attributional and social comparison processes in depression. *Journal of Personality and Social Psychology*, 52(3): 605–10.

Weinberg, R. S., Gould, D. and Jackson, A. (1979) Expectations and performance: an empirical test of Bandura's self-efficacy theory. *Journal of Sport Psychology*, 1: 320–31.

Weinberger, M., Hiner, S. L. and Tierney, W. M. (1986) Improving functional status in arthritis: the effect of social support. *Social Science and Medicine*, 23(9): 899–904.

Weiner, B. (ed.) (1974a) *Achievement Motivation and Attribution Theory*. Morriston, NJ: General Learning Press.

Weiner, B. (1974b) A conceptual analysis of locus of control, in B. Weiner (ed.) *Achievement Motivation and Attribution Theory*. Morriston, NJ: General Learning Press, pp. 105–13.

Weiner, B. (1975) 'On being sane in insane places'. A process (attributional) analysis and critique. *Journal of Abnormal Psychology*, 84: 433–41.

Weiner, B. (1980) A cognitive (attribution)-emotion action model of motivated behaviour: an analysis of judgments of help-giving. *Journal of Personality and Social Psychology*, 39: 186–200.

Weiner, B. (1985) An attributional theory of achievement motivation and emotion. *Psychological Review*, 92(4): 548–73.

Weiner, B. (1990) Searching for the roots of applied attribution theory, in S. Graham and V. S. Folkes (eds) *Attribution Theory: Applications to Achievement, Mental Health, and Interpersonal Conflict*. Hillsdale, NJ: Lawrence Erlbaum Associates, pp. 1–13.

Weiner, B., Amirkhan, J., Folkes, V. S. and Verette, J. (1987) An attributional analysis of excuse-giving: studies of a naive theory of emotion. *Journal of Personality and Social Psychology*, 52(2): 316–24.

Weiner, B., Heckhausen, H., Meyer, W. and Cook, R. E. (1972) Causal ascriptions and achievement behaviour: a conceptual analysis of locus of control. *Journal of Personality and Social Psychology*, 21: 239–48.

Weiner, B. and Litman-Adizes, T. (1980) An attributional, expectancy-value analysis of learned helplessness and depression, in J. Garber and M. E. P. Seligman (eds) *Human Helplessness: Theory and Applications*. Orlando, FL: Academic Press, pp. 35–57.

Weiner, B., Nierenberg, R. and Goldstein, M. (1976) Social learning (locus of control) versus attributional (causal stability) interpretation of expectancy of success. *Journal of Personality*, 44: 52–68.

Weiner, B. and Sierad, J. (1974) Misattribution for failure and the enhancement of achievement strivings: a preliminary report, in B. Weiner (ed.) *Achievement Motivation and Attribution Theory*. Morriston, NJ: General Learning Press, pp. 140–50.

Weiner, B. and Sierad, J. (1975) Misattribution for failure and enhancement of achievement strivings. *Journal of Personality and Social Psychology*, 31: 415–21.

Weinert, C. (1987) A social support measure: PRQ85. *Nursing Research*, 36(5): 273–7.

Weinert, C. and Brandt, P. (1987) Measuring social support with the PRQ. *Western Journal of Nursing Research*, 9: 589–602.

Weinert, C. and Tildern, V. P. (1990) Measures of social support: assessment of validity. *Nursing Research*, 39(4): 212–17.

Weiss, R. L. (1974) The provision of social relationships, in Z. Rubin (ed.) *Doing Unto Others*. Englewood Cliffs, NJ: Prentice Hall.

Weisz, J. R. and Stipek, D. J. (1982) Competence, contingency and the development of perceived control. *Human Development*, 25: 250–81.

White, C. B. and Janson, P. (1986) Helplessness in institutional settings: adaptation or iatrogenic disease? in M. M. Baltes and P. B. Baltes (eds) *The Psychology of Control and Aging*. Hillsdale, NJ: Erlbaum, pp. 297–313.

White, R. W. (1959) Motivation reconsidered: the concept of competence. *Psychological Review*, 66: 297–323.

Whitehead, G. I. III and Smith, S. H. (1974) The effect of expectancy on the assignment of responsibility for a misfortune. *Journal of Personality*, 44: 69–83.

Whitehead, J. R. and Corbin, C. B. (1988) Multidimensional scales for the measurement of locus of control of reinforcement for physical fitness behaviours. *Research Quarterly for Exercise and Sport*, 59(2): 108–17.

Whitley, B. E. and Frieze, I. H. (1985) Children's causal attributions for success and failure in achievement settings: a meta-analysis. *Journal of Educational Psychology*, 77: 608–16.

Whitman, L., Desmond, S. M. and Price, J. H. (1987) Development of a depression locus of control scale. *Psychological Reports*, 60: 583–9.

Wiedenfeld, S. A., O'Leary, A., Bandura, A. *et al.* (1990) Impact of perceived self-efficacy in coping with stressors on components of the immune system. *Journal of Personality and Social Psychology*, 59: 1082–94.

Wiener, C. L. (1975) The burden of rheumatoid arthritis: tolerating the uncertainty. *Social Science and Medicine*, 9: 97–104.

Wigal, J. K., Creer, T. L. and Kotses, H. (1991) The COPD self-efficacy scale. *Chest*, 99: 1193–6.

Wilcox, B. L. (1981) Social support, life stress and psychological adjustment: a test of the buffering hypothesis. *American Journal of Community Psychology*, 9(4): 371–86.

Wilkin, D., Hallam, L. and Doggett, M.-A. (1992) *Measures of Need and Outcome for Primary Health Care*. Oxford: Oxford University Press.

Wilkinson, R. G. (1999) Putting the picture together: prosperity, redistribution, health and welfare, in M. Marmot and R. G. Wilkinson (eds) *Social Determinants of Health*. Oxford: Oxford University Press, pp. 256–74.

Williams, C. B. and Nickels, J. B. (1969) Internal–external control dimensions as related to accident and suicide proneness. *Journal of Consulting and Clinical Psychology*, 33: 485–94.

Wilson, G. T. (1979) Perceived control and the theory and practice of behaviour therapy, in L. C. Perlmuter and R. A. Monty (eds) *Choice and Perceived Control*. Hillsdale, NJ: John Wiley, pp. 175–89.

Winefield, H. R. (1982) Reliability and validity of the health locus of control scale. *Journal of Personality Assessment*, 46: 614–19.

Winemiller, D. R., Mitchell, M. E., Sutcliff, J. and Cline, D. J. (1993) Measurement strategies in social support: a descriptive review of the literature. *Journal of Clinical Psychology*, 49(3): 639–47.

Wong, P. T. P. and Sproule, C. F. (1984) An attribution analysis of the locus of control construct and the Trent Attribution Profile, in H. M. Lefcourt (ed.) *Research with the Locus of Control Construct. Volume 3, Extensions and Limitations*. New York: Academic Press, pp. 309–60.

Woodward, N. J. and Wallston, B. S. (1987) Age and health care beliefs: self-efficacy as a mediator of low desire for control. *Psychology and Aging*, 2(1): 3–8.

Worell, L. and Tumilty, T. N. (1981) The measurement of locus of control among alcoholics, in H. M. Lefcourt (ed.) *Research with the Locus of Control Construct. Volume 1, Assessment Methods*. New York: Academic Press, pp. 321–36.

Wortman, C. B. (1975) Some determinants of perceived control. *Journal of Personality and Social Psychology*, 31: 282–94.

Wortman, C. B. (1976) Causal attributions and personal control, in J. H. Harvey, W. J. Ickes and R. F. Kidd (eds) *New Directions in Attribution Research, Volume 1*. Hillsdale, NJ: Lawrence Erlbaum Associates, pp. 23–51.

Wortman, C. B. and Brehm, J. W. (1975) Responses to uncontrollable outcomes: an integration of reactance theory and the learned helplessness model, in L. Berkowitz (ed.) *Advances in Experimental Social Psychology. Volume 21, Social Psychological Studies of the Self.* San Diego: Academic Press, 277–336.

Wortman, C. B. and Dintzer, L. (1978) Is an attributional analysis of the learned helplessness phenomenon viable? A critique of the Abramson–Seligman–Teasdale reformulation. *Journal of Abnormal Psychology*, 87(1): 75–90.

Wortman, C. B. and Dunkel-Schetter, C. (1979) Interpersonal relationships and cancer: a theoretical analysis. *Journal of Social Issues*, 35(1): 120–55.

Wurtele, S. K., Britcher, J. C. and Saslawsky, D. A. (1985) Locus of control, health value and previous health behaviours among women. *Journal of Research in Personality*, 19: 271–8.

Ziegler, M. and Reid, D. W. (1983) Correlates of changes in desired control scores and in life satisfaction scores among elderly persons. *International Journal of Aging and Human Development*, 16: 135–46.

Ziff, M. A., Conrad, P. and Lachman, M. E. (1995) The relative effects of perceived personal control and responsibility on health and health-related behaviours in young and middle-aged adults. *Health Education Quarterly*, 22(1): 127–42.

Ziller, R., Hagey, M., Smith, M. and Long, B. (1969) Self-esteem: a self-social construct. *Journal of Consulting and Clinical Psychology*, 33: 84–95.

Zindler-Wernet, P. and Weiss, S. J. (1987) Health locus of control and preventive health behaviour. *Western Journal of Nursing Research*, 9: 160–79.

Zuckerman, M. (1960) The development of an affect adjective check list for the measurement of anxiety. *Journal of Consulting Psychology*, 24: 457–62.

Zuckerman, M. (1991) One person's stress is another person's pleasure, in C. D. Spielberger, I. G. Sarason, Z. Kulcsar and G. L. van Heck (eds) *Stress and Emotion, Volume 14*. New York: Hemisphere, pp. 31–45.

Zuckerman, M. and Biase, D. V. (1962) Replication and further data on the validity of the affect adjective check list measure of anxiety. *Journal of Consulting Psychology*, 26(3): 291.

Zuckerman, M. and Gerbasi, K. C. (1977) Dimensions of the I–E scale and their relationship to other personality measures. *Educational and Psychological Measurement*, 37: 159–75.

Zuckerman, M., Knee, C. R., Kieffer, S. C., Rawsthorne, L. and Bruce, L. M. (1996) Beliefs in realistic and unrealistic control: assessment and implications. *Journal of Personality*, 64(2): 435–63.

Zuckerman, M., Lubin, B., Vogel, L. and Valefius, E. (1964) Measurement of experimentally induced affects. *Journal of Consulting Psychology*, 28(5): 418–25.

Zung, W. W. K. (1965) A self-rating depression scale. *Archives of General Psychiatry*, 12: 63–70.

Zuroff, D. C. (1980) Learned helplessness in humans: an analysis of learning processes and the roles of individual and situational differences. *Journal of Personality and Social Psychology*, 39(1): 130–46.

Index

RETHINKING HEALTH PSYCHOLOGY
Michele L. Crossley

- What are the main theories, methods and applications relevant to the study of health and illness from a psychological perspective?
- In what ways can contemporary health psychology be critically 'rethought'?
- What are the implications of this 'rethinking' for the future of health psychology?

This introductory text presents a coherent overview of prevalent theories, methods and applications within contemporary health psychology. In particular, it provides a critical analysis of mainstream health psychology by drawing on newer approaches such as discourse, narrative, postmodernism and material discursive analysis. In this way, the largely decontextualized, individualist and cognitively-orientated field of health psychology is brought up to pace with critical developments in other areas such as social psychology. These theoretical ideas provide the basis of the book's main thesis: that contemporary health psychology needs to be rethought.

After presenting an overview of the different theories and methods associated with mainstream and newer approaches within health psychology, the application of these approaches is logically and critically pursued across a range of substantive areas. These include: 'risky' health-related behaviours such as eating, alcohol and drug use, exercise and sex; health promotion related to these 'risky' behaviours; living and coping with chronic illnesses; mental health and illness; communicating and relating with health professionals; and living with dying. Finally, this book locates the growing popularity of health psychology within the contemporary social and political context, particularly in relation to recent changes in the way health care is organized and the commodification and commercialization of health and lifestyles.

Contents
Approaches to health psychology – Health and illness in contemporary society – Rethinking psychological approaches to health promotion – Mainstream health psychology's study of pain and disease – Critically reformulating the study of pain and disease – Approach to mental illness – 'Managing' illness: relationships between doctors and patients – Living in the face of death – Concluding comments – References – Index.

198pp   0 335 20430 9 (Paperback)   0 335 20431 7 (Hardback)